Alias SIMON SUGGS

JOHNSON JONES HOOPER

From a Portrait in the Alabama State Department of Archives and History, Montgomery

Alias SIMON SUGGS

THE LIFE AND TIMES OF
JOHNSON JONES HOOPER

By W. STANLEY HOOLE

UNIVERSITY OF ALABAMA PRESS
Tuscaloosa

Tuscaloosa, Alabama 35487-0380

Manufactured in the United States of America

∞
The paper on which this book is printed meets the minimum requirements of American National Standard for Information Science—Permanence of Paper for Printed Library Materials, ANSI Z39.48-1984.

First paperback printing, 2006

Library of Congress Control Number 52008066

TO

ELIZABETH STANLEY HOOLE

age SIX

without whose constant collaboration
this biography could have been completed
in less than half the time

FOREWORD

W. STANLEY HOOLE strikes a challenging note in this study of Johnson Jones Hooper and his racy, realistic story-telling, immortalized in *Some Adventures of Captain Simon Suggs* and other tales, when he says, "If the literary Old South has been too long reflected in the glorious fuss-and-feathers of old-line make-believers—Simms, Kennedy, Caruthers, Poe, Augusta Evans Wilson and their ilk, to say nothing of foreigners like Thackeray, Mrs. Hemans, Bulwer, and Sir Walter Scott—it is indeed time to lift their veil of smug respectability for a refreshing view of the real thing. Perhaps the Old South wasn't Sir Walter Scottland, after all." For *Alias Simon Suggs* is a study of realism and folk literature, of the sources and the techniques of story-telling, earthy and redolent of the early American frontier. It is fresh in its findings and rich in its delightful discoveries. Although extensively documented with illuminating footnotes and revealing references, its style is direct and captivating—so much so, indeed, that everyday human beings, those who enjoy entertaining biography for its own sake, will relish the privilege of reading it. As a study of the life and writings of Johnson J. Hooper of Alabama, it is a masterful contribution to American biography and to American literature. One glance will tell the reader that it is largely a labor of love, revealing hundreds of hours of ardent, painstaking research in newspaper and periodical files, in holograph letters and documents, in excessively rare histories as well as reminiscences.

But now, at long last, and thanks to Doctor Hoole, we can

enjoy the opportunity of meeting and learning to know the many-sided "Jonce" Hooper in all his facets, including his absorbing interest in politics, editing, lawyering, and horse-racing. We have known so little about him up to now, except from folklore and gossip, that this full-length study seems a veritable Niagara of fascinating information. Of Hooper the humorist we have known something, but now we have added to that knowledge new insights into his many other roles: Hooper the lawyer, the newspaper editor, the politician, the businessman, the state solicitor, the author, the first Secretary and first Librarian of the Provisional Congress of the Confederate States of America. Doctor Hoole has done an amazingly competent job of drawing together the network of these many activities, with hundreds of details relating to persons, places, things—all carefully footnoted with the sources of his information. Among other things is revealed the contents of the rare Tuscaloosa imprint of Hooper's second book, *A Ride with Old Kit Kuncker* (1849), and at last the reader and bibliophile have a chance to appreciate the ramification and delights of this unique volume for the first time.

Hooper's *Adventures of Simon Suggs* (1845) is recognized throughout the English-speaking world as one of the great masterpieces of American humor and satire. These lush tales were undoubtedly known to Thackeray and Dickens; and they were known to Lincoln as a part of the robust humor of the flush times of Alabama and Mississippi. This vigorous, virile humor was the very breath of life on the westward-moving frontier of which Abraham Lincoln and Mark Twain were so natively, so naturally a part. In his chief character, Hooper achieves a powerful personal study, bringing to a focus in one man all the virulent forces of frontier life. Suggs is a sharp, shrewd swashbuckler whose whole philosophy "lies snugly in his favorite aphorism—'it is good to be shifty in a new country'—which means that it is right and proper that one should live as merrily and as comfortably as possible at the expense of others; and of the practicability of this in particular instances, the Captain's whole life has been a long series of the most convincing illustrations."

Hooper's stories under the titles *Some Adventures of Simon Suggs* and *Widow Rugby's Husband,* and others which appeared in newspapers and periodicals, were of course not alone in the pre-Civil War humorous tradition of the Old South. Indeed, they were a part of a very general movement in this kind of writing which had its beginning much earlier, in both the North and in the South. To be true, in the North humorous writing had taken a somewhat different turn. It comprised more nearly political and economic satire in the form of what purported, for example, to be letters of advice to the President—prototypes of the Will Rogers techniques of our time. A great deal of the Northern material dropped also into the polite pattern of Irving, Curtis, Holmes, and other literary gods so nostalgically embalmed by Barrett Wendell. These were conventional things, mostly in the vein of social satire, delicate, genteel, and consequently pale in their points and ineffectual. The writers prided themselves on being "gentlemen and men of taste," and consequently no vigorous, male literature resulted.

But in the ante-bellum South less settled conditions existed. There, in that part of the new nation, especially, was felt the rapid expansion of a country growing and crowing lustily. Inevitably, then, the South with its many attitudes, so different from those of the North, produced another kind of writing. Some of these differences were suggested by "Marse" Henry Watterson, when he intuitively observed in *Oddities in Southern Life and Character* (1882) that, "In the Southern states the humor turns upon character and incident. We body forth a personage out of the odds and ends of comic thought and memory, the heel-taps of current observance; we clothe this image appropriately, and then put it through a series of amusing adventures. Thus it is that our humor is anecdotal, producing such figures as Ned Brace, the practical Georgia joker; Major Joseph Jones, Esq., of Pineville, Georgia, famous lover and traveller; Captain Simon Suggs, of the 'Tallapoosy Vollantares'; Ovid Bolus, Esq., of the flush times in Alabama and Mississippi; Sut Lovingood, 'ornary' hell-raising mountaineer of the Great Smokies; and the Rev. Hazekiah Bradley, who discoursed on the 'Harp of a Thousand Strings.' "

This special kind of story-telling was hailed by that great American authority who knew his *literati,* Edgar Allan Poe. In a review of the "Big Bear of Arkansas" in the *Broadway Journal,* May 24, 1845, Poe wisely pointed to this literature as a "species of writing." Here and in other reviews of similar titles, he reiterated his observance of the uniqueness of the *genre.* It is significant to remember that it was Poe also who first gave resounding applause to the appearance of Longstreet's *Georgia Scenes* (1835), which he reviewed in the March, 1836, issue of the *Southern Literary Messenger* (Richmond).

The distinctiveness and the importance of this "new" literature was also recognized by Bret Harte in his lecture on "American Humor," as Doctor Hoole has stated (Chapter I), and although Mark Twain was not in the habit of referring professionally to his predecessors in humor, he too, subsequently acknowledged and paid tribute to them in his *Autobiography* and in his anthology, *The Library of American Humor,* published in 1888. In the latter he devoted considerable space and emphasis to the humor of the Old South to which he himself was so indebted. Doctor Hoole has carefully discussed and clearly emphasized this indebtedness, particularly the significance of Simon Suggs in the development of *Huckleberry Finn,* but the complex problems of the relationships of Clemens to other earlier Southern humorists needs to be studied with great care. Indeed, it may very well be said that Mark Twain, in the art of telling a humorous story, comes at the END of an era instead of at the beginning of a new one. Clemens marks the culmination, the climax of a period of story-telling. His famous "Jumping Frog" story, instead of opening up a new vein of American humor, revived a native American folk art of story-telling that had its origin earlier in the Old South before the Civil War, in the writings of Longstreet, Thompson, Hooper, Baldwin, and Harris.

In the United States there developed from the beginning an art of story-telling, of spinning native yarns first told orally and later carried over into print. These tales were told by all classes of men—not professional authors, but lawyers, doctors, actors, hunters, sporting gentry, army officers, breeders of blooded stock, horse-race fans, frontiersmen, steamboat captains, preachers, newspapermen, editors, and others. To all of them writing was subordinate to living; they lived what they wrote, and they wrote the way they lived, colorfully and enthusiastically. Often their tales appeared in local newspapers and often in that most famous of all sporting journals, the New York *Spirit of the Times*, a weekly which had an extremely wide circulation, particularly in the Old South and West.

Consequently, a new technique, an art of story-telling, was developed that was largely conditioned by its oral origin. These tales were anecdotal, realistic, and were told with directness and gusto; they vividly depicted striking characters in their native settings, as for example, Hooper's Simon Suggs. There are in these colorful tableaux of American life sparkling characterizations that make you "snigger right out," native images and intonations of speech, with "meaning, rhythm and expression flowering in a poetic image." This art of story-telling so charmingly characteristic of the Old South, may very well be thought of as the "sub-soil of American literary humor," as noted by Andrew Lang, British author and acute observer, while traveling in the United States. Said he, in his book, *Lost Leaders* (1889), "The contrasts, the energy, the mixtures of races in America, the overflowing young life of the continent, doubtless give its humorists the richness of its vein. All over the land men are eternally 'swopping stories' at bars, and in the long endless journeys by railway and steamer. How little comparatively, the English 'swop stories' . . . The Englishman has usually a dignified dread of dropping into his 'anecdotage' . . . The stories thus collected in America are the subsoil of American literary humor . . ."

As has been indicated, Johnson J. Hooper's writings were not alone in this tradition, but they were a tremendously significant contribution, not only to the literature of the Old South but to the folk literature of the United States generally. The tradition had its inception some years before in the stories of Augustus Baldwin Longstreet with his *Georgia Scenes,* published in Augusta in 1835, a book which was really the cornerstone, not only of that period and place, but actually of American realism in general. It was the first in this mood and manner, and therefore gave pattern and shape for the literature that was to follow. A second edition of *Georgia Scenes* appeared in New York in 1840, illustrated with a series of etchings, appropriately expressing the nature and the feeling of the stories. By contrast, Hooper's *Simon Suggs* and other stories may be thought of in sharper contrasts of strong blacks and whites, so characteristic of the woodcut technique. Darley's frontispiece portrait of Simon Suggs, drawn for the original edition of the *Adventures,* illustrates strikingly these sharp masses of black and white, and helps convey the feeling of Hooper's stories.

Longstreet and Hooper were among the forerunners of this type of yarnspinning. Contemporary with them were several other famous writers whose books were much in a similar mood and manner: Longstreet's friend and associate on his newspaper, William T. Thompson, the author of the Major Jones tales; Joseph G. Baldwin, painter of the *Flush Times in Alabama and Mississippi;* and George W. Harris, creator of the *Sut Lovingood* yarns. These titles, these books, and these authors are only a handful and only the most famous. In addition to them there were literally hundreds of story-tellers and thousands of tales, in newspapers and magazines, often published under less formal circumstances than in boards and paperbacks. This vast and exciting field may be set apart as something basically new and unique in American letters and may very well be called the beginnings of a true American folk literature.

Especial emphasis is placed upon this characterization of American "folk literature," since it furnishes the framework and points the place of Hooper's stories in terms of a general concept. Hooper's stories are true to the pattern: they are a part of this stream of national folk expression. Their significance can best be understood in terms of the whole American scene to which they contributed so much. The nature of the literary *genre* is such that it lies between oral folklore on the one hand and literature with a capital "L" on the other. Because it is thus "in between" it partakes of some of the qualities of both extremes—it resembles both forms, yet differs radically from both. Characteristically, this folk literature was a printed literature. The stories, like Hooper's tales, usually got into print quickly and usually close to the source —in the local newspaper, a booklet, or a pamphlet—or farther away in almanacs or weekly papers, such as the *Spirit of the Times* or the *Yankee Blade* of Boston. They were reprinted frequently in newspapers, almanacs and magazines from coast to coast. Consequently, in a very short time an author like Hooper became a national rather than just a local figure. The story-teller-writer became all important. He generally used oral materials which he, in turn, wove into a pattern of his own. Thus he became a creative artist in his own right, fashioning tales—both oral and his own—into the written story. Hooper's stories reflect exactly this process and achieve a new high level through his artistry.

Particularly was this folk literature episodic. The stories dealt with experiences in everyday life, particularly with incidents experienced, witnessed, recalled or retailed, or life on the Alabama frontier, its variety forming the basis of Hooper's first-hand yarning. He did not need to go far for his materials. They were all about him. Sometimes these tales or sketches, often of a fragmentary nature, were woven together to revolve about a central character, such as in Simon Suggs, and as other writers developed in such characters as Sut Lovingood, Mike Fink, and their kindred high spirits.

Again, this folk literature was generally informal. It was not written by great literary figures whose interest was to produce a Great Literature. It was written by men like Hooper, themselves a product of a homespun environment and everyday life, for the sake of entertainment or immediate necessity in meeting newspaper or other requirements. Consequently, because of its informality, this literature has been largely overlooked and mostly lies buried in old files. Its importance is only now, within recent years, beginning to be appreciated and properly developed by American literary scholars.

In the encouragement and development of American folk literature the *Spirit of the Times*, 1835-60, played a tremendously important role. Indeed, its editor, William T. Porter, may be characterized as the "father" of the movement. His *Spirit* was a twelve-page weekly aimed generally at a "sporting" public, before the differentiation of sports periodicals had taken place. Its subtitle ran in the masthead, "A Chronicle of the Turf, Agriculture, Field Sports, Literature and the

Stage." It was not a professional paper, certainly not a professional literary paper like its contemporary, *The Knickerbocker,* or later, *Harper's.* Rather, it appealed to the man on the turf, the sportsman in the field, the farmer, the actor, the river pilot, the country gentleman. It regarded man from a sporting point of view rather than an aesthetic one, it considered down-to-earth values rather than abstractions in art, literature or anything else. In other words, it dealt with life in its everyday phases, with an emphasis upon what men *did.* It was the kind of journal in which professional literary men, like Poe and Irving, could "take down their hair" and write as they damned pleased and for their own pleasure. In its columns story-telling came to be looked upon as a good sport, and was accepted and honored as such.

Although printed in New York City the *Spirit* circulated extensively throughout the United States—from the swank cafes and bars in New York City, from the capitol in Washington over western waterways to the camp fires on the plains, to the music halls in the Rockies, to the mining camps in California. Through its exchange relations with newspapers throughout the country, it gave stories a national circulation. But it did more than that; it provided an opportunity for getting into print stories that might not otherwise have appeared locally for lack of editorial appreciation or unhappy local allusion, and it stimulated an enthusiasm and a rivalry in story-telling that produced a native American folk literature.

After Porter's death, George Wilkes, associate editor of *Porter's Spirit of the Times,* on July 24, 1858, wrote the following interpretative sketch of Porter and his *Spirit*: "William Porter," he said, "moved among the Livingstons, Hamptons, Stevenses, Stocktons, Jones, Waddells, Longs, etc., making all happy by his cheerful spirit and distributing favor by his presence, rather than receiving patronage. The merit of his paper, and the high character of these voluntary associations, not only drew around him the most distinguished writers and correspondents of the time, both at home and from foreign lands, but brought out a new class of writers, and created a style which may be denominated an American literature—not the august, stale, didactic, pompous, bloodless method of the magazine pages of that day; but a fresh, crisp, vigorous, elastic, graphic literature, full of force, readiness, actuality and point, which has walked up to the telegraph, and hardly been invigorated or improved by even the terse and emphatic lightning. This literature was not stewed in the closet, or fretted out at some pale, pensioned laborer's desk, but sparkled from the cheerful leisure of the easy scholar—poured in from the emulous officer in the barracks, or at sea—emanated spontaneously from the jocund poet—and flowed from every mead, or lake, or mountain—in the land where the rifle or the rod was known."

Seven years after the publication of *Simon Suggs* in book form, Thomas Chandler Haliburton, famous Canadian (and later English) humorist, included some of Hooper's tales in his anthology, *Traits of American Humor,* published in London, 1852. A year later William Jerdan, noted British *littérateur,* issued a volume of *Yankee Humour, and Uncle Sam's Fun,* most of which was devoted to the *Simon Suggs* tales. Thus, in less than a decade, Johnson J. Hooper became internationally known as one of the great humorists and storytellers of the Old South.

If Longstreet started the pattern and tradition of telling the Southern humorous story *in print,* "Jonce" Hooper carried on this carnival of story-telling with adroitness and zest. In the character of Simon Suggs he depicted a folk "hero" and developed the picaresque tale in America. To his story-telling he brought an intensity of feeling and the contrasts of the bold black-and-white lines of the woodcut. Hooper thus became a unique figure in the procession of realistic humorists of the Old South from 1830 to 1860.

But he is not so simply typed. His books and his newspaper stories brought him great renown. To this was added the distinction of having been one of the intimate friends of William T. Porter and one of the inner group of correspondents of the *Spirit,* an honor which brought him into that princely fellowship of American writers which included, in addition to Porter, Frank Forrester, Thomas B. Thorpe, and many others who were creating a great American humorous literature. These men, whatever their pursuits and interests, were great men, great American sportsmen—and in their society Hooper naturally took his foremost place.

Franklin J. Meine

Chicago, Illinois
Fall, 1951

ACKNOWLEDGMENTS

WRITING THIS BOOK has indebted me to many people, all of whom I cannot mention here. But I do want especially to thank President John M. Gallalee of the University of Alabama and the members of the University Research Committee, whose grant-in-aid made possible the necessary travel and research, and the Committee's gracious executive secretary, Mrs. Kathrina B. James, for her many courtesies.

I owe a special debt of gratitude to librarians, archivists, and other researchers in many places whose kindnesses have greatly facilitated my work. Some idea of their generosity may be got from the footnotes throughout and from the list of correspondence recorded in the bibliography.

In 1934 Mr. Marion Kelley completed a thesis, *The Life and Writings of Johnson Jones Hooper,* in partial fulfillment of the requirements for the Master of Science in the Graduate School of the Alabama Polytechnic Institute, Auburn. With his permission I used this work as a point of departure and, although I have already personally acknowledged my appreciation to Mr. Kelley, I want again to state that I am beholden to his earlier efforts.

Mr. Joe O. Naylor, president, The Naylor Company, San Antonio, I thank for permission to quote from my own *Sam Slick in Texas* (1945); Probate Judges C. J. Coley and J. V. Chambers of Tallapoosa and Chambers counties, respectively, and their staffs, and Grand Secretary Charles H. Stubinger of the Masonic Grand Lodge, A. F. & A. M. of Alabama, I thank for their generous cooperation; and Mr. W. B. Wood.

Jr., Lafayette, Alabama, Mr. C. S. Johnson, Jacksonville, Florida, and Miss Anne Heard Augustus, Macon, Mississippi, a niece of Mary Brantley Hooper, I thank for their sympathetic assistance and for the use of family papers and other materials. I am likewise indebted to Dr. W. A. Evans of Aberdeen, Mississippi, now deceased, who personally collected much Hooper material, willing it to the Evans Memorial Library of his city. His Johnson Jones Hooper Collection contains, besides the family Bible and Mary Brantley Hooper's *Autograph Album*, several other books and miscellany which once belonged to various members of the family. And I am thankful to Miss Frances M. Hails and Mrs. Mary L. Akin of the Alabama State Department of Archives and History, Montgomery, for their continued interest and friendly assistance in my efforts.

In the laborious task of locating Hooper's grave I am much obliged to the following citizens of Richmond: Mr. H. Fred Pace, caretaker, Shockhoe Hill Cemetery; Miss Katherine Garland, City Home; Mr. John H. Johnston, Comptroller's Office, Virginia State Capitol; Mr. H. P. Wilson, assistant superintendent, Hollywood Hill Cemetery; Mr. L. T. Christian, Christian Funeral Home; Father Herman H. Branderis, St. Peter's Church; and Mr. Vernon J. Birkhimer, superintendent of cemeteries, City of Richmond.

Professors Charles G. Summersell and James B. McMillan, University of Alabama, have obligingly read my manuscript and made invaluable suggestions. For their kindness I am very grateful.

Without the help of Mr. Franklin J. Meine, of Chicago, I could not have completed this study. I am grateful to him, not only for the use of his delightful personal library of American humorous literature, but also for his guidance and his willingness to lend this volume the prestige of his name.

To Mrs. Betty Austin Gober, my erstwhile secretary and

research assistant, I am also deeply obligated. She helped me stalk my subject up and down the land and through the smelly, musty pages of piles of old newspapers, magazines, documents and manuscripts, copying and typing and chasing down the minutiae of bibliographical data. I owe much to her good-humored efficiency.

And, finally, to my wife, Martha Sanders Hoole, I am grateful in more ways than I can possibly record. For years she smilingly tolerated a usurper named Simon Suggs, a wily, arrogant rascal who cluttered up her household and all but monopolized her existence. Surely, in the broad and blessed realm of historico-literary scholarship there is a place for those like her who only listen and encourage and listen and wait. Had it not been for her calm endurance I am sure this book would never have been more than a mere wishful idea.

W. Stanley Hoole

University, Alabama
Thanksgiving Day, 1951

CONTENTS

Alias SIMON SUGGS

PROLOGUE

SPRING CAME EARLY to Cape Fear in 1830. All up and down the narrow, humid peninsula yellow jasmine and azaleas tinted the sandy countryside. Palmettos, windswept and scraggly, rattled and rustled from Corncake Inlet to Old Topsail and magnolias for miles along the river were white-splotched with blossoms.

The day was perfect for a ship-launching. And folks from all around, from far off Holly Shelter Swamp, the Town Creek settlements and the uppermost reaches of the divided, wandering Cape Fear River had come, like Spring itself, to Wilmington for the celebration. They had arrived in stylish carriages, on horseback, in the stages, in wagons and afoot. Throughout the night songs of wagoners had filled the air and their pine-pitch torches outlined the plank roads as far as eye could see. By morning the quiet, sleepy little North Carolina seaport had sprung to life. The crowd that filled the streets and wharves and overflowed into the surrounding hills knew that the launching of a ship was a historical event. Everywhere in the little town of thirty-five hundred expectancy hung by a thread.

Fashionable, parasolled ladies in wasp-waisted dresses of satin and cabriolet bonnets clung to the arms of gentlemen planters, gay and tall in their green walking suits and black beavers. Rubbing elbows with them were hordes of plain dirt farmers, the dust of the wagon roads still on their jackets, and bare-footed po' whites from the backwoods dressed, as they seemed always to dress, in their coarse, dingy yellow linsey-woolsey. From beneath their flopping broad-brimmed hats came mostly silence or sullen glances. Impish boys, screaming a game of tag, weaved in and out among their elders. And away off, down on the river banks, Negroes laughed.

At three o'clock the throng pushed slowly toward the docks on the southern outskirts of the town. To the platform at the water's edge climbed the dignitaries, the mayor and his party, the shipbuilder, the owner, the crewmen and last but by no means least His Majesty's rotund representative, the British Consul at the Port of Wilmington.

Now, everyone knew the Consul, Mr. Anthony Milan. He was an educated gentleman, to be sure, and he was arrogant. During his long service in Wilmington he had become familiarly friendly with no one. Apparently, he took no pains to conceal his haughty, aristocratic mien, considering himself, or so everyone said, several notches above Americans in general and North Carolinians in particular. Always pompous, dogmatic, overbearing and always severely "British," he had succeeded in becoming the butt of young boys' jokes and a source of scorn for Wilmingtonians who somehow never forgot that only a generation before they had chased British Redcoats ragged all up and down the Tidewater and sent their fine ships to the bottom of Cape Fear harbor. But the contemptuous Consul, with a growl for everything and everybody democratic, saw no virtue, except himself, west of the London Foreign Office.

Today, as he labored up the christening platform, the Consul was at his arrogant best. From one fine broadcloth lapel to the other and across his spotless ruffled shirt swung an array of massive gold seals and medals (whence they came or why no one ever knew) and his gold-framed spectacles dangled from a gold chain around his neck. Below, but considerably out front, a curiously woven gold pendant graced the end of his watch fob. So prominent was the corpulent

Consul that spectators, unaccustomed to the routine of ship-launching, might well have wondered whether the schooner *Hatteras* was to be launched—or Anthony Milan . . .

As the sun bore down and the speeches wore on, "Sir" Anthony, sweating like a tea-kettle but eager to represent His Majesty to the conspicuous fullest, slowly maneuvered his way across the platform toward the flag-draped bow of the *Hatteras.* Once there, he propped his weight, medals and all, against the bunting-decorated bannister and threw his gaze over the spectators who fanned out on all sides from the water's edge.

For a simmering while all went well. The speeches droned to an end and the crowd cheered. The mayor's wife with one hefty swing smeared the *Hatteras'* bow with wine. Workmen, joyous in their final duty, pulled the stays and the creaking schooner began her slow slide down the greased runways.

At that instant the dignitaries, doubtless forgetting themselves in the excitement, stepped forward suddenly as one man toward the departing *Hatteras.* The platform swayed and groaned, decorations were shattered, everyone screamed, the bannister was ripped from its moorings, and frog-like into the river plunged His Britannic Majesty's immaculate Consul.

As if by magic cheers changed to laughter. Thousands of eyes, a moment before fixed on the *Hatteras,* now turned to bobbing Consul who, sucked in the wake of the rolling schooner, floated out to deep water, his bald head glistening in the sun and his bemedalled belly rising and falling with the waves. Amid cries of "Call George the Fourth!" and "Let him *stay* launched!" workmen towed the dripping Britisher to shore.

By now the crowd was in an uproar. Scores of small boys, devilish members of the "Muscat Club," screaming for joy, rushed down to the water's edge. There they formed a circle about the bedraggled official and, taunting him unmercifully, escorted him up the cobble-stoned street toward his "castle," at every step yelling, " 'Sir' Anthony's launched! *'Sir' Anthony's launched!"*

The next day one of the boys, little Johnson Jones Hooper, 15-year-old son of Archibald Maclaine Hooper, editor of the *Cape-Fear Recorder,* wrote the following poem, honoring the historic occasion:

Anthony Milan's Launch

Ye who pretend to disbelieve
   In fixed degree of fate
Give, I beseech your listening ear
   To what I now relate.
It is about the launching
   A stately ship I tell,
And of a fearful accident
   That then and there befell.

To one well known to all in town,
   A man of portly size,
Who carries watch seals in his fob
   And glasses in his eyes.

He holds a high position from
   His Majesty Britannic,
And claims to be a member
   Of the breed aristocratic.

He looks with sovereign contempt
   On those whose daily toil
Brings out in rich abundance
   The products of the soil.

He does not care a pin for him
   Who weareth not fine clothes,
And he uses linen cambric
   With which to wipe his nose.

He has no need for comb or brush,
  For his cheeks are rosy red,
And a microscopic lens can find
  No hair upon his head.

His boots are always polished bright,
  His beaver sleek as silk,
His ruffled shirt is clean and white
  As a bowl of new-skimmed milk.

But to our fate—the morning sun
  Shone bright upon that day
When all our people through the streets
  Most gaily took their way.

Down to the docks where on the stocks
  The gallant ship was seen,
Decked out in brilliant colors
  Of blue and red and green.

A monstrous crowd was gathered there,
  In feverish excitement,
To see the ship glide off the ways
  Into the watery element.

The British consul with his glass
  Stuck in his nether eye,
Was there in force, for could the ship
  Be launched, and he not by?

She starts, she's off, a shout went up
  In one tumultuous roar,
That rolled o'er Eagles' Island and
  Was heard on Brunswick shore.

Full royally the ship slid down
  Towards the foaming tide,
While cheer on cheer from every lip
  Went up on every side.

She passed along towards the stream,
  Majestically grand –
When suddenly she stopped, Alas!
  She grounded in the sand.

And there she would have always stuck
  And never more have stirred
Had not the scene I now relate
  Most happily occurred.

Just at that moment when she stopped,
  With many a shake and shiver,
The pompous British consul slipped
  And tumbled in the river.

The Cape Fear rose three feet or more
  As Anthony went under,
The waves they beat upon the shore
  In peals of living thunder.

The ship was lifted from the sand
  And like the lightning's gleam,
She glided out into the deep,
  And floated in the stream.

"All honor then to Anthony!"
  Was heard on every side.
And should we build another ship
  And scant should be the tide

May he be there, and gently drop
  His carcass in the sea;
That ship will float, it matters not
  How low the tide may be.[1]

Folks who knew the Hooper family in 1830, and that was about everybody on Cape Fear peninsula, in North Carolina and, for that matter, all up and down the twenty-four United

States of America, were not surprised at little Johnson's wit and wisdom. The poem, they admitted, was—well, first-rate for a lad of fifteen, to be sure; and it most certainly bespoke an early affinity for the art of self-expression. But that was usual, too, coming from a Hooper. As far back as anyone could remember a Hooper of one generation or another had been orating or writing, preaching or publishing—it was in their blood. The boy Johnson, they agreed, had got his urge honestly.[2]

A century before, his great-grandfather, William, the first American Hooper of the line and a master's graduate of Edinburgh University, had quit his native Scotland to become first pastor of Boston's West Congregational Church.[3] Because of a desire for "a more liberal theology," however, he had soon adopted the Episcopal faith and, after voyaging to England for ordination, had returned to Boston to accept the rectorship of famous Trinity Church, a post he had held for twenty years. Highly revered as a minister and theologian, he had died suddenly but quietly in his sixty-third year while strolling in the church gardens.

Three of the beloved old gentleman's sons—William, George, and Thomas—had left Boston shortly before their father's death and together moved south to the thriving little thirty-three-year-old seaport town of Wilmington. Of little Johnson's great-uncle Thomas not much was remembered, except that he had married Mary Heron, moved to South Carolina and died in the prime of life, without issue. Not so with William, Johnson's other great-uncle, and with George, his grandfather. From these brothers, one a tense, aloof, fearless Whig, the other an assiduous Tory, had descended two long lines of Hoopers, several of whom had won renown in North Carolina and elsewhere in the nation as statesmen, educators, editors, authors and ministers.

Without question, William, the eldest of the three brothers

who had made their homes in the South, was the most famous.[4] A graduate of Harvard College, he had studied law under James Otis, one of New England's most fiery patriots, and upon his arrival in Wilmington in 1764, had been quickly recognized as an able attorney and a liberal and liberty-loving statesman. In 1771, as Deputy Attorney General, he had marched side by side with General William Tryon against the North Carolina "Regulators." Two years later he had been elected to the Assembly and in 1774 had been one of the five "projectors" of the first Provisional Congress. From that date until 1777 he had represented the Old North State in the Continental Congress, and on July 4, 1776, had put his signature in bold letters on the Declaration of Independence. Afterwards, as "the prophet of American Independence," he had retired to Wilmington to resume his law practice and to serve his borough several times in the House of Commons.

Meanwhile, George, the second brother and Johnson's grandfather, had become one of Wilmington's most successful and well-to-do merchants. But as his brother William had stormed the state in behalf of independence and grown to national stature, George had quietly stood by his business and his honest convictions—he could not, it was said, "find it in his heart to imbrue his hands in the blood of his neighbors." Respect for his high character and rigorous intellect had been general throughout the Cape Fear country, however. In spite of his strong Loyalist sympathies, he had maintained intimate and cordial relationships with the most rabid Whigs, including his fellow-citizen, Archibald Maclaine,[5] the distinguished North Carolina congressman and Federalist, whose only daughter, Catherine, he had married on the eve of the Revolutionary War.

To George and Catherine Maclaine Hooper three children had been born—Mary, Spence, and Archibald Maclaine, the eldest, who, forty years later was to become the father of

Johnson Jones Hooper, the youthful author of "Anthony Milan's Launch."

Archibald Maclaine Hooper, like his uncle, "the Signer," had begun the practice of law in early manhood and had soon been elected solicitor of the Wilmington Circuit. On June 8, 1806, he had married Charlotte DeBerniere, daughter of Lieutenant-Colonel John A. DeBerniere, of Charleston, and great-granddaughter of the heroic Huguenot Jean Antoine DeBerniere who had fled France after the revocation of the Edict of Nantes.[6] Between 1809 and 1815 she had given birth to six children, George DeBerniere, Maclaine, John DeBerniere, Louisa, Mary, and Johnson Jones.

Upon inheriting from his father a large estate, including Maclaine's Bluff, a plantation, and a salt works in Cape Fear Sound, Archibald Hooper had quit the profession of law to become cashier of the Wilmington branch of the North Carolina State Bank. That position he also found unattractive and in 1826, at the age of fifty-one—when his youngest son, Johnson, was but eleven—he had accepted the editorship of Wilmington's only newspaper, the *Cape-Fear Recorder*.

Those who knew the father of Johnson Hooper declared him morally unqualified for financial success, though "intellectually equal to any effort." He was amiable, hospitable, honorable; but he was also irresponsible, childlike in simplicity, and "had but little idea of the value of money." Moreover, it was said, he possessed "a fondness for polite letters" and was believed to have been the author of several literary essays—facts, one gathers, in those days deadening to a legal reputation. However that may be, as editor of the *Recorder*, he gave full vent to his talents, enlivening the paper's columns with interesting historical and current contributions—as his biographer put it, "the flowers which he carelessly strewed along the way will well reward with their perfume the friendly hand, that shall gather them together."

But by 1832 Archibald had lost his position as editor and, having run through his patrimony, found himself suddenly "reduced from wealth to poverty."[7] He accepted a place in the Wilmington Customs House but, shortly thereafter, was discharged by the Collector. Over the signature of "Caius Victor" the ex-lawyer-banker-editor immediately published a pamphlet attacking his former employer, embellishing it "with portraits of the different gentlemen who successively filled the office of Collector, from the foundation of the Republic to that day." Suffice it to say that, while the pamphlet made fascinating reading for Wilmington's citizens, it did not replace the author's name on the Customs' payroll and he, aging and without income, was forced to retire to his daughter Louisa's home in nearby Pittsboro. There, and in Alabama, whence George, his eldest son, had moved in 1833, the "old man eloquent," blind and sorrowful, passed his last four years, talking over old times and writing anecdotes and "revolutionary memoirs."[8] He died September 25, 1853, in Crawford, Alabama, in his seventy-eighth year.

Three sons of Archibald and Charlotte DeBerniere Hooper, George DeBerniere (1809-1892), John DeBerniere (1811-1886), and Johnson Jones (June 9, 1815-June 7, 1862), lived to carry on honorably and usefully the traditions of their antecedents. Maclaine, the fourth son, died in childhood.[9]

George and John, reared during the days of the family's affluence, while yet their father's fortune lasted, were sent to college. The former, appointed a cadet at the United States Military Academy, resigned before graduation on account of ill health. He returned to Wilmington, served an apprenticeship in law and in his early twenties was practicing in Charleston, South Carolina. John was graduated from the University of North Carolina in 1831. Five years later he returned to accept a professorship of language. He was considered "the most accurate Greek and Latin scholar of his age and day."

Johnson, the youngest of the three boys, suffered the misfortune of reaching maturity at about the time of his family's reduction from "wealth to poverty," and, consequently, he could not or did not attend college. His formal education was therefore limited by the meagre offerings of the Wilmington public school. Informally, however, as the facts of his later life testify, his youth was spent in learning. To his father, the sincere though erratic lawyer, banker, editor, author and "one of the most accomplished scholars of his day," the boy went daily to school.[10] His mother, herself an "amiable and estimable lady," and a direct descendent of Jeremy Taylor, the eminent seventeenth century English divine, lent him charm and a generous share in the art of happy living. And George, whom he dearly loved, gave him the guidance that only an elder brother can give. Together, these three were Johnson's tutors. At home he doubtless listened eagerly to arguments of the law, its fine points and finesses, that came from father and brother, and between the formative years of eleven and seventeen worked as printer's devil on his father's newspaper, setting and cleaning type and from time to time amusing himself with such youthful poetic outbursts as "Anthony Milan's Launch." Otherwise, it may rightly be supposed, he led the life of any normal youngster who grew up in the small-town South of a century ago, playing along the streets and wharves of Wilmington, swimming, boating and fishing in the Cape Fear, taking his fun where he found it. Certainly, he was an active member and the "honored poet" of the "Muscat Club," a gang of barefoot boys organized for no good purpose.[11] Withal, he was an observant lad and in later years, as he himself followed his father's professions of law, letters and journalism, he must have been reminded often of a successful apprenticeship served, as it had been, under the stern if erratic master of his boyhood days.

In 1830, the year "Sir" Anthony was launched, George

Hooper, Johnson's eldest brother, who was twenty-one and a rising young attorney, moved from Wilmington to Charleston.[12] Three years later, discontented, he travelled on, westward across Georgia to the frontier town of La Fayette, in newly-created Chambers County on the Chattahoochee River in East Alabama, there to practice law in a land which only twelve months before had been ceded to the United States by the Creek Indians.[13]

In 1835 Johnson, then but twenty, joined his brother and the scene of the distinguished Hooper family, which within a century had changed from Scotland to Massachusetts to the Carolinas, shifted once more—this time to the rough-and-ready pioneer state of Alabama.

CHAPTER ONE

"... people is more like hogs and dogs ..."

WILLIS BREWER says that in going from his father's home in Wilmington, North Carolina, to his brother's home in frontier La Fayette, Alabama, Johnson Jones Hooper "journeyed through the Gulf States, and remained in Tuscaloosa several months."[1] To have reached this West Alabama community, on the opposite side of the state from Chambers County, he would have had to come by ship from Wilmington, *via* Charleston and Savannah, to Mobile, and thence up the Mobile, Tombigbee and Black Warrior rivers—a long, slow and circuitous voyage which would have ultimately deposited him yet many miles from his known destination. As Alabama's capital, Tuscaloosa doubtless held a charm and opportunities not to be expected in the county-seat of La Fayette, and Hooper might well indeed have wished to "look the field over" from that vantage point.[2] But this is not likely, in view of subsequent facts. Another writer, obviously following Brewer's lead, romantically states that Hooper "set out on a journey of the Gulf States, living by his wits, a few months here and a few there, until 1840 when he settled in La Fayette . . . and read law under his brother, already a resident of seven years' standing."[3] Another possible though highly improbable route would have been the Fall-Line Road all the way across the Carolinas and Georgia, a tedious stage-coach journey of approximately six hundred miles.[4] And still another, even more improbable, would have been the northern road through western North Carolina, Knoxville, Huntsville and Tuscaloosa.

None of these routes seems plausible. As will be seen, Hooper was in East Alabama much earlier than 1840. Moreover, the logical and most attractive route for him to have followed from Wilmington to La Fayette was certainly not the longest way round.

By taking passage on one of the regularly scheduled schooners from Wilmington, Hooper could have reached Charleston in less than two days. There he could have boarded the newly-constructed, 136-mile South-Carolina Rail-Road, then the longest in the world, and have arrived in Hamburg, across the Savannah River from Augusta, in a matter of hours.[5] In Augusta, Georgia's principal stagecoach terminal, he could have taken the Fort Mitchell route directly west, through Sparta, Milledgeville, Macon and Columbus, across the Chattahoochee River to Fort Mitchell, Alabama, and thence to Opelika and La Fayette, a distance of but two hundred and sixty miles.[6] This route, from Middle Georgia westward a part of the old Washington-New Orleans Federal Road and because of surveyors' markings commonly called the "Three Chopped Way," was the most frequented southwestward highway of its time. Immigrants from the Carolinas and Georgia who settled in Alabama, as well as those who pushed farther on, to Mississippi, Louisiana and Texas, had used it extensively and long.[7] Moreover, Chambers County, one of Alabama's most easterly counties, strategically situated near famous Fort Mitchell on a chief pioneer thoroughfare, was widely known as one of the state's gateways. It is wholly logical to assume, therefore, that Hooper journeyed this way, rather than the longer and more circuitous route *via* Tuscaloosa.

At the time of Hooper's arrival, La Fayette was a mere

frontier crossroads, a muddy-streeted, log-cabin village of scarcely two hundred inhabitants. Chambers County, of which it was the "chief city," contained not more than twenty settlers to each of its 620 square miles, almost one-half of whom were Negro slaves, and an unknown quantity of Muscogee Indians of the Creek Nation who still roamed the countryside, frightening women and children and in general adding no pleasure to an already rugged pioneer existence. Scarcely three years old, the county had been created December 18, 1832, carved out of territory ceded to the United States at the Treaty of Cusseta the preceding March. Already, however, settlers from Georgia, the Carolinas, Tennessee, Virginia and the older counties of Alabama to the west were pouring into the new land, staking claims, clearing the piney-woods, building log houses and trading posts, planting crops, and otherwise slowly converting the backwoods wilderness into a livable outpost of civilization.[8] By 1840, five years after Hooper's coming and the year of Chambers County's first census, 17,333 had arrived.[9] Within another decade thousands more were to come, dotting the red clay hillsides with better and better homesteads, cultivating the bottomlands along Osanippa and High Pine creeks and the rich valleys that eastward led into the historic Chattahoochee River and westward to the Tallapoosa.[10]

Hooper, doubtless through the good offices of his brother George, now one of the county's leading attorneys, adjusted himself quickly to East Alabama's pioneer life. He moved about the region easily, sharing his time between La Fayette and the nearby villages of Dudleyville, Dadeville and Wetumpka, making friends wherever he went. The Indians especially fascinated him, their councils, ball games, sham battles, dances, and hilltop camp-fires remaining sources of unending pleasure. "It was a right beautiful sight to look at," he once stated, "the camp fires of five thousand Indians, that burned at every point of the circular ridge . . . and it was thrilling to hear the wild whoopings, and the wilder songs of the 'natives,' as they danced and capered about their respective encampments."[11]

Quick to see the Indians' many faults, their drunkenness, stupidity and general undesirability as citizens in a white man's country, Hooper nevertheless lamented the ill-treatment these naive and unlearned people received at the hands of land-sharks, speculators and traders. "There are few of the old settlers of the Creek territory in Alabama," he wrote, "who do not recollect the great Indian Council held at Dudley's store, in Tallapoosa County, in September of the year 1835. In those days, an occasion of the sort drew together white man and Indian from all quarters of the 'Nation,'—the one to cheat the other to be cheated. The agent appointed by the Government to 'certify' the sales of Indian lands was always in attendance; so that the scene was generally one of active traffic. The industrious speculator, with his assistant, the wily interpreter, kept unceasingly at work in the business of fraud; and by every species and art of persuasion, sought—and, sooner or later succeeded—in drawing the untutored children of the forest into their nets. If foiled once, twice, thrice, a dozen times, still they kept up the pursuit. It was ever the constant trailing of the slow-track dog, from whose fangs there was no final escape!"[12]

According to contemporary accounts, however, the Creeks were as a whole a revengeful, lazy lot of individuals who mostly lurked on the edges of the forest, a constant menace to the settlers. With "whiskey too much" they either lay about the piazzas of the village stores or, accompanied by "miserable-looking squaws" and filthy, naked children, begged food from white house-wives, "gobbling up their supper of hominy" and sneaking off into the shadows.[13] Easily persuaded and largely controlled by intriguing settlers with the smoothest tongues, they remained constantly a disturbing element of Alabama's backwoods civilization. For years, until the Creeks were finally transported, the white man never dared let down his guard.[14]

Yet the catalogue of the white man's frauds against the Indians was long, too, "as long almost, as the catalogue of Creek wrongs." He exploited them in every way, seduced their maidens, married them to get titles to their lands and left them, cheated and tricked them and laughed in their faces, refusing them at last even the beneficence of a horse and wagon in which to travel to the promised new lands in the West. Many a Creek, once self-sufficient and, after his fashion, proud, "was compelled to wait until the Government removed his people; and then he went in one of the 'public' wagons, among the '*poor*' of his tribe."[15]

Against these unscrupulous, conniving settlers Hooper, the "Champion of the Creeks,"[16] vented his special anger. With apparent great glee he rejoiced when "those lords of the soil!—the men of dollars—the fortune-makers who bought with hundreds what was worth thousands!" fell victims of "retributive justice." Within ten years, he declared, nine out of ten of the cheaters had "lost money, lands, character, every thing! And the few who still retain somewhat of their once lordly possessions, mark its steady, unaccountable diminution, and strive vainly to avert their irresistible fate—an old age of shame and beggary. They are cursed, all of them—blighted, root and trunk and limb! The Creek is avenged!"[17]

As he moved about the countryside in these early, formative years, when life itself leaned heavily on the rifle, the axe and the froe, Hooper observed not only the white man's treatment of the Indians, but also the white man's treatment of himself.

To begin with, the old Southwestern frontier was a mecca for every sort of American, the good, the bad and the indifferent. Some who came, the large majority, no doubt, were hard-working, honest pioneers who desired more than anything else to exchange their old, worn-out soils back east for fresh, to build homes, churches, schools and to better themselves and their families for all time to come. They were steady, sturdy farmers, carpenters, mechanics, blacksmiths, merchants, printers, saw-millers—the numerous little people, largely unlearned but, like true pioneers everywhere, God-fearing folks filled with zeal to carve a homeland out of a wilderness. With them of course travelled some few already well-to-do planters and their families who rode in comfortable carriages, their slaves trailing behind in wagons sagging with Sheraton and Hepplewhite.[18] Doctors, lawyers, editors, teachers, surveyors and other professional men came too, partly for adventure, perhaps, but largely because of man's eternal faith in the pot at the other end of the rainbow. Many were college graduates, men who had flung aside profitable careers and enviable reputations to join the southwestward caravan. Once on the frontier, however, they pitched eagerly into the practice of their professions, posting their shingles, opening schools or starting newspapers. Frequently they also tried their hands at farming or trading, but always they found that the last river they crossed had been their Lethe . . .

But not all who came were angels on horseback. A loud-voiced minority were shiftless ne'er-do-wells, the parasites of progress, hangers-on to whom the other fellow's grass seemed always greener and freer. Not a few were fugitives from justice. For reasons never discussed they somehow felt that Alabama's climate might be particularly healthful. Convicts emptied from the bowels of prisons in the old states cut paths westward, also. Indeed, some of all the flotsam and jetsam of a fabulous America, for one reason or another stifled by the too-sweet aromas of organized society, found their way to the backwoods of Alabama in the 1830's.[19]

Once this adventuresome medley of the clean and the unclean reached their destination, they were strangely bound together by a common denominator of necessity. The frontier was America's greatest leveller. There were Indians to master and forests to clear, homes to raise and roads to build, crops to plant and food to gather. From sun-up to sun-down—from *can* to *can't*—was a day and each was hard and sombre. The unlearned farmer plowed around his stumps and shot the panther on his doorstep. The learned doctor, forced to spend the night on a shuck-and-straw mattress in a settler's chinked-and-daubed cabin, remote and not infrequently filthy, or the learned lawyer, obliged to hobnob with ignorant, drunken, tobacco-spitting clients or rascally land speculators, or the learned politician, making merry over a pewter piggin full of red-eye in a crowded, itchy, foul-smelling roadside tavern, came face to face with a happy breed he might possibly have considered many notches beneath his dignity. If he did, he could not afford to have the fact known. And so it came to pass that, for all his homespun jeans, his rawhide galluses and his bare feet a man was accepted for what he was, not what he had been, and no questions raised. It might have been frontier etiquette to ask a settler whence or even how he came to Alabama—but never *why*.

If life was bleak and rough, it also had its fun and frolics. Like the Pilgrim two hundred years before him, Alabama's pioneer shouldered old Silver Heels and trekked through the virgin forest to take part in a neighbor's log-toting, house-raising, wood-chopping, corn-husking, picking-bee, or that most social of all socials, the break-down. Funerals, too, though solemn to tears, were eagerly anticipated as gala occasions, important both to business and society. Usually they were preached weeks or months after the actual burial and were publicly advertised in the press and by widely distributed announcements. Few people passed up the opportunity for such get-togethers: at them office-seekers saw votes, horse-traders horses, creditors uncollected debts, farmers land, oxen or mules. All saw a good, rowdy time. "Brethering, as being as I'm here," announced one preacher as he opened a service for a colleague, "I'll open the meetin' fur Brother Buncomb, an' then he'll preach the funeral sarmint accordin' to previous a-p'intment. But while I'm before you, I want to say as how my main business over here is a-huntin' of some seed peas, and if anybody here has got any to spar', I'd like to know it after meetin'."[20]

Like funerals, weddings were all day or all night affairs where corn whiskey flowed freely down the throats of celebrants of both sexes, including the Man of God who frequently relied upon a dram or two for added inspiration. Homemade white-lightning was as common as homemade cornbread. There were week-long religious camp-meetings held under the trees, quilting parties, cock and dog fights, shooting and cotton-picking bees, horse-racings, wrestling matches, militia musters, house-warmings, goose jousts and gander-pullings—all keyed more or less to the tune of frontier rowdyism. Every crossroads had its "tippling house," "confectionary" or "grocery" where rot-gut and bust-head licker, peach brandy and other "sperrits" were sold by the keg, jug or dipperful. Along with their men-folks women smoked, chewed or dipped unceasingly, so much so that ministers railed from their make-shift pulpits against the evil of the "filthy weed." But to no avail. For it was considered quite an art to hit the bucket at twenty feet: apparently few were so accomplished, however, judging from the sluices of tobacco juice that found the floors or trinkled down the walls of stores, homes and public buildings.

Yes, Hooper's Alabama was a rough, tough, swearin', gamblin', heavy drinkin', fist-fightin' country and physical prowess, not mental, was usually its own reward. The "champeen" of any activity, be it shooting, wrestling or corn-shucking, easily crawled up the ladder of social prestige—and not the least affluent was the champion drinker, the man who could take on the most and walk away. It was, as the oft-quoted Henry Watterson once stated, "the good old time of muster days and quarter-racing, before the camp-meeting and the barbecue had lost their power and their charm; when men led simple, homely lives, doing their love-making and their law-making as they did their fighting and their plowing, in a straight furrow; when there was no national debt multiplying the dangers and magnifying the expenses of distillation in the hills and hollows, and pouring in upon the log-rolling, the quilting, the corn-shucking, and the fish-fry an inquisitorial crew of tax-gatherers and 'snoopers' to spoil the sport and dull the edge of patriotic husbandry."[21]

Crude and lewd though it was, Alabama's backwoods society had its virtues. Chief among these was a deeply ingrained sense of friendliness, or better still, of neighborliness. When trouble threatened, as it often did, a community became instantly a big family: it was a poor dog indeed that wasn't worth whistling for. Withal his roughness the real frontiersman was at heart an altruist, quick to come to the aid of his friends. Independence of thought and action he had, to be sure, and frankness and forthrightness and a lightly borne spirit of belligerency, but seldom did he covet a reputation in his region higher than that of being a staunch friend. Fist fights were routine affairs, along with drinking and churchgoing, but it was against the frontier's code of ethics for a man to carry concealed weapons, fight with a gun or a knife or attack an opponent smaller than himself. Locks on cabin doors, even in remotest sections, were taboo, and untaught pioneers had to take them off. It was insulting not to have the latchstring always on the outside. Man's faith in man was abiding and everyone was accepted as four-square until proved otherwise. Then, it often happened, it was too late.

In this simple but austere life, where free thought, speech and action was the unwritten law, American democracy found its finest testing-ground. Nowhere was ever more completely democratic, more wholly American than the frontier.

For Hooper, the young, aristocratic North Carolinian, who saw this pioneer Alabama during its most uncouth era, the illiterate, tough settler was a source of wonder and amusement. As the brother of an established attorney and a neophyte lawyer in his own right, Hooper had access to the homes of the affluent, slave-holding and not infrequently aristocratic planters, some of whom maintained, as far as was possible on the bewildering frontier, the standards of refinement once enjoyed in the old states. But these families were few and far between. The majority of associates with whom Hooper was of necessity thrown were small farmers, storekeepers, blacksmiths and their like, backwoodsmen all, a curious motley of men, crude, unpredictable and incongruous.[22] Their society, so numerous throughout the Old South's ever-shifting frontier, instead of oppressing Hooper and his kind, however, served as comic relief in an otherwise bleak and boring existence. As a result, the peckerwood, cracker, sandlapper, hill-billy, red-neck, tar-heel, clay-and-dirt-eater, and piney-woods tackey, to list but a few of the well-known synonyms for the Southern poor-white, became soon and have been for more than a century a stock-in-trade for countless humorists, down to and including the renowned latest, William Faulkner and Erskine Caldwell.[23]

If this seems incongruous, it must be remembered that the writing man on the frontier was himself recording the incongruous. Hooper and his fellow humorists in the antebellum Southern hinterland, had at best only three or four levels from which to choose their subjects—the wealthy, cavalier-minded landowner, his Negro, the Indian, or the po' white.[24]

Withal his fine feathers, the planter-aristocrat offered nothing particularly unique. His chattel, the slave, was at best but chattel, and if his songs and antics were comic, as they doubtless were, he was after all hardly worthy of literary effort. His time in American letters, as well as that of his master, was to come in the romantic future. The Indian, of course, was mildly exciting, but not book-worthy, except for such hair-raising episodes as "captivities" (of which there were many) or for slushy, "noble-savage" sentiment.

The po' white, on the contrary, the illiterate, shiftless, malaria-ridden backwoodsman was a real find, coarse, native, a comic of the first water and a perfect subject to laugh *either at or with.* He was in short a social anomaly.[25] Whether seen as a scheming politician, a big-muscled bully, a Hard-Shelled Baptist preacher, a mock-heroic Davy Crockett, a conniving, shiftless rogue, a ludicrous horse-trader, a crooked faro dealer or, at his worst, a lazy, vermin-ridden squatter in his windowless, floorless, doorless and filthy log-cabin in the hills, he was the Great Common Man. If he belonged to the "half-agricultural, half-piscatory . . . sinewy, yellow-headed whiskey-loving set" in Tallapoosa County,[26] or dwelt in Butler where "ther is no society nor no nothing . . . [and] the people is more like hogs and dogs than they are like folks,"[27] or in Barbour County where "we hain't ben eatin' nothin' but dried beef so long we've wore ur corn-grinders down to the gums, and we want suthin' else by way of change,"[28] he was nevertheless appealing as a pioneer, and Americans have always loved the pioneer. He was ignorant, but not pathetic and mainly he was *odd.* He was typically "Southern," unlike any class in any other section of the nation. But most of all he was humorous, a primitive comic, and as such he became the main stock of humor in the South for a hundred years, from Thomas Singularity to Jeeter Lester.[29] Out of him or by means of him sprang a truly American literature, the most indigenous this country has ever produced. No doubt, Bret Harte, himself famous as a humorist throughout the English speaking world, had him in mind when he declared, "It is to the South and West that we really owe the creation and expression of that humor which is perhaps most characteristic of our lives and habits as a people. It was in the South, and among conditions of servitude and the habits of an inferior race, that there sprang up a humor and pathos as distinct, as original, as perfect and rare as any that ever flowered under the most beneficent circumstances of race and culture. It is a humor whose expressions took a most ephemeral form—oral, rather than written. It abode with us, making us tolerant of a grievous wrong, and it will abide with us even when the conditions have passed away. It is singularly free from satire and unkind lines. It was simplicity itself. It touched all classes and conditions of men. . . ."[30]

The writers who so naively portrayed the ludicrous aspects of frontier life were not professional humorists. Rather, they were respectable doctors, travellers, surveyors, schoolmasters, preachers, printers, planters, merchants, politicians, soldiers, actors, country squires, or—like Hooper—lawyers or country editors who had keen eyes for the grotesque and the knack for putting it down. Crackerbox philosophers they have been called, amateurs who had the skill to blend horseplay with horse-sense to make horse-laughs and by so doing to create, unconsciously, a distinctly national type of literary expression, the so-called Big Bear School of American Humor.[31] As Franklin J. Meine has admirably written, they "were quick to seize upon the comic aspects of the rough life about them, and graphically sketched the humorous and colorful happenings, the oddities in rustic or pioneer character, and the tall tales that were going the rounds of the locality. These spontaneous, hilarious pencillings, from an academic point of view, may indeed be considered nothing more than rather charcoal sketches. Yet in their way they are masterpieces: realistic, racy, written in a vein of rollicking humor, and thoroughly characteristic in tone, color, and action of that forgotten era. The age, one of the most vivid of American experiences, has no other authentic record in our literature. Nothing is more essentially American than the frontier; and these sketches, humble enough in intent, were the earliest literary realization of the frontier, and, remain its most revealing expression."[32]

Many of the recorded yarns and tales were doubtless apocryphal, first heard on horseback in the wide open spaces or around the fireplaces of isolated taverns on winter evenings. Their *locale* was the country store, the village courtroom, the river steamboat, the squatter's cabin, the backwoods camp-meeting, the stagecoach or the hunter's camp. Their *subject matter* was the teller himself and his neighbors, the uncultured, unsophisticated Common Man. And their *style* was the frank, leisurely and often irreverent vernacular of the comic backwoodsman, spiced with anecdotes, repetition, trick-endings and crude, homespun dialogue. As a result, the stories are strongly provincial, genuinely Southern and in most respects wholly unlike the humor produced in other parts of the nation. Certainly, their authors staked no claim to academic respectability. But nowhere in American letters is there anything more really American. Their eyewitness portrayals of life and character on the ante-bellum Southern frontier, exaggerated though they may be, are quite likely to be nearer the truth than those of the better-known Lavender and Old Lace School. From them American literature has inherited a realism, an earthiness and balance which has helped it steer a middle course these many years. As William T. Porter stated in his 1845 Preface to *The Big Bear of Arkansas,* "a new vein of literature, as original as it is inexhaustible in its source, has been opened in this country within a very few years, with most marked success . . . [The authors are mainly] country gentlemen, planters, lawyers, &c., 'who live at home at ease' . . . . Most of them are gentlemen not only highly educated, but endowed with a keen sense of whatever is ludicrous or pathetic, with a quick perception of character, and a knowledge of men and the world: more than all, they possess in an eminent degree the power of transferring to paper the most faithful and striking pictures with equal originality and effect. In this respect they have superiors on neither side of the Atlantic."[33]

To these tongue-in-cheek raconteurs, of whom Hooper is a recognized example, everything was grist for the mill. Without them our social history would be but dull drivel of a pseudo-chivalric past, a ruffled record of dyspeptic lords and crinolined ladies—as *un*-American as five o'clock tea. With them is an almost inexhaustible treasury of information about the early frontier—gambling, horse-racing, courtroom scenes, hunting and fishing, backwoods courtships and weddings, murders, burlesque revivalists' meetings, camp life, descriptions of the weather and the country, local customs, and hundreds of subjects typically American. "They rubbed elbows daily with the vigorous life of their times and reported it with shrewdly humorous insight. In laughing at the hurly-burly of America, *they knowingly laughed at themselves as part and parcel of it.* That is the core of our native sense of humor."[34]

Nearly always these authors wrote anonymously, not for profit but for fun, publishing their products in local newspapers wholly for local consumption. If, as in the case of Hooper, their efforts were somehow forced upon a wider audience, they were frankly astonished. "If what was designed, chiefly," Hooper stated in the Preface to his first book, "to amuse a community unpretending in its tastes, shall amuse the Great Public, the writer will, of course, be gratified. If otherwise, the mortification will be lessened by the reflection that the fault of the obtrusion is not entirely his own."[35] Several of the humorists, including Hooper, either tried later to suppress their works or denied having written them, fearing that such fame was detrimental to their rightful pursuits of politics, law, medicine, or preaching.[36]

A few of them are well-known: Davy Crockett, George Washington Harris ("Sut Lovingood"), Augustus Baldwin Longstreet, whose *Georgia Scenes* (1835) has been called "the cornerstone of this early humorous literature," William Tappan Thompson ("Major Joseph Jones"), Joseph Glover Baldwin ("Ovid Bolus, Esq."), Sol Smith, George W. Bagby ("Mozis Addums"), Thomas Bangs Thorpe ("Tom Owen, the Bee Hunter") and William Trotter Porter who, although not a humorous writer himself, admirably served by collecting and publishing many tales in his *Big Bear of Arkansas* (1845), *A Quarter Race in Kentucky, and Other Tales* (1846), and—most important—in the *Spirit of the Times*, a weekly sporting journal of which he was for many years editor and proprietor. And of course Samuel L. Clemens, who unquestionably owed a great debt to his predecessors in the field of American humor, satire and realism.[37]

Until lately the contribution of these homespun stalwarts to the literature of the region and, for that matter, of America, has been pretty much overlooked, "elegantly ignored," as Meine put it a decade ago, "by most of our writers on American history . . . and students of American literature, who have been, for the most part, either ignorant of the field or superior to it."[38] More recently, however, they have attracted increasing attention as a highly important element of our native literary heritage.[39]

And it's high time. If the literary Old South has been too long reflected in the glorious fuss-and-feathers of old-line make-believers—Simms, Kennedy, Caruthers, Poe, Augusta Evans Wilson and their ilk, to say nothing of foreigners like

Thackeray, Mrs. Hemans, Bulwer and Sir Walter Scott—it is indeed time to lift their veil of smug respectability for a refreshing view of the real thing. Perhaps the Old South wasn't Sir Walter Scottland, after all.[40]

Then, in ever clearer outline the predominant literature of the ante-bellum South slowly comes into focus—a simple, homemade literature, but a complete one because it is folk-literature of the people themselves and native to the core. In it is embodied the many aspects of society from the high-and-mighty cavalier to the wooden-nutmeg pedlar, a coarse, colorful, satirical, climactic literature, extremely masculine and frequently as funny as all *git-out*. It was the frontier in action, a literature as indigenous as camp-meetings-with-dinner-on-the-ground, corn-shuckings or house-warmings. It is the old Southern frontier looking at itself, laughing at itself, and talking about itself. It is as near as America has come to a literature all its own.[41]

CHAPTER TWO

". . . Yonder goes the chicken man!"

YOUNG HOOPER'S FIRST YEARS in and about the monotonous little village of La Fayette were uneventful and, it may well be imagined, uninspiring. Day after day he read law in his brother's office and met his brother's friends, familiarizing himself with Alabama's legal procedures as well as its people and laying the foundation for the partnership George had proffered him once his apprenticeship had been served. George was by now an "old-timer" in the region, a man of family,[1] a respected land- and slave-owner,[2] a justice of the peace,[3] an attorney who frequently served as administrator of estates and guardian, and in general a highly regarded businessman.[4] In addition to his practice in Chambers County he frequently worked in the neighboring towns of Dadeville and Dudleyville in Tallapoosa County, twenty-odd miles to the west, where he was known as a competent lawyer, especially in the defense of clients in chancery court.[5] His friends soon became Johnson's friends: Charles Stone, Edward Hanrick, Isaiah Perry, John J. Holly, and Bird H. Young, all original settlers of Dadeville,[6] and in La Fayette and Dudleyville J. A. and A. Holifield, P. T. Richardson, T. M. Baugh, J. Henry Kellam, Joseph A. Johnson, James Moore, Green D. Brantley, John Wood and others[7]—all of whom apparently liked the Hooper brothers, especially jolly, fun-loving Johnson.

Friends though he had, Johnson Hooper's life in the piney-woods settlements of East Alabama in the late 1830's could not have been too joyous, certainly not the type a young man just out of his teens would have preferred. Of "Houses of Entertainment" La Fayette and Dadeville had plenty, to be sure (so many, in fact, that the County Commissioners were forced to regulate prices on lodging, meals, whiskey, brandy and rum),[8] but even the excitement of their gambling and drinking and rowdiness could not stay the wanderlust of the young North Carolinian. In September, 1837—he had been in the state slightly more than a year—he chucked the law and struck out on a foolhardy horse-and-wagon trip with his friend Joseph A. Johnson (who was then clerk of the Circuit Court of adjoining Tallapoosa County) across the wilds of Alabama and Mississippi to Lake Caddo on the yonder side of newly-founded Shreveport, Louisiana, "near the line of Texas." Johnson, who was several years Hooper's senior had been engaged by his father-in-law, the well-to-do James Moore of Dudleyville, whose half-Indian son Jackson had died *en route* to Texas, to look after Jackson's affairs, and Hooper had elected to go along, perhaps just for the ride. At any rate he bought a "fine saddle," a pair of "fine shoes," a silk handerchief and other commodities from a Dadeville merchant and made ready for the journey.[9]

For the footloose and fancy-free Hooper the trip was only a lark, but to his companion it was a sad and serious mission. Early in June Jackson Moore had left "Talapsy Count Dudleyville P. O. Alabam," as he put it, accompanied by his sister Peggy, his wife Catherine and their children, a white man named Murray and several Negro slaves. From Jefferson County, Mississippi, on June 28 he had advised his family that he had been unwell and, on August 1 from Ouachita Parish, Louisiana, Catherine had told of the "distressed situation" that had fallen the party "in 4 days ride of Shreveport." There nearly all had been attacked by fever and "bowel complaint" and on July 25 Eliza, Catherine's child, had died. Exactly a week later, as Catherine stated, "Jackson at this time is a corpse . . . He died about 3 oclock this evening [August 1]." Both bodies were buried at "Richard Dickerson's grave yard" and, added brave Catherine, "As soon as able to travel we expect to hunt out a home and then I will write you immediately to let you know where and how we is and I would bee very glad for you to let us know what are your wishes for us to do . . ."

The elder Moore's wishes were quickly made. At eleven o'clock on Sunday morning, September 10, Joseph A. Johnson and Johnson J. Hooper left Dudleyville on horseback with a wagon loaded with supplies and, after a circuitous route of 678 miles *via* Montevallo, Tuscaloosa, Pickensville (Alabama), Madisonville, Clinton, Rodney (Mississippi) and Copenhagen, Minden and Russellville (Louisiana), on September 27 reached "the place where poor Jackson died." Six days later they arrived at a Dr. Scott's where they at last caught up with Catherine and Peggy, who, wholly undismayed, were busily building a house on the banks of Lake Caddo. From Russellville, September 30, Johnson wrote back to Moore in Dudleyville that after Jackson's death the ladies had "had a great deal of trouble about the negroes" and Murray (who is never otherwise described) had stolen "Jackson's riding horse and made his escape to Mississippi but in the race lost his hat and vest . . ." Later, November 18, Johnson again addressed a long letter to his employer, this one mailed from Shreveport, in which he declared that he and Hooper had arrived in Texas and started the slaves "to clearing a piece of land to make a crop next year" and thought that he ought to remain with the ladies "till next spring." "Hooper and myself," he added, "are well."

From the beginning to the end of their 24-day trip from

Dudleyville to Lake Caddo Johnson kept a detailed daily diary, including an itemized account of his and Hooper's expenses. Several times is the latter mentioned, including the occasions Johnson lent him money and one entry, dated September 14 (later struck out), in which he purchased Hooper a $3 umbrella in Tuscaloosa.[10]

Whether Johnson or Hooper or both remained in Texas until the spring of 1838 is unrecorded. But, the mission over, they returned to East Alabama where Hooper once again began the study and practice of law under his brother's tutelage, simultaneously earning his way by working at various jobs, one of which included a trip to South Carolina to purchase merchandise for an unidentified merchant, probably the affluent James Moore whom he described as "the Old Man." On October 3, 1838, he wrote his friend Johnson from Charleston that he had been sick and delirious with yellow fever and had been "so far unsuccessful in getting Goods & am waiting for a letter of Credit from old Mr. Sanders." Obviously unhappy, he continued, "God damn the Goods to Hell. You may know I hate going back to Tallapoosa without the damned Goods, but I can't help it. When do you go to Texas. I will go with you by God, if the Old Man will give me Milley [Moore's beautiful blonde daughter, aged twenty] and I shall ask him soon as I get back . . ."[11]

Hooper was back home in Tallapoosa County in time to appear in the 1838 fall term of court,[12] however, and by May 27, 1839, two of his Dadeville friends, Isaiah Perry and John J. Holly, signed his $2000 bond of appointment as an authorized "Notary Public in, and for Tallapoosa County." Meantime, Hooper had again taken time off to see some of his adopted state. How widely he travelled is conjectural, but by early 1838 he had again paid his respects to the Capital City of Tuscaloosa.[13]

Apparently, Dadeville offered greater opportunity for the

ambitious young attorney than did the rival community of La Fayette. At any rate, early in 1840, when the United States government began its sixth "enumeration of the Inhabitants," William L. Justice, clerk of the Tallapoosa Circuit Court, and Job Taylor, census marshall, selected and deputized Hooper as an assistant marshall, gave him a proper quantity of blanks and sent him forth, as he later recorded it, "to count the noses of the men, women, children, and chickens resident upon those nine hundred square miles of rough country which constitute the county of Tallapoosa." This work, afterwards so pleasantly remembered, took Hooper into every nook and corner of the hilly, muddy county and gave him ample opportunity to see Alabama frontier life at its crudest. To say the least, as "Chicken Man" he was not always welcomed. Almost everyone was suspicious of him, feeling that a "tremendous tax would soon follow the minute investigation of the private affairs of the people." Showering the census-taker with "taunts, threats and abuse," the inhabitants gave scantily of their information. "The dear old souls," Hooper wrote, "could not bear to be catechised about the produce of their looms, poultry yards, and dairies; and when they did 'come down' upon the unfortunate inquisitor, it was with a force and volubility that were sure to leave an impression." Some residents "sicked" their dogs on him, others could not know what "a man wanted to be so pertic'lar about gals' ages for, without he was gwine a-courtin'," children yelled, "Yonder goes the chicken man!" and men said, "Yes, d--n him, he'll be after the *taxes* soon." One woman, Elizabeth Wyatt, actually refused to describe the persons in her family, insisting on returning a whole number only.[14] All in all it was "very difficult work." "Glorious sport," Hooper had thought in the beginning, "but it didn't turn out so."[15]

By October the task was completed. Hooper had counted 2,318 white males, 2,106 white females, 2,013 slaves and 9 free colored persons—6,444 in all. Moreover, he had recorded the name of the head of each family, the number of deaf, dumb and blind persons as well as those employed in various pursuits and, at the end, had solemnly sworn that "the number of persons set forth in the return made by me . . . had been ascertained by an actual inquiry at every dwelling house, or a personal inquiry of the head of every family . . ." A certified copy of his tabulation was duly posted "at two of the most public places within the Division open to the inspection of all concerned." However, Hooper, dissatisfied with the rate of pay, persuaded his employers to write and attach the following statement to the last sheet of his report: "This is to certify that the subscribers are well acquainted with Tallapoosa County; and they willingly state that [it] is a large and very hilly county—that it being very thinly populated, and the Tallapoosa River running thro' it, makes any business like that of taking the Census peculiarly difficult. The extreme length of the County is 48 miles, and its breadth 24 m. We do not think that less than the highest compensation would adequately repay the Census Taker for his trouble and expense—the families generally in the County are very small, averaging only eight and a fraction."[16]

Whether Hooper succeeded in his demand for immediate "highest compensation" is not known. But there is no doubt that his "official pereginations," laughably recorded three years later in the *Spirit of the Times* and afterwards in book form, brought him national renown as one of America's leading humorists.[17]

Three months after the completion of the census, on January 16, 1841, Hooper and another friend, Charles Stone, "entered into and formed a copartnership in the practice of Law," with office in Dadeville. It was mutually agreed that each party to the contract would share equally in both profits or losses, and that the partnership should continue until January

1, 1848, "unless sooner dissolved by mutual consent."[18] Although the firm of Hooper and Stone is known to have been employed soon after its formation by at least five clients in the fall of 1841 and spring of 1842,[19] it was very shortly dissolved and, by mid-1842, Hooper had gone into business with his brother George, under the name G. & J. Hooper, Attorneys at Law. This partnership practiced in both Tallapoosa and Chambers counties,[20] but the office was in La Fayette, George's home, and there Johnson again—in the Fall of '42—made his headquarters.

Law, it appears, was not the only attraction of La Fayette. For in that village lived a merchant, Green D. Brantley, one of the earliest settlers, a well-to-do man and planter who had several children, among them two attractive girls, Ann E. and Mary Mildred.[21] And to Ann, the elder daughter, Hooper had been for some time paying court. Suddenly, however, when she decided to marry another, Hooper, broken-hearted—or so the story goes—turned his attention to Mary, who in few ways resembled her sister. Ann, a magnetic personality, was the cheerful, vivacious type, easy of friendship and always the gracious hostess, a lover of books and intellectual companionship, while Mary, a quiet, pretty but reserved girl sought her amusement more or less in the family circle, an excellent seamstress, a good cook, an enthusiastic and interesting devotee of "small talk" and a loyal home body.[22]

Be that as it may, Ann married Thomas R. Heard on November 13, 1842,[23] and one month later, Thursday, December 15, Johnson was married to sixteen-year-old Mary—in the same church and by the same pastor, the Reverend T. P. C. Shelman, "ordained minister of the Gospel of the Methodist Episcopal Church" of La Fayette. George Hooper, the faithful, posted his brother's $200 marriage bond.[24]

Just how sudden or uncalculated was Ann's marriage to Tom or Johnson's to Mary will in all probability continue to remain the enigma that it is—an unsolvable figment of family history. Suffice it to say, however, that Green D. Brantley, the firm, commanding father was not too happy on Christmas Day, 1842, a few weeks after the two ceremonies. ". . . And now dear Thomas and Ann," he wrote in a long, parental-toned letter, "another and quite different matter to both of you—Your sister Mary and Mr. Hooper is *[sic]* married & as there was bad feeling among you all before you separated, I desire on my part that all the bad feelings & animosity among the whole of you may be forgotten, for it is (must be) a very desirable thing for peace & Harmony to prevail in every family . . . ." Further pleading for "harmony," he added, the whole matter "must never be made a subject of correspondence on neither *[sic]* side."[25] That the obedient daughters—in all probability he wrote a similar letter to Johnson and Mary—followed their father's wishes cannot be questioned. But Johnson Hooper and Tom Heard evidently saw the "whole matter" in another light, remaining coolly indifferent to each other and at unpleasant odds for at least seven years, until their father-in-law's death in December, 1849.

When Green D. Brantley fell ill in the fall of that year, he called his large family to his bedside. Ann, who was then living in Mobile, came up to La Fayette and stayed with her sister, Mary, remaining as a guest well into the new year. On January 21, 1850, she wrote to her "Dear Sister," perhaps Sarah, "You will understand from my being with my sister Mary—that the unpleasant difference between Tom and Mr. Hooper is adjusted. Father requested them when, he was dying, *[sic]* to be friends and brothers—& they pledged themselves to each other, in his presence. This was extremely gratifying to us all."[26]

But Ann, though happily married to Tom, the wealthy cotton factor and commission merchant and later major in the Confederate Army, never forgot Johnson and Mary. Her childless home, first in Mobile and then New Orleans, was a mecca for them as well as for all her kin and numerous in-laws. With them she carried on copious correspondence,[27] and in her diary she frequently paid them one by one loving tributes. "My mind," she wrote on August 31, 1858, "has been full of my sister Mary—whom I have not seen for seven long years. Dear girl, how I long to see her!" Three weeks later, September 19, when Johnson was sick in Montgomery, she told her diary, "Grieved to see in the paper a notice of Mr. Hooper's ill health. I love him, & have always entertained for him the most delicate regard. How I should like to live near them *[sic]*!"[28] And among the many papers and books she left upon her death, November 23, 1898, one is a praiseful newspaper account of Hooper's death, another a humorous poem by him,[29] and a third is a manuscript poem, "The Sea: In Calm and Storm," by A. B. Meek, across which is written in her own hand: "Copied by Johnson J. Hooper—*Alias Capt. Simon Suggs* . . . ."

Never, perhaps, was man more closely wedded to a family than was Johnson Jones Hooper. Partly was this a fact because the Brantleys and the George Hoopers had been on friendly terms for several years—indeed, one of the Brantley girls was named Caroline Hooper. But largely was it true because Johnson Hooper was obviously an open-hearted man, one possessed of a magnetic personality which somehow drew others into his immediate confidence. From the day of the marriage, Green D. Brantley became his son-in-law's fast friend and three years later, when the older man became a state legislator under the Whig party banner, he and Hooper developed strong political affinities. Meanwhile, Hooper served as his attorney, handled his legal business, prepared his will and during his last illness and after his death attended to his large estate.[30] Hooper's friendship for other members of the Brantley family was equally unique. When Alsea and Ben, Brantley's sons, moved to Union County, Arkansas, in 1849, to manage a new plantation their father had purchased, Hooper corresponded with them, passing on to them such advice as the following concerning the handling of cotton crops: "It is your father's request that you push on with the gathering. Ben mentioned having been offered ten cents for cotton—your father's instructions are that you sell at *no* price, nor do any trading of the sort. There is every probability that if the crop be well handled and *early* gathered, and properly baled, it will command a price largely over what you are likely to be offered for it. You will see from what I have said, how anxious your father is about the cotton being properly and well taken care of."[31] When Sarah J., a daughter, got a job teaching school in a girl's academy at Pontotoc, Mississippi, Hooper kept her posted on affairs at home and advised her as follows: ." . . let me congratulate you on the return of your cheerfulness; for I see pretty plainly that you are getting quite to like your work at Pontotoc. I am sorry your time is so fully engaged, for you ought to have plenty for exercise and intellectual recreation. Any way, you must learn to control your temper. I do not mean to control outbursts, for you are not given to them—but to control it, so that there is no internal corrosion of the affections, no impairment of the tone of mind. Cold water I find a great soother of morbidly irritable nerves- tho' Lord knows I get little enough of it here."[32] But his most interesting correspondence was carried on with the Ann of his first love, who by now, as Mrs. Thomas R. Heard, had become one of Mobile's most highly respected matrons. Ann had no children of her own but kept open-house for all her many nephews and nieces. On one occasion she offered to have Hooper's son William as a guest and Hooper wrote her: "I very much desire it, and if the next *riding* [of the circuit court] pays me $600, shall certainly carry or send him down . . . . Will is anxious to go—

of course—and I verily believe it would be of the greatest possible advantage to him."[33]

Mary Hooper, Johnson's wife, was herself a remarkable woman, spirited, loyal and generally beloved by all who knew her, including her mother-in-law and father-in-law who, in 1849, had moved to Crawford, Alabama, from North Carolina. "Mary, Dolph and I," Hooper wrote in the above letter, "went down to Russell [County] the other day and stayed one afternoon and night. We found my mother confined to bed, with a billious attack. They were much disappointed at not seeing Willie again. Mary 'took to' my father very much, I believe." For twenty years, until her husband's untimely death in 1862, she was a good wife and a good companion. Except on rare occasions, such as when she and Mrs. Leroy Pope Walker guided the destinies of Montgomery's society in the late 1850's and when poet Alexander B. Meek dedicated his "Rose of Alabama" to her in 1846,[34] she remained always in the quiet background of her husband's busy life. Of her Hooper wrote to Ann, "Mary has very sore finger from quilting. I don't myself see the use of making what she never uses. She and I both have whooping cough, but it does no material damage except . . . spoiling my very pretty temper."[35]

Fourteen months after their marriage, on February 28, 1844, a first child, William DeBerniere, was born to Johnson and Mary Mildred Hooper, and twenty-one months later, November 12, 1845, a daughter, Annie Brantley, named for Mary's sister, who lived but one year and eight months. On October 29 [19?], 1849, a second son, Adolphus S., was born. During these early years the Hoopers continued to make their home in La Fayette. But as time went on and her husband's work as attorney, solicitor, editor, fiery secessionist and, finally, as secretary of the Provisional Congress of the Confederate States of America called him more and more away from her, Mary was drawn deeper into the recesses of domesticity, finding her joy in her children and, one supposes, in the reflected glory of her husband. For several years while Hooper lived in Wetumpka and in Montgomery as editor of the *Mail,* she remained with the children in La Fayette, taking pride, it is said, in her home, her needles and crochet hooks, a quiet woman "who gloried in making beautiful things."[36]

But sadness followed Mary to the end of her days. When the Civil War began, she saw her husband immediately enter government service and soon thereafter, before the conflict had got well under way, lose his job and his health and die at the early age of forty-seven. Meanwhile, Will, the older son—he was but seventeen—had joined the Confederate Army and gone to Mobile, leaving her alone at home with Dolph, who was twelve.[37] Seven of her brothers entered the service, too: Edward, Randall, Charles W., Green, Jr., Benjamin, Alsea and John, enlisting in Alabama and Louisiana companies and in the Confederate Navy. But it was the death of John, at Columbus, Kentucky, September 30, 1861, that brought first grief. At twenty-two, he had left home only six weeks before to enlist in the Beauregard Fencibles, 12th Louisiana Regiment—"Island Ten" was his first and only battle. Her two nephews, George's son, Charles M. and George W., also went to war—George as captain in the Sixth Alabama Regiment, Charles in the Fifth. At Seven Pines, the former, at the time a major, received a wound in the side, suffered two broken legs and lost the use of his right hand. For his gallantry in action he was promoted to lieutenant-colonel and "was highly complimented by Gen. Rodes for his courage and ability." Charles was likewise heroic, receiving special mention for gallantry at Second Manassas by Brigadier-General J. J. Archer, was promoted to lieutenant-colonel on the battlefield and afterwards "awarded a medal of honor authorized by the Confederate Congress, and made Colonel on the recommendation of General Lee himself."[38]

After the war and during the tragic period of Reconstruction, Mary lost her home and was shuttled about from pillar to post, living an unsettled existence with relatives—with her sister Ann, who had before the war moved to New Orleans, with other sisters in Tuscaloosa, Alabama, and Artesia and Macon, Mississippi. From time to time she visited her son William who, in 1868, had married Carrie Yokely Smith and was practicing law in Aberdeen, Mississippi,[39] and Dolph, who never married but who worked as a railroad accountant with headquarters in New Orleans.[40]

Even in her old age tragedy stalked her. On July 27, 1875, her son Will was brutally assassinated on the steps of the Aberdeen County Courthouse by Bradley Jones. No cause could be assigned to the tragedy, stated the Aberdeen *Examiner,* other "than that ill-feeling had for some time existed between the parties in reference to an estate matter about to come on for trial," but the affair "created the most intense excitement in the city, and there can be but little doubt that the formalities of a trial would have been dispensed with had not the murderer been consigned to the jail before the crowd commenced to assemble."[41] As a result of this shock, Mary suffered a stroke of paralysis and was a semi-invalid for the twenty-four remaining pain-wracked years of her life, though she fought heroically against her infirmity and finally succeeded in walking again with the aid of a cane.

A few years later she suffered a second stroke and a broken hip and was bed-ridden for months—but again she stoically accepted her reverses, recovered, and continued to enjoy the companionship and correspondence of friends and the chatter of little children who listened to her stories.

Once more, on April 14, 1895, misfortune came to her—this time through Dolph, the younger son, who was run over by a railroad train in the New Orleans [Algiers] yards.[42]

Mary lived on, with relatives but mostly with Will's wife

in Aberdeen, past the age of usefulness, thirty-eight years beyond her husband's death, until May, 1899, an old, silently unhappy but outwardly cheerful lady, "a fine brave soul—proud and highstrung—yet enduring with tremendous courage the vicissitudes of war, the privations of reconstruction days, the dependence of widowhood, the mental torture and grief in losing her only children both in such a tragic way, and almost constant bodily pain." Her days were passed in reading to her grandchildren, Johnson II, Nancy, and William and others in the family and in teaching them, in corresponding with her relatives and friends and in visiting with many callers who came to talk over "old times."[43] Through it all she remained financially dependent upon her sons, and, after their deaths, upon her relatives, but she never wanted loving care and affection. To those who knew her best she was until the end a lover of little children,[44] affectionate and approachable and "always busy making with her trembling hands handsome counterpanes knitted with perfect stitches, beautiful quilts, and exquisite embroidery."[45] She was indeed a courageous woman, one whose quiet latter years were steeped in a becoming sadness and leavened over with joyful memories of the good old days before the war and Reconstruction, before the death of her husband and children, days that reached back across half a century to that crisp December morning in La Fayette's little Methodist Church, pastor Shelman, a host of happy, carefree friends of Johnson.[46]

CHAPTER THREE

"... good to be shifty in a new country..."

ON SATURDAY DECEMBER 17, 1842, two days after Hooper's marriage, John F. Gilbert & Son, enterprising job-printers of La Fayette, published what is believed to have been the first issue of Chambers County's first newspaper, the *East Alabamian,* a small weekly dedicated in principle to American Whiggery and especially to Henry Clay.[1] Hooper, who had obviously never forgotten the smell of printer's ink of his father's *Cape-Fear Recorder* and who now more than ever needed to increase his income, was persuaded to accept the editorship of the new hebdomadal.[2] Almost simultaneously, he withdrew from the law partnership with his brother (who soon formed another),[3] and entered business alone, advertizing in his newspaper that he would "Practice law in the Courts of Chambers and the adjoining Counties" and that he could "be found at the office of the *East-Alabamian,* La Fayette, Alabama."[4] Thus began his dual interest, like his father's before him, in law and journalism,[5] professions between which he was to vacillate for more than a decade, pursuing first one and then the other and from time to time both at the same time.

Hooper's choice of the Whig party evidently displeased his old and good friend Joseph A. Johnson, who at first subscribed for but then suddenly discontinued the *East Alabamian.* From

La Fayette Hooper wrote that "I cannot tell you how much [cancelling the subscription] hurt my feelings, not on account of the money . . . but because it seems to indicate a decrease of kindly feeling and affection." He then recalled the "old-time" they had had together, saying that he valued their friendship more than "politics or any other damn stuff." He concluded: "Joe, if I have a feeling which is altogether free from any alloy of interest, it is my love for you, and it would gratify me beyond measure, that you should tell me that I am the same to you, that I have always been."[6]

Be that as it may, into the columns of the *East Alabamian* Hooper continued to pour his Whig-tinged editorials and, doubtless for comic relief, the fruits of his creative imagination. Soon he was known far and wide as an "accomplished" and crafty editor of "signal ability" and a "facetious gentleman," and his paper as "handsome." Mostly, however, he used scissors and paste, only occasionally printing original comments. News in the semi-wilderness of the old Southwest was not easy to come by and paying subscribers were few. For the owner the *East Alabamian* was an extremely doubtful venture, therefore. "I must have money, or I cannot get along with my paper," frankly announced Gilbert. "All who are in arrears for the Lord's sake, come and pay up, for I want paper *now*—NOW—and cannot publish without it."[7]

In the summer of 1843, most probably on August fifth or twenty-eighth, Hooper ran in the columns of the *East Alabamian* a little tongue-in-cheek yarn of his own making and based on his own experience, entitled "Taking the Census in Alabama," and signed "By a Chicken Man of 1840."[8] If it is possible to put a finger on the one effort of his life which proved to be an open sesame to fame and immortality in the realm of American humorous literature, this was it, undoubtedly.

Up in New York, William T. Porter, genial and fun-loving editor of the *Spirit of the Times, A Chronicle of the Turf, Field Sports, Literature and the Stage,* and from 1843 until his death in 1858 Hooper's firm friend and Maecenas, picked up "Taking the Census" and reprinted it in his widely-circulated weekly on September 9, 1843. Thus, overnight, Hooper left the ranks of the purely local "funny-men," of which there were hundreds, especially throughout the South and Southwest, to become a nationally-read humorist. For, once a story found its way into the *Spirit,* whose circulation even in this early day was more than 16,000 and soon was to be thrice that number, it was reprinted again and again in weeklies all over the country, large and small, frequently bringing a national reputation, not only to the author himself but also to his oftimes remote newspaper. For this famous weekly, besides inaugurating a new style of writing, "through innumerable Southern and Western correspondents, brought together the most truly original and genuine American humor that the literature of the country can boast."[9]

Besides editing the most popular sporting-humorous journal prior to the Civil War,[10] on which the *Knickerbocker Magazine* claimed had no "superior in *any* country, for various merits, sporting, literary and pictorial," William T. Porter himself was one of the most admired journalists of his time, a man of "peculiar genius" whose writings sparkled "like diamonds with the light of his wit and good humour." In addition to "an inimitable pen, a playful fancy, and a heart all kindness and sincerity," said the *New York Mirror,* he possessed "all the requisites of an able and skillful caterer for the public taste," and had "no fellow in the literary firmament."[11]

Porter was, indeed, according to all accounts, a genuinely fine personality, a highly respected gentleman and a credit to his profession.[12] Into the columns of the *Spirit,* which had subscribers as far away as England, India and Australia,[13] he drew articles and stories from men of "all walks of life, lawyers, explorers, doctors, journalists, river boatmen, officers of frontier posts, editors, and even members of Congress,"[14] each of whom regarded him as an editor without equal and a personal friend.[15] As he himself put it, "we believe that our correspondents comprise more men of genius—disciples of Momus, we mean, than any mere newspaper or magazine ever had. To be sure very few of them [are designated] from the signatures they adopt in their correspondence with this paper, nor are we at liberty to designate them. Disguised under signatures as quaint and novel as the scenes they describe, are some of the most brilliant writers of the day, who have been read and admired the world over, Albert Pike, Henry Wm. Herbert, Willis, Hoffman, Noland, Thorpe, Dr. Irving, and others of kindred genius. The writers of articles like 'The Quarter Race in Kentucky,'—'Jones's Fight'—'That Big Dog Fight at Myers's'—etc. etc. are retired country gentlemen, with very rare exceptions. Four of them are planters in Alabama and Mississippi, one a North Carolina lawyer, another a leading man in the government of Canada, and two are Ex-Governors of cotton growing States. Though unknown to the world and not to be detected by their respective signatures, how much of brilliant wit and fancy, of fun and humor is embodied in Dunbar, January, Brougham, Aimsworth, Skinner, Grathan, Waddell, Oaks, McClure, Durivage, Williamson, and others. Though named above, no one can 'tell the other from which,' or designate a single article written by either."[16] The *Spirit* thus became a magnet for the freshest and best humor in the nation, yarns by such outstanding writers as Thomas B. Thorpe, William Tappan Thompson, Sol Smith, Joseph M. Field, George W. Harris, John S. Robb, "Madison Tensas, M.D.," C. M. F. Noland, and scores of others, many of whom have yet evaded identification, throughout the Old South and Southwest from Virginia to Texas. In addition to original contributions, Porter combed the newspapers of the nation for reprints, as he did when he "discovered" Hooper, picking the liveliest stories available from the big-city dailies—the New Orleans *Delta* and *Picayune*, the St. Louis *Reveille*, the Louisville *Courier*, for examples—down to the smallest weeklies like the *East Alabamian*.

If Porter was a competent editor and the finest exponent of early American humor, he was also the most altruistic of men. Never did he fail to encourage talent of promise. When he spotted "Taking the Census," for instance, he told his readers that "The following graphic description of the denizens of a remote district of country, is copied from the 'East Alabamian,' . . . edited with signal ability by Johnson J. Hooper, Esq. . . . This Hooper is a clever man, and we must enlist him among the correspondents of the 'Spirit of the Times.' His sketch reminds us forcibly of the late Judge Longstreet's 'Georgia Scenes,' and the 'Adventures of Thomas Singularity,' by the late Prof. Nott, of S. C. Hooper's 'Sally Higgins' and the famous 'Cousin Sally Dillard' should be near relatives."[17]

Hooper, obviously delighted by his sudden leap to national recognition, replied in the *East Alabamian* two weeks later, "Porter . . . , republishing our sketch of 'Taking the Census,' pays us some handsome compliments which would be more easy of digestion, if we were conscious of digesting them. We suspect that we know our own calibre pretty well—and we are small in the Bore—though we believe our hind sight is where it ought to be, and our head all right. That very 'delekit insinuation' about contributing to the 'Spirit of the Times' shall be attended to."[18]

On December 2, 1843, Hooper published in the *East Alabamian* a lengthly story called "Our Hunt Last Week," embellishing it with a one-column cut of a wild boar. Immediately, Porter, now on a sharp lookout for anything from

Hooper's pen, copied it, changed the title to "A Three Days Hunt in Alabama," and added: "The writer of this 'report' is the same facetious gentleman who recently favored us with the amusing account of his adventures while engaged in 'Taking the Census' . . . He is the accomplished editor of the 'East Alabamian,' a handsome paper published in La Fayette, in that State."[19]

Four months later, not having heard from Hooper meanwhile, Porter again reprinted excerpts from "A Three Days Hunt" which dealt especially with duck shooting on Oachumhatchie Creek, entitling them "The Biters Bit." These he prefaced with the following praise: "Col. Hooper, of the 'East Alabamian,' has a dog named 'Ponto' whose sagacity and exploits deserve to be hauled down to posterity in 'perpetual verse,' as much as the exploits of Achilles or the intrigues of Paris."[20] Hooper, not displeased, reciprocated by stating in the *East Alabamian* that "the 'Spirit of the Times' is the most complete original Sporting Intelligence, Theatricals, and the Fun, Flash and Fashion of the day."[21]

During 1844, following the appearance of "Taking the Census" and "A Three Days Hunt," only infrequent references were made to Hooper in the *Spirit* and no original stories by him appeared. It may be supposed that he was too busy with editing the *East Alabamian* and practicing law and dabbling in local politics to devote much time to creative effort.[22] His first son, William, it will be remembered, had been born on February 28, and shortly afterwards he and his family had moved to new quarters, leaving the town limits of La Fayette and taking the old Samuel Spence house, a mile in the country.[23]

Meanwhile, he continued to advertise his law practice in the *East Alabamian* in the following facetious manner:

L-A-W—L-A-W.

The undersigned not having been elected by the Legislature now in session to any office whatsoever, notwithstanding there were several which he might be induced to accept; and being extremely desirous to earn a subsistence by some Lawful means; announces to the public, that from and after this date, he will hold himself in readiness to serve all of his fellow citizens who choose to entrust to him their

LAW BUSINESS,

to the extent of his ability. And as the times are very hard and he is very necessitous - and moreover, as members of the Bar will under-bid privately - he offers to bring collection suits for whatever he can get; and to do all other business from a Justice Court case, up to - yes, e'en up to - "Chancery" cases, at whatever may be agreed on.

He will execute commissions to take testimony to be given in any of the courts at moderate charges.[24]

However, it must not be assumed that during this period Hooper was unproductive, for in December, 1844, there appeared in the *East Alabamian* the first of several stories which were destined further, along with "Taking the Census," to help win for him his high place in the annals of American humor—those devoted to the remarkable Captain Simon Suggs of the Tallapoosa Volunteers, a shrewd, brazen, farcical backwoodsman whose whole ethical system was snugly summed up in his favorite frontier aphorism, *"It is good to be shifty in a new country."*

The ready-witted Captain, "the Shifty man," was not entirely a figment of Hooper's imagination. Rather, his prototype was a young man "of medium height . . . raw-boned and of angular build . . . high cheek bones, bright blue eyes, and rather pleasant expression of face" whom Hooper had known fairly intimately during his early meanderings in Tallapoosa County—Bird H. Young.[25] Young, it will be recalled, was one of Dadeville's first settlers and property owners, a well-known man in his community and a friend of George Hooper.[26]

To say the least, Young was most surely a contradictory character, a perfect "type" for Hooper's vivid imagination and the epitome, a subject *summum bonum,* of all that a writing man could have hoped for on the old Southwest frontier. On the one hand he was a responsible family man, the father of six children, who owned a 600-acre farm near Youngsville (now Alexander City in Tallapoosa County) and with the help of his wife, *nee* Annie McDonald, lived a long and prosperous life as one of his community's best-remembered citizens.[27] According to all accounts he had been born in Greene County, Georgia, in 1803, had migrated to Alabama as a lad of sixteen and spent several years roving in Montgomery, Pike and Monroe counties before finally settling in Tallapoosa in 1833. He served as Tallapoosa County's first tax collector, was a justice of the peace and a constable and on several occasions acted as guardian or administrator of estates,[28] facts which substantiate the belief that Hooper's humorous "pen pictures" of him did him great injustice.[29] "He was," according to one who knew him, "a plain man of much vitality and of native talent, but of fair standing as a citizen," who upon his death left "a number of descendants of much respectability."[30]

On the other hand it is a recorded fact that Young, especially in his early days, was a gay blade who in many ways admirably fitted Hooper's facetious description of Simon Suggs. In less than a year after he had moved to Tallapoosa County he was hauled into court for gambling ("State *vs.* Bird H. Young, Gaming, capiases ordered"), the following spring he was fined $20 costs for the same offense and in early 1836 he was arrested for "Betting at Faro," a charge from which he was later exonerated by jury.[31] If gaming and drinking seem to have been his greatest faults, at least one merchant found his credit poor;[32] but the legends about him that still persist in the region center chiefly around his prowess as a practical joker and genuine horse-play artist.[33]

On one occasion, for example, Young is reputed to have stopped at Coosa Hill, a Wetumpka hotel and, just prior to leaving, sneaked his saddle-bag and blankets out and hid them nearby. He then returned, politely asked the proprietor to assemble his belongings and prepare his horse for departure. After searching in vain for his guest's baggage, the inn-keeper was forced to deduct $12 from the bill and Young, of course, promptly paid the reduced bill and as promptly retrieved his "lost" property. On another occasion, or so the story goes, Young was one day fined $10 for contempt of court by Judge Robert Dougherty. That night the "culprit" and his cronies held a "mock trial" in a local tavern and fined the Judge $10 for having worn his hat in the courtroom! The good-natured Judge Dougherty paid the "fine" to "Judge Young" who immediately used the "fee" for a spree for all.[34]

However much truth there may be in these "Young legends," certainly he was a well-known citizen in early East Alabama, a popular man among his fellows and one who, as he attended the court sessions in Chambers, Coosa, and Tallapoosa counties and on visits to such communities as Wetumpka and Montgomery never failed to attract "a group about him to gratify their curiosity in looking at and listening to the chat of this noted character."[35] Such was the man Hooper frankly designated as "the Mad Bird" and used as the basis for his immortal Capting Simon Suggs of the Tallapoosy Vollantares.[36]

That Young was highly indignant at being so ridiculously immortalized is not difficult to understand. Once, it is said, he threatened to bring suit against Hooper for defamation of character,[37] but realizing that the stories had been written in fun and, incidentally, enjoying the notoriety of being identified with such a "noted character" as Simon Suggs, he finally laughed the whole matter away with a shrug of his shoulders.[38] Hooper himself obviously got great fun out of the affair. He wrote Porter that "the original of 'Simon' will be 'lifted kleer off the ground,' when he learns that he has been embalmed in the columns of the 'Spirit.' He will not believe it, however, unless he have ocular demonstration." To this Porter replied that he would send "ocular demonstration," if Hooper would furnish his address.[39] A month later a long letter from Hooper to Porter, containing the following sentences, was printed in the *Spirit*: "If you will send the next 'Spirit' to Capt.——, of ———, Tallapoosa County, Alabama, 'Suggs' will believe—else not, 'though one should rise from the dead.' If he catches me and flogs me next week at Court—as he swears he will—the 'Spirit' shall have the particulars . . . ." Porter answered by saying that he did "not exactly cotton to the idea of Captain Suggs' flogging you 'on sight'" but that he was "still anxious to hear more of him."[40]

With the Captain Suggs yarns Porter was—to put it mildly—overjoyed. What a "great pity," he proclaimed, in a long prefatory announcement to the reprint of the first installment, January 11, 1845, that Hooper should hide his "light under a bushel" by writing for a small, local newspaper. "What a correspondent he would make for the 'Spirit!' What a 'choice spirit' among that circle of 'jolly good fellows'" who have made the *Spirit* "famous for original wit and humor." Among the *Spirit's* contributors, he continued, "we intend to enroll Hooper . . . whose 'Simon Suggs, *the Shifty Man*,' late Captain of the Tallapoosa Volunteers, [he] introduces to the world with an exordium as ornate, graphic, and fanciful as Wirt's on the occasion of the trial of Aaron Burr." Reminding his readers of "Taking the Census," which had appeared sixteen months previously, Porter added that the new story was "by this same Mr. Hooper, of whom we merely know that he is a young lawyer of repute, and editor, *en amateur*, of the 'East Alabamian,'" a gentleman of "sterling intellectual ability," and one whose "well written editorials are mainly confined to political themes, and it is only once in a long while that he indulges his readers with a sketch like the one annexed—thrown off probably, at a heat."[41]

Two weeks later the *Spirit* carried the second installment of Hooper's story under the title of "Simon Suggs, the Shifty Man," a week afterwards the third, "Simon Leaves Home—His Last Operation," both copied of course from the *East Alabamian.* Meanwhile, Hooper wrote Porter a letter, thanking him for his courteous treatment and agreeing to serve as a writer "expressly for the *Spirit.*" Editorially, he also thanked him "for the very complimentary notice of ourself and 'Simon Suggs' . . . . It is not the first time," he added, "that Mr. Porter has given us more by far, than our deserts; and we shall be glad to show our appreciation of his kind notices, at our earliest leisure."

Porter hastily announced with pride that he had engaged the author of these "sketches unsurpassed for their wit and humor" as an "occasional correspondent" and that readers of the *Spirit* and "the world of letters" had yet another "great treat in store for them . . . as great joy as that afforded to Pedro (in Cinderella) by the 'wonderful news' of the 'royal proclamation,' brought 'by royal post,' which was 'proclaimed about the city by sound of trumpet *and* drum.'" In short, Porter announced, Hooper had agreed to send him an original story, "Daddy Biggs's Scrape at Cockerell's Bend." "There won't be a button left on the jackets of the readers of the *Spirit,*" he added, "if we scare up many more correspondents like Hooper! Our private opinion is that the 'Spirit' can just naturally beat the world, in the way of correspondents! 'It takes us, and we can't hardly!'"[42]

Meanwhile, Hooper's fame spread across humor-loving America. Readers of the *Spirit* began to write in to ask for information about the new author and papers in all sections copied the Suggs yarns, prefixing such praise as this inelegant but typical example from the Nashville (Tennessee) *Daily Gazette*: "He is a rare genius—worth a horse-lot full of your common ladies books and gingerbread magazine 'contributors.'" The New Orleans *Picayune* referred to the stories as "worthy enough to take a man's life if laughing could bring about such consumption." The Carroll (Louisiana) *Watchman* declared: "We laughed so heartily on reading the following Alabama scene, and entered so fully into the spirit of the author, that, for once, our good humor entirely overcame our antipathy [for long articles and] we gave it to the compositors with directions to go the entire figure. If our readers enjoy its perusal half as much as we did they will not regret the space it occupies. Simon is 'some.'" And Porter himself recorded that "Hooper sketches of 'Simon Suggs,' etc., are the theme of unqualified praise all over the country."[43]

But Porter did more than praise his friend Hooper editorially. Realizing that he had "discovered" a yarn-spinner of rare ability, he stopped the presses, as it were, on *The Big Bear of Arkansas,* a volume of American humor he himself was at the time editing for Carey & Hart, Philadelphia publishers, in order to include one of Hooper's stories. Then he wrote to the same firm, urging them to get in directly behind Hooper to write a book of his own.

Both plans worked. When the *Big Bear* appeared in May 16, 1845, it contained twenty-one masterpieces by the best-known humorists in the country, all of which had previously appeared in the *Spirit,* including the title-story by Thomas Bangs Thorpe and Hooper's "How Simon Suggs Raised Jack," all fittingly illustrated by Felix Darley.[44] And in less than no time Carey & Hart had signed a contract with Hooper and set their type for a first edition of 3,000 copies of a book to be entitled *Some Adventures of Simon Suggs, Late Captain of the Tallapoosa Volunteers; Taking the Census; Daddy Biggs' Scrape at Cockerell's Bend; and Other Alabama Sketches.*[45]

Porter evidently took great pride in fostering Hooper.[46] On March 3 he wrote Carey & Hart, congratulating them on having made "an arrangement" with the author, adding "who knows but I may have been or be the means of making his 'fortune?' 'Tall oaks from little acorns grow, etc.'" He also thanked the publishers for their "offer of Hooper's sketches in advance." Ten days later he wrote again, saying "Lord bless him, he can have anything connected with the '*Spirit*', the editor included, if he wishes." Meanwhile, Porter apparently kept up a correspondence with Hooper also, urging him to keep to his pen—he was anxious, he wrote, to get advance chapters for printing in the *Spirit*.[47] On April 10 he begged Carey & Hart, "Do send me a chapter or two of Hooper. I have seen an intimate friend of his today very fortunately and learned 'a heap' of him which I will give you 'by word of mouth' as soon as I can have the pleasure of paying you my respects in person."[48]

Meanwhile, as promised, Hooper wrote Porter a letter, enclosing the new yarn, "Daddy Biggs's Scrape at Cockerell's Bend," which Porter jubilantly printed on March 11 under the heading, "Another Crack Original Story." "We have read nothing superior to it for many a day," Porter stated, "and doubt not our readers will agree with us in our estimate of the writer's extraordinary ability. His keen perception of the ludicrous and the comic, is only excelled by the facility with which he displays in bold relief, striking features in character of incident. His style is forcible, playful or ornate, by turns, and he possesses, in an eminent degree, the happy faculty of rendering his portraitures instinct with life . . . Daddy Biggs's *Scrape*' . . . will not 'set him back any' in general estimation, and like . . . other inimitable sketches by our correspondents at the South and South-West, will go the rounds of the press."[49]

Throughout the spring and early summer of 1845 Hooper kept constantly in touch with Porter and Carey & Hart and as the latter received a chapter of *Simon Suggs,* they would forword proofsheets on to the *Spirit*.[50] On May 17 Porter used "Simon Becomes Captain," and on July 19 "Captain Suggs and Lieutenant Snipes 'Court-Martial' Mrs. Haycock," in both instances acknowledging his indebtedness to Carey & Hart.[51] And from time to time Porter would pick up other editorials, notes and comments from the *East Alabamian,* giving them national publicity in the *Spirit.* Once, for example, he quoted Hooper as writing, "Divers applications having made to us for complete copies of 'Simon Suggs,' . . it is proper we should state that . . . we . . . have no complete copy, but 'Simon,' with some other sketches, in a small volume with illustrations, is probably out of press about this time." On another occasion, Hooper was quoted as saying that his copy of the *Big Bear of Arkansas* had arrived but "the 'boys' got it immediately, and since then I have been unable to recover it. *They* say 'it's a sight.' Suggs was sent a copy by Carey & Hart, which was opened . . . on the supposition that it was the Capting's own history . . . He is greatly pleased with the 'Bear' . . . "[52]

On July 19, 1845, Carey & Hart announced in a large advertisement in the *Spirit* that the first edition of *Some Adventures of Captain Simon Suggs, Late of the Tallapoosa Volunteers; Together with "Taking the Census" and Other Alabama Sketches,* would be published on July 30. Evidently, the plan did not materialize, however, for six weeks later the book had not yet appeared,[53] and it was not until September 20 that Porter was able to review it. "This is the best half dollars worth of genuine humor, ever enclosed between two covers!," he declared. "The writer is so well known to our readers as a correspondent, that we are confident there are very few of them who are not 'snatching and eager' to secure a copy. . . ."[54] His prediction was literally correct. "Who has got Simon Suggs?" asked the Montgomery (Alabama) *Journal.* "Two copies of the immortal Captain, in circulation here, have been read into lint and have vanished; not, however, until they had given some half hundred the side ache . . . it is impossible to find a copy in the South and West."[55] Up in New York *The*

Harbinger commended the volume to "all lovers of fun" as "a pleasing contrast to the crowd of shabby and worthless publications with which the literary world is infested," its humor "rich and genuine, and its scenes true to life."[56] Thomas Bangs Thorpe, editor of the New Orleans *Commercial Times* and author of "The Big Bear of Arkansas," found *Simon Suggs* not only humor of the "first order . . . and promise of great future excellence," but also evidence of Hooper's outstanding ability as writer on more serious themes. Comparing one of Hooper's sketches to the "Story of Litka and Her Lover" in *Inkle and Yarico*, he declared that "Mr. Hooper has written, evidently, very unconscious of his own ability, [combining] pathos along with the commonplace . . . *Simon Suggs* is a curious work, displaying much humor, and we doubt if any one could be more successful in portraying his character; but the episodes which occasionally show themselves in this volume, betray the genius which, if cultivated would attract lasting attention, and place Mr. Hooper among the first writers of our country."[57] Porter, continuing to ride the band-wagon of *Simon Suggs's* popularity, reprinted two chapters in one issue of the *Spirit*, "copied from Carey & Hart's new work, just published."[58] Meanwhile, Carey & Hart, sensing that their new title would enjoy great popularity, made plans for a second, larger edition and by late fall had an additional 5,000 copies in the presses.[59]

Amidst this national recognition which, it must be assumed, Hooper found not unappealing, he kept up his day-by-day writing for the *East Alabamian*, now and again exchanging editorial messages with Porter. His every movement seemed to have attracted attention: one "Reader" from Montgomery wrote to tell the *Spirit* that Hooper was planning a deer-hunting trip in Coosa County, another regretted that "an attack of 'dumb ague'" had prevented his participating, and yet another declared that the party did go and "killed seven deer."[60]

But Hooper was having troubles too. If he had had difficulty in earlier appeasing Bird H. Young, the prototype of Simon Suggs, he now embarrassingly encountered that gentleman again—this time on behalf of his wife. Under the simple caption, "Apology," Hooper publicly cleared himself thus: "We have received a letter from the individual who is generally considered to have been the original of 'Suggs,' requesting us to say . . . that no disrespect was intended to his wife, by the occasional mention of the name of 'Mrs. Suggs,' in the pamphlet. We certainly did intend none, and say so most willingly, for the lady referred to is highly respectable and estimable; and moreover, we doubt not that the captain has received as hard raps at home from his wild frolics, as ever he caught in 'Suggs,' or any where else."[61]

Then suddenly, for reasons one may only surmise, in the mid-summer of 1845 Hooper resigned his position on the La Fayette *East Alabamian* and moved fifty miles southwest, to Wetumpka, an ambitious little town near Montgomery,[62] to accept the editorship of the *Whig*, a new but "very capable paper, reflecting the highest credit on the country press of Alabama."[63] Whatever the motives behind his leaving may have been, the move most certainly reflected Hooper's personal interests.[64] At Wetumpka he was within fifteen miles of Montgomery, the new capital of Alabama, nearer than ever the center of the state's political arena—and into that arena he was soon to march, holding the Whig banner high.

CHAPTER FOUR

". . . a rough road to travel . . ."

"PLEASE SEND US the back numbers of the 'Whig' from the date you have been connected with it," Porter wrote Hooper early in September, 1845. "The first . . . we have received is that for the 2d inst."[1] A month later he quoted a lengthy *Whig* editorial in the *Spirit,* and in November again reminded his readers that the *Whig* "is now edited by the author of *Adventures of Simon Suggs.*"[2] Meantime, he continued to reprint chapters of *Simon Suggs,* to quote frequent favorable criticisms of the volume, and to maintain personal contact with Hooper by means of editorial questions and answers, as was the custom among the journalists of the day.[3] But no more original sketches of Hooper appeared, obviously indicating that the humorist was too deep in the routine duties of his new position in Wetumpka to devote time to creative work.

Simon Suggs, however, was still in demand the country over and Hooper continued to enjoy the fruits of his humor. Carey & Hart, with two editions of the little book behind them, in February, 1846, made plans for another—the third within ten months.[4] As a volume in the publishers' "American Works of Humor" Hooper's *Simon Suggs* was selling rapidly and being widely noticed, even in far-off St. Louis, where Joseph M. Field, editor of the *Reveille* and a humorist himself, wrote,

"The 'library' of Western life and fun which these gentlemen are now engaged in publishing, continues to grow in popularity with every issue; and their enterprise should be a sufficient challenge to other houses to come out and avail themselves of the material which so abundantly exists among us. Porter, Hooper, Thorpe, Sol Smith, Corcoran, 'Solitaire' [John S. Robb], and others, now busy, are but pioneers upon a road, the track of which bends through a region rich in romance and peculiar character.[5]"

But Porter was not yet happy. He was discontent to let his witty and competent friend Hooper rest on his laurels. "Why in the world doesn't he write more?" Porter asked editorially in the *Spirit*. "He has done nothing worthy of his reputation for months, that we have seen; it may be, though, that he is at work on some 'Sketches of the Alabama Legislature,' which were talked of last winter." Graciously, he added, "He has few equals in his peculiar style."[6] The prodding brought doubtful results: Hooper wrote Porter a long personal letter indicating that he would "be himself again soon," and the New Yorker hoped on the strength of this "to receive something from him equal to his "Daddy Biggs's Scrape at Cockerell's Bend.' "[7] Nothing, however, was forthcoming.

Hooper's failure to produce during this period was not a lack of energy. For at least two years prior to his resignation from the *East Alabamian* he had simultaneously been practicing law in Chambers County. Indeed, as late as the fall of 1845, when he accepted the editorship of the *Whig*, he had appeared in the Circuit Court there to defend a client.[8] Upon his transfer to Wetumpka, however, his law practice ceased and for a while he devoted his entire time to journalism. But not for long. For when the state legislature met in Tuscaloosa for the December-February, 1845-1846, session, Hooper was there, employed by W. C. Bibb as an "Assistant Engrossing Clerk" of the House of Representatives at "five dollars per diem . . . for the time during which . . . he continues to be employed."[9] It was during this fiery session that the moving of the capital from Tuscaloosa was so hotly concluded and the decision ultimately reached to transfer the seat of government to Montgomery.[10] On January 21 five commissioners were elected by the General Assembly to examine the newly built State House and to report to the Secretary of State whether it was "equal in every respect, if not superior, to the one now occupied." Hooper, though neither a legislator nor a senator, was honored by being selected as one of the examiners.[11] Meanwhile, he continued his editorship of the *Whig*, of course, reporting political events to his paper by mail.

After the legislature adjourned in early February, Hooper returned to Wetumpka, remained three months, abruptly tendered his resignation, moved with his family to Montgomery and become associate editor and part owner with John C. Bates and E. Sanford Sayre of the *Alabama Journal*, a powerful Whig organ and one of the oldest and best newspapers of the Southwest.[12]

Porter, obviously unconcerned about Hooper's political ambitions (the *Spirit* made no mention of his service as engrossing clerk or State House commissioner), was delighted with his transfer to the *Journal*. "Our old correspondent, J. J. Hooper, Esq.," he announced, "the author of 'Simon Suggs,' etc., has retired from the Wetumpka 'Whig,' and associated himself with our friends Bates and Sayre, of the 'Montgomery *[sic]* Journal.'" A few days later in the *Spirit* he re-printed the following "hint" from the *Journal*, undoubtedly written by Hooper himself: "The newly induced associate editor of the 'Journal' has not heretofore made his acknowledgement to his brethren of the press in this State and elsewhere, for the courteous and in many instances too flattering terms in which they have noticed his connection with this paper."[13] No mention was made by either editor of the important fact that the firm name of the *Alabama Journal* had now become "Bates, Hooper & Company, Editors and Proprietors," and that the humorist, after four years of valuable experience on the La Fayette *East Alabamian* and the Wetumpka *Whig*, had at last bought himself into partnership on one of Alabama's leading newspapers.[14]

During his two and a half years with the *Journal* Hooper was charged with varying responsibilities.[15] Almost from the beginning his activities consisted of such prosaic duties as purchasing a new printing machine, acquiring much-needed paper (which his friend Porter secured for him in New York on commission),[16] travelling about the state in search of subscribers and advertisements, and contributing column after column of monotonous political news and comments.[17] In December, 1846, he wrote Porter to ask if the *Spirit* would be interested in publishing an "original song . . . by the Hon. A. B. Meek, of Alabama, which [had been] respectfully dedicated to Mrs. J. J. Hooper, of Montgomery,"[18] and otherwise kept in touch with his patron. Once Porter obtained and sent to him "an exercise and three race saddles" and two suits of clothes, on other occasions the New Yorker acted as his agent for the purchase of books and other "packages," and at least once shipped the Alabamian a crate of fancier's breed fowls called Dorkings.[19] All the while Porter continued to encourage his friend to put his talents as humorist to work. The gifted Alabamian's failure to write more pieces like "Taking the Census" and the Simon Suggs yarns was to Porter positively unthinkable. "Hooper," he declared in the *Spirit* of April 10, 1847, "is 'held to answer' why he does not continue his inimitable sketches," and to a mutual friend in Montgomery, "An Old Subscriber," he addressed this public note: "Now that the author of 'Simon Suggs' has become a neighbor of yours, why don't you 'stir him up' for that new story?" And Samuel Lover, the Irish humorist, whom Hooper had met earlier, wrote, "Johnson J. Hooper *alias* Capt. Suggs . . . all luck say I to Johnson J. Hooper."[20]

But again Hooper was not idle. In the fall of 1847 he tried once again to get his old job back as engrossing clerk in the 1847-1848 session of the state legislature—"Principal Secretary" of the Senate was the exact title sought—but his Whig affiliations were apparently unacceptable to the Democrats.[21] The Wetumpka *State Guard,* however, approved his appointment by stating the "natural 'Simon Suggs' of Tallapoosa county is in the field. We are confident, that should it be the will of the Legislature to elect him, they will find 'Simon' 'one of 'em.' " W. C. Bibb, the chief engrossing clerk, he who had hired Hooper in 1845-1846, also rushed to his defense, claiming that Hooper's duties had once been "performed faithfully," that he could again serve successfully and that he had not attempted in any way "to deceive the Legislature in regards to his politics." In fact, Bibb added, in 1845-1846 "he was known to be a Whig out and out" and that his political affiliations had not prevented his doing a good job. But the Huntsville *Democrat* saw nothing good in either Hooper or Bibb. "Why all the fuss about Hooper's serving as Clerk?" Editor Woodson asked. "There might have been members of the Legislature, who were aware that J. J. Hooper was sailing, or rather scuttling under different colors than that of Wetumpka or Montgomery Whiggery, while he was counting the old lady's chickens in Tallapoosa county for a Democratic administration." But what of it? As far as the *Democrat* was concerned, neither of the men would get a job "higher that that of 'yardsweeper' in the next Legislature . . . and Bibb can 'rest at home' and Hooper retire 'beautifully-less' to the shades of the 'simmon trees of 'Noth Calina.' "[22]

During this time of political controversy and on through 1848 ill health and his travelling responsibilities had forced Hooper to spend more and more time away from the *Alabama*

Journal office, frequently out of Montgomery, rendering his connection with the paper "only nominal."[23] Then, too, he had other irons in the fire: creative writing, law, and politics. For neither could he find much time amid the hackwork and dull literary responsibilities of the *Journal.* On January 1, 1849, therefore, he resigned his position,[24] sold his interest, withdrew from the partnership of "Bates, Hooper & Co." and returned to La Fayette, in Chambers County, where seven years before he had begun his editorial career on John Gilbert's *East Alabamian.* Learning of Hooper's withdrawal, the editor of the Mobile *Register and Journal* declared: "[His] connection has been for sometime merely nominal. He would be a fine acquisition to any journal which could afford to compensate him for the employment of his whole time."[25]

Back in his old home town once more, Hooper immediately resumed the practice of law, advertising that he was available "in the courts of Chambers, and adjoining counties" for executing commissions or taking testimonies—his fees "per witness, if more than one, $2.50—if only one, $5.00."[26] And as a "side line," he announced, he had been persuaded by his erstwhile friend and partner, John C. Bates, to contribute by mail to the *Alabama Journal* a weekly column, called "Chambers Gossip," on whatever subjects his fancy directed. To a contemporary observer it must have seemed obvious that at last the author had got what he wanted: the law and leisure to "free lance" as he wished for one of the state's most widely read and reputable newspapers.

Once again, then, Hooper was back where he started, in La Fayette following his chosen professions. Yet this time he was a beginner in neither. His name, synonymous now with "Simon Suggs" was recognized the nation over—just a few months earlier, in the summer of 1848, a fourth edition of the book had been published by one of the nation's most highly respected book companies, Carey & Hart of Philadelphia.[27]

And as an ardent Whig and shrewd and witty attorney he was known from one corner of Alabama to another. Within a few months he was to capitalize on both reputations, the literary and the legal.

On January 23, 1849, the first "Chambers Gossip" column appeared in the *Alabama Journal,* dated La Fayette, January 19. Significantly enough, as will be later seen, it contained a long section on "The Judgeship of the 9th," and paragraphs on the "La Fayette Brànch Rail Road" and "The Next Legislature." A week later the "Chambers County Court" was described, on February 6 the "Circuit Judgeship of the 9th, and County Judgeship of Chambers," and on February 12 "The Judgeship Again." As weeks went by, practically every type of subject was covered by the "roving contributor"—railroads, duels, weather, political addresses, banks, faro, schools, murder cases, and women—some seriously, some humorously, but few so excellently as he was capable.[28] The author's loyal friend Porter evidently thought otherwise, however, for as the *Journal* began to print the "Gossip," so did the *Spirit* to reprint excerpts from it—such pieces as "An Alabama Lawyer," "The Elephant in La Fayette," "Captain Stick and Toney," and "Captain McSpadden, the Irish Gentleman in Purshute of a Schule." These sketches, Porter joyously stated, are from the pen of "the most graphic delineator of scenes in real life, J. J. Hooper, so favorable known as the 'Chicken Man of Alabama.'"[29] At last, Porter pondered, the humorist had again hit his stride.

Most heartening of all, however, was the fact that Hooper, now that he had more time for creative effort, was once more to contribute *directly* to the *Spirit.* "Our readers will be gratified to learn," Porter wrote on March 10, "that the author of 'Simon Suggs' has sent us that 'Muscadine Story,' which beats 'Daddy Biggs's Scrape at Cockerell's Bend.'"[30] Two weeks later the yarn, sub-titled "The Unwritten Chapter in the Biography of Captain Suggs," and "written for the *Spirit,*" appeared,[31] and immediately began to make the rounds of the newspapers and magazines.[32] Early in June Hooper penned another "dozen lines of nonsense" for Porter, entitled "A Veritable Mare's Nest," adding that he had recently tried his wings in Chambers County politics by suddenly running for the House of Representatives—but with no success. "I have a little item anent racing that my modesty *almost* forbids me to talk about," Hooper wrote. "This year the Whigs of the county determined to select their candidates by voting for them at a regular election, and just a week before the thing came off, your correspondent 'put his name in the pot.' Four were to be nominated for the House—ten in the field—here we go. For some time I didn't know anything, and when I did come to, found I was a *slow seventh!* Reason—*'too d---d knowin' about Suggs to be honest himself!'* . . . after all, there is but little harm done."[33]

Unsuccessful in his trial flight into politics, throughout the summer of 1849 Hooper continued his weekly "Gossip" column for the *Journal* and practiced law in and about Chambers and the adjoining counties—one of the state's strong Whig areas. Apparently, he was leaving no stone unturned in his effort to ingratiate himself into the good legal and political graces of his community. Then, again suddenly, his plans changed almost overnight and once more he pulled up an editor's chair.

On Sunday, August 19, 1849, as usual he sent from La Fayette the twenty-second weekly number of his "Chambers Gossip" to Bates, a long *pot pourri* about Chambers County conditions which contained the significant information that his old friend Joseph A. Holifield and [?] Williams, "a practical printer," had purchased the La Fayette *Sun,* a local weekly, changed the name to *Chambers County Tribune* and employed him as editor. "Perhaps you haven't heard," the columnist continued, "that next Friday week [September 1], there will be issued at this place the first number of a new [Zachary] Taylor paper, to be called the 'Chambers Tribune' . . . [the owners] have capital to sustain the new paper for the first year or two; and, doubtless, after that, it will be about to 'stand alone.' 'This infortunate' will be, until better can be done, the editor of the 'Tribune.' That will not, however, interfere with his weekly 'inflections' upon your readers."[34] Two weeks later Bates acknowledged receipt of the first two numbers of the new paper, "edited by our old ally and *fidus*, Hooper, of La Fayette," adding that "to say it is 'rich, rare and racy,' is but faint praise. It could of course, in such hands, be 'nothing else.' We trust that this new attempt to establish a Whig paper in the strong Whig county of Chambers will be amply sustained. The spirited Whigs there cannot fail to see its importance to the party."[35]

Within a month after the beginning of the *Tribune* and in spite of his statement to the contrary, Hooper discontinued his "Gossip" column for the *Journal*,[36] and began earnestly to apply his talents to his own paper, to writing and to politics—thus again riding his favorite horses.[37] For the *Tribune* he wrote such sketches as "More Silence," "The Widow Rugby's Husband," "An Editor Off His Foot," "In a Disagreeable Fix,' and "Jim Wilkins and the Editors.'"[38] To the *Spirit* he contributed "The Res Gestae a Poor Joke," which Porter proudly announced as "an original contribution by the author of 'Simon Suggs.'"[39] And for the first time he sent original pieces to the new *Daily Delta* of New Orleans: "Dick McCoy's Sketches of His Neighbors," the famous "A Night at the Ugly Man's," and "Col. Hawkins and the Court."[40]

As if all this were not enough to keep him busy, in early October he announced himself a candidate for the solicitorship of the Ninth Circuit, consisting of six East Alabama counties, contracted with M. D. J. Slade, a Tuscaloosa printer, for the publication of his forthcoming new book to be entitled *A Ride With Old Kit Kuncker and Other Sketches,* and became the father of a second son, Adolphus Sanford, who was born on the twenty-ninth of the month.

The Ninth Judicial Circuit—better known as the "Bloody Ninth"—comprised the counties of Chambers, Macon, Randolph, Russell, Talladega and Tallapoosa, all new, having been but a few short years earlier Muscogee Indian territory. Against Hooper in the race for the four-year term as solicitor were four competitors, at least two of whom were or were later to become quite prominent men, Milton S. Latham of Russell and Alexander W. Bowie of Talladega. Latham, who moved to the West Coast in the early '50's, was there elected a state congressman, governor of California, and in 1860 to a six-year term as United States senator.[41] Bowie, a graduate of the University of South Carolina, was a distinguished Alabama state legislator and attorney, a trustee of the University of Alabama, and for several years "presided on the Chancery bench" of the state. He was widely known for his "graceful elocution, independent judgement, and scholarly attainments."[42] "You know, I believe," Hooper wrote on October 7, 1849, to his brother-in-law, Alsea K. Brantley, who was living in Arkansas, "that I am running before the Legislature for the solicitorship of this Circuit. I consider my chances very good, as several leading Democratic members are going to vote for me. If I am beat, however, I shall come out among you some where, as soon thereafter as I can 'raise the wind.'"[43]

Upon a joint ballot of the Senate and House Hooper defeated his opponents handily in the November elections,[44] and soon thereafter began his duties around the circuit, representing Alabama as prosecutor in all legal matters in which the state was concerned—at an annual salary of $1500, plus such fees as were "allowed by law."[45] During court seasons he rode on horseback from county seat to county seat, La Fayette in Chambers,[46] Tuskegee in Macon, Wedowee in

Randolph, Crawford in Russell, Talladega in Talladega, and Dadeville in Tallapoosa, a round robin distance of approximately 160 miles, trying cases for "murder, arson, burglary, . . . gaming, retailing liquor without license, adultery, and so forth."[47] Most prolific were cases of "assault and batteries, assaults with intent to murder—[and] (sometimes the intent was executed!)"[48] In all the counties of the circuit Hooper's prowess as a wit and humorist was well known and in two of them he had lived and worked—Chambers and Tallapoosa.

While in Dadeville, the seat of the latter county and, it will be recalled, the home of Bird H. Young, the prototype of "Simon Suggs," Hooper lived at the Union Hotel,[49] and held court in the small, two-story, four-room brick-and-log Court House built atop a "Dungeon room . . . eleven feet by fifteen feet made secure with Iron . . . ."[50] And in Russell County he frequently stayed at his brother's home, visiting him and their mother and father, who had moved to Alabama from North Carolina in 1849 to be with the older son, George, then a prominent attorney in the town of Crawford.[51]

As solicitor of the "Bloody Ninth" Hooper, as he later declared, "had a rough road to travel." The people of this region of Alabama were for the most part unrefined, difficult, impudent and in spite of the "law and testimony" were rascally, ingenious and subject to "devilish device [to] clear the well-arranged meshes of legislative enactments." His predecessors had helped the situation little. "They had, in 'tender commisseration' of the *freshness* of the country . . . ," Hooper wrote, "exhibited great leniency towards those who claimed to be arraigned for mere misdemeanors . . . . In truth, the Judges themselves liked toddy, and whist, *per se,* and did not perceive that the flavour of the one was regulated by the legal competency of the vender."[52] To make matters worse, he admitted, he was but "a novice in the prosecuting line."

Nevertheless, his experiences on the circuit supplied him

with rich material for his pen and enabled him to improve his financial condition considerably. So much so, in fact, that within a year he was able to buy half interest in the *Chambers Tribune* (which during his term of solicitorship he continued to edit),[53] and in so doing to form a long-lasting partnership with Joseph A. Holifield, the man with whom four years later he was to move to Montgomery and begin the greatest newspaper venture of his life.[55]

During October and November, 1849, in the midst of his election campaign for the judgeship, Hooper was simultaneously preparing copy for his new book, *A Ride with Old Kit Kuncker,* sending chapter by chapter to Slade, the Tuscaloosa publisher. In December the volume was issued, a thin, paper-backed brochure of 120 pages containing, besides the title yarn (which was sub-titled "Part Third of 'Taking the Census' "), "The Muscadine Story" (sub-titled "The Unwritten Chapter in the Biography of 'Captain Suggs' "), "The Widow Rugby's Husband" ("Another Story of 'Suggs' "), copied from the Cincinnati *Great West,* and nineteen other stories and sketches of varying length.[55] Three of the stories ("Colonel Hawkins and the Court," "A Night at the Ugly Man's," and "Dick McCoy's Sketches of His Neighbors") were credited to the New Orleans *Delta,* two ("An Involuntary Member of the 'Temperance Society' " and "An Alligator Story") to the *Alabama Journal,* and one ("Captain McSpadden") to the *Spirit of the Times.* "Jim Wilkins and the Editors" and "Montgomery Characters" were reportedly copied from the *Chambers Tribune,* but for the others no source was indicated. Except for "Our Granny" and "The Good Muggins," both labeled "original," they doubtless also were first printed in Hooper's own paper. The *Alabama Journal* stated the *Ride* "embraces within its covers as much hearty, genuine humor as would have made the reputation of a dozen sketch-writers . . . . Hooper's writings have been read with delight by thousands of the purest and most cultivated intellects of the land. . . . 'Simon Suggs,' alone, passed through eight editions, and was read by immense numbers." Replying to the Mobile *Tribune,* which had accused Hooper of inelegant language, the *Journal* added, "Hooper, in the language which he puts occasionally in the mouths of some of his characters, may have been more faithful to nature than many approve— perhaps, in some instances, to a fault; but these are minor defects which do not dim the acknowledged and transcendent merits of most of the descriptions . . . we know of no writer with more ability to draw deeply and use effectually from the 'pure well of English undefiled.' "[56]

Of greater significance is the fact that the author "respectfully inscribed" the volume of humorous sketches to "his friend" the Honorable Alexander B. Meek, "Alabama's leading man of letters in the antebellum period," editor, poet, and historian.[57] It must be added, however, that Hooper was evidently not ungrateful for the poet's earlier dedication of his "The Rose of Alabama" to Mrs. Hooper, "the accomplished lady of our occasional correspondent, the author of 'Capt. Simon Suggs.' "[58]

The faithful Porter, always glad to foster Hooper's talents, gave *A Ride with Old Kit Kuncker* national publicity in the *Spirit* by immediately reprinting "Jim Wilkins and the Editors," "A Ride with Old Kit Kuncker," "The Erasive Soap Man," "Our Granny," "The Colonel," and "Jim Bell's Revenge" (under the title, "Fun on the Circuit"),[59] and by advertising the volume as "mailable, and can be had by enclosing half a dollar (post paid) to M. D. J. Slade, Tuscaloosa, Alabama."[60] He also went back in the files of the *Spirit,* unearthed and reprinted the first part of Hooper's "Taking the Census," which had first appeared on September 9, 1843, seven years before.[61] And not yet satisfied, Porter copied from the Augusta (Georgia) *Republic* (which had in turn copied from the *Alabama Journal*) a lengthy, unflattering and humorous personal description of Hooper, written by one of his friends, signed "Big Ugly." Grasping the opportunity to tease his friend into productivity, Porter prefaced the thumbnail sketch with a challenge to Hooper to come to his own defence, permitting "neither an 'especial ally' nor any body else to take such liberties with [your] physiognomy or corporsity. No person should with 'malice afore-thought' talk thus about [your] peculiar features. You must speak out, friend Jonce. We shall give you one month to show cause why you are not as thus represented, and, if in this time you do not plead 'Not Guilty,' we shall send the description to Barnum. 'The Philistines' will then be upon you."[62]

Hooper, meantime, continued to ride the "Bloody Ninth" and to edit the *Tribune*, as time would allow,[63] making his home in La Fayette with his wife and two sons.[64] As the nationally-known author of two humorous volumes, a successful editor, a state solicitor and an ardent local attorney and politician,[65] he had come a long way in the fifteen years he had lived in Alabama—and he was still a young man, only thirty-five. *Simon Suggs* was at its popularity peak. A fifth edition of 1,000 copies had been issued in March, 1850, by A. Hart,[66] successor to Carey & Hart, and six months later a sixth, of another 1,000.[67] Two publishers, Getz & Buck of Philadelphia and Stringer & Townsend of New York, had in 1851, doubtless with permission of Hart, simultaneously "collected and formed into a handsome little book" an illustrated edition of the stories, entitled *Some Adventures of Simon Suggs*, and the following year Getz & Buck had issued yet another edition.[68] *A Ride with Old Kit Kuncker* was being quoted across the nation and already A. Hart had contracted to republish Slade's Tuscaloosa volume in Philadelphia, under the new title, *The Widow Rugby's Husband*.[69] Excerpts from it and from *Simon Suggs* were still going the rounds of the newspapers,[70] occasional pieces were appearing in widely distributed magazines,[71] and in *Polly Peablossom's Wedding,* a collection of notable humorous stories itself dedicated to Hooper "as a Token of Respect, and a Slight return for the many favors which the editor is proud to acknowledge at his hands," and edited by Thomas A. Burke, one of Hooper's own yarns was included—"Shifting the Responsibility—A Hard Shell Story," which had originally appeared (unsigned) in the *Spirit* a few weeks earlier.[72] And shortly he was to see his own humorous Simon Suggs given even further notoriety in "Simon Suggs, Jr., Esq., a Legal Biography" in *Flush Times in Alabama and Mississippi,* by the renowned Joseph G. Baldwin.[73]

Meanwhile, Hooper himself was noted in the local press, wherever he went. "It is a matter of congratulation to his many friends, to see our old friend and ally, Jonce, of the 'Tribune,' down here on a visit," stated the *Alabama Journal,* "after having accepted the perils [of] field, flood and fire in the 'Bloody Ninth,' and with whole bones, as large as life, and much more natural."[74] Earlier the editor of the *Macon Republican* (Tuskegee) had written "Jonce Hooper is about some this week, and, if Big Ugly's description of him was correct, he has improved upwards of considerable. Both his shoes are now blacked every morning, one or the other of them is tied semi-occasionally, and we never see more than one or two pieces of tape hanging about his heels at a time . . . . In a word, Jonce is playing gentleman and Solicitor about this time with remarkable success, and we advise the b'hoys to look out, for he is after them with a 'sharp stick.' "[75]

Hooper, now enjoying the well-earned prestige of his position and sufficient income for a more comfortable life,[76] turned his attention to the great outdoors. In the winter of 1852 he asked his friend Porter to order for him from London a "9 bore double Gun . . . 40 inches in the barrel," suitable for "bird shooting . . . , $95." A year later he ordered another, "made to order" in New York for $150, and a bird dog, "a well-broken Pointer or Setter," at $75.[77] By July, 1853, his enthusiasm for hunting had encouraged him to question whether Porter would be interested in printing a series called "Suggestions to Sportsmen." "For some little time I have been thinking that, if it pleased you, I would undertake to furnish for your columns, at *slightly* irregular intervals, such notes of birds, beast, and men, in this region, as might seem worthy of preservation . . . down 'pon de branch!'" The letter was signed "*Number Eight*"—Hooper's first use of a pseudonym,[78] (the source of which he failed to clarify until six months later, after his defeat for reelection to the solicitorship of the Ninth District): "Since I have lost the number of my mess (Circuit) and can no longer write myself of the 'Ninth,'" he informed Porter, "perhaps I shall oftener have occasion to subscribe myself, Yours truly, *Number Eight*"[79] Porter apparently had no objections and Hooper supplied the *Spirit* with quite infrequent hunting stories during the next several months, all written over his new pen-name.[80] Porter, obviously not too pleased with these sporting anecdotes, reached back into the files of the *Spirit* and reprinted "A Visit to the Ugly Man's," which had first appeared four years earlier.[81]

Late in 1853, as his four-year term as solicitor drew to an end,[82] Hooper began to make plans for reelection by visiting the Capitol "to learn the state of matters for himself." The usual fall term of court in Tallapoosa County was thus dismissed, and Hooper took temporary leave of the editorship of the *Chambers Tribune* in order to devote more time to politics during the potboiling season.[83] The *Alabama Journal* had several weeks earlier announced that Holifield and Hooper had sold out their paper to Phillips and Prather, practical printers of La Fayette.[84] Hooper, however, obviously continued as contributing editor, for in November J. C. Bates wrote: "We had the pleasure of seeing for several days our old friend and 'fides Hooper of the Bloody 9th.' He was in tolerable health though somewhat worn by the fatigues of the circuit. Though we have not been able exactly of late years to trace our old confrere's position in politics, we know him to be the same, genuine hearted—unchanged and unchangeable as ever. In the absence of the usual court in Tallapoosa Hooper took the opportunity to make a trip down here for a few days, to learn the state of matters for himself. He gives in the last *Tribune* some of the results of his observations . . . ."[85]

But Hooper's success as lawyer, editor, humorist and staunch Whig, all of which had stood him in such good stead in 1849, did not carry over to the campaign for reelection. In the fall of 1853 he was summarily defeated for the solicitorship of the Ninth District by John Jefferson Woodward, a lawyer of Talladega, erstwhile member of the House of Representatives (1847-1849), editor of the newspaper, *Democratic Watchtower,* and a "high-toned" gentleman of much "legislative capacity."[86] Hooper explained his defeat by saying that he was on the wrong side of the political fence, "while Judge Woodward was a prominent member of the dominant party, backed by extensive and influential family connections." Even as a Whig, however, he admitted, he was not a "a 'good' Whig. According to the latest test, *I am not.* But I do entertain and cherish the sentiments of the *Clay Whig* Party, and I have no concealments about what I approve or condemn . . ."[87]

Be that as it may, at the year's end Hooper went back to La Fayette to take up again the full editorial responsibilities of the *Chambers Tribune* and to plan for the future. His return to the paper he humorously and boldly heralded: "*Cirkelate! Cirkelate!* The subscriber has agreed with the publisher of the 'Tribune' to act as its editor, and on consideration of the arduous labors and momentous responsibilities of that position, he becomes entitled to a considerable portion of the funds arising from *new* subscriptions. To those, therefore, of his friends who would like to see his rations increased, he would exclaim in the pointed language of the lamented Wagstaff—'cirkelate! cirkelate!' . . . Letters containing remittances for *new* subscriptions (except for Chambers County) may be addressed to the subscriber, who will take especial pleasure in pocketing the contest."[88]

During the next two or three months Hooper edited the hebdomadal with marked success, contributing such humorous pieces as "The Speatch of Mr. Twyster, of Bunkum, Alabama, on Stait Ade," and short sketches.[89] Early in March, however, word was going the rounds that he was quitting the *Tribune* and moving back to the capital of the state to commence a new paper, this time, his own, to be called the Montgomery *Mail*. "We hope that [Hooper's] *Mail* will not be so slow, irregular, and inefficient, as Uncle Sam's is under the management of Mr. Postmaster Campbell," opined the *Macon Republican* of Tuskegee,[90] and the *Dallas* (Alabama) *Gazette* credited the forthcoming new sheet as "Simon Suggs' . . . literary and family paper at Montgomery."[91] Hooper himself wrote his sister-in-law, Sarah Brantley, that he recently had been passing through an interval 'of much pressure and anxiety . . . on account of the unforseen delays in getting out my paper—which, however, will be issued next Wednesday [April 12] after a vast deal of trouble and perplexity to all concerned . . . I can never write you a very long [letter], because I am written to death, Joe [Joseph A. Holifield] leaving all the business correspondence on my hands."[92]

Hooper was not too busy, however, to write his friend Porter about his new venture and to ask that the *Mail* be put on the *Spirit's* mailing list—the need for frequent use of scissors and paste might be urgent. Porter replied that he would not only send "a copy to the 'M.M.'" but that he would also mail one to Hooper personally, "for your private tooth."[93]

Thus, in the spring of 1854, Hooper moved again to Montgomery to shoulder the heaviest editorial responsibility of his career. At thirty-nine, he was already Alabama's best-known newspaperman, a fearless political writer, an ex-judge of the Circuit Court, and a humorist whose Simon Suggs was a household word across the nation. Everything indeed, augured well for the success of the Montgomery *Mail* and its distinguished editor.

CHAPTER FIVE

". . . *dead—as dead as a mackerel . . .*"

AT THE TUMULTUOUS Baltimore convention of 1852, when the pro- and anti-slavery delegates came to a final parting of the ways, the death warrant of the American Whig party was finally signed.[1] The beginning of the end had indeed long been foreseen. Hooper himself, who had tenaciously clung to Whiggery since his arrival in Alabama in 1835, realized early that a common denominator of understanding between the Southern and Northern factions could never be reached. In 1851 he had publicly declared his party "dead—as dead as a mackerel!," adding that within a year it would be difficult to find "a specimen of the Whig family" in the state or nation.[2] His prediction, though somewhat exaggerated, in essence proved true.

For a time hope had been held out for a peaceful settlement of the burning slavery question under terms of the Compromise of 1850, but when this last chance failed and the Whig party all but collapsed in 1854, the abolitionists of the North sought refuge in the Republican party while the "slavers" of the South, bitter and frustrated, made common cause, sooner or later and in one way or another, with their arch rivals, the Democrats. For the Southern group this was a most embarrassing, uncertain, and bewildering period. Many a Whig accepted willingly the principles of the States

Rights wing of the Democratic party and some few aligned themselves with the Union Democrats. Others were of course driven willy-nilly to the decision. But the majority, unready yet so soon to cooperate with their long-time opponents, slowly drifted into the new American or "Know Nothing" party, which first became evident in Alabama politics in 1854. Then, too, there was a minority who in effect saw equal or no good in either and for the nonce elected to remain independent of all party affiliations.

Of these last-named, political "free thinkers" and middle-of-the-road mavericks, Hooper was one. Thus, on Thursday, April 13, 1854, when the first issue of his Montgomery *Weekly Mail* appeared, it announced no adherence to any party, proclaiming, rather, that "independence" lay in prudence, that one should look cautiously before he leapt.[3]

Although the *Mail* was often referred to as "Hooper's paper," it was in its earliest months actually not that at all. The humorist was indeed "Principal Editor," but ownership was vested in the hands of "Joseph A. Holifield & Co." – Holifield, Hooper, and a third proprietor, doubtless the printer, P. A. Knight. With Holifield, it will be remembered, Hooper had formerly been associated as co-owner of the *Chambers Tribune,* and it was together that they had moved to Montgomery to establish the *Mail.* Since Hooper editorially referred to his partner as "the Senior," designating himself consistently as "the Junior," it is likely that Holifield owned controlling interest in the company at its beginning. Of some significance also is the fact that Holifield was able to bring his wife to Montgomery with him and take in Hooper as a boarder. Mrs. Hooper and the two boys, Will and Adolph, meanwhile, remained temporarily in La Fayette. By late summer the family was together again, however, and on November 30, 1854, Hooper and his wife had their sons baptized in Montgomery's St. Johns Episcopal Church by Bishop Nicholas H. Cobbs.[4]

For twelve years—since 1842, when he had begun his editorial career on the *East Alabamian*, and throughout his service on the Wetumpka *Whig*, the *Alabama Journal* and the *Chambers Tribune*—Hooper had been everywhere identified as a rabid Whig. By the Democrats he had been severely condemned as a Whig for obtaining the position of engrossing clerk in the Democratic legislature of 1845-1846, and again for trying to repeat the process two years later. As a Whig he had been elected solicitor of the "Bloody Ninth" in 1849. It was also a well-known fact that his father-in-law, Green D. Brantley, had served two terms as a Whig congressman from Chambers County. Thus was it not easy, therefore, for Hooper to sever associations so quickly and easily by simply proclaiming from the masthead of the new *Mail* that he was an "Independent," especially when his principal rivals in Montgomery, the *Journal* (edited by his erstwhile "friend and 'fides' ", John C. Bates) and the *Advertiser* (edited by P. H. Brittan, who had once worked on the *Chambers Tribune*), delighted in frequently reminding their readers of Hooper's first love.

In addition, Hooper and his partners were experiencing a hard time financially. The *Mail's* competitors were old, established papers and in Montgomery, a county of but 11,000 white citizens, it was obviously difficult for three major newspapers to flourish.[5] For several months, however, everything apparently went smoothly along, thanks to Hooper's pen, and the *Mail* continued to gain in prestige and patronage, receiving contributions from such writers as Joseph G. Baldwin, author of *Flush Times in Alabama and Mississippi.*[6] On June 10, two months following the beginning of the *Weekly Mail*, the owners, in an attempt to give their patrons more frequent coverage of the news, inaugurated a *Tri-Weekly Mail,* which was published on Tuesday, Thursday, and Saturday.[7] Besides writing many political essays, Hooper livened both papers with humorous sketches for which he was famous—such pieces as "An Irish Demurrer," "A Very Slight Difference," "Fluttering," "Cut Loose Again, Mister," "From 'A' to 'Ampezant,'" "A Sharper Meeting One Keener," and "The Distinguished Dan Hickok of New Orleans," all of which were immediately copied and given national distribution by Porter's *Spirit.*[8] It must have been heartening indeed for the struggling editor to come upon such praise as was recorded him in the Macon *Republican*: "[The *Mail*] is a handsome sheet, tastefully gotten up, and its matter, original and selected, admirable. We have no doubt that there is room in Montgomery for just such a paper as the 'Mail,' and Hooper and his partner are just the men to fill it. We wish them abundant success."[9] Even dignified *Harper's Magazine,* copying a piece called "Sloshin' About," declared, "the Montgomery (Alabama) Mail, seems to have a fund of humor on hand, and gives occasionally a Southwestern sketch by a few touches, that are as telling as Hogarth's."[10]

In the early fall of 1854, however, misfortune struck Montgomery in the form of a yellow fever epidemic and the *Mail,* which had been in business but six months, was forced to cease publication temporarily, missing four weekly and twelve tri-weekly issues.[11] Hooper himself went down with the disease, though his attack was evidently mild. "We are rejoiced," exclaimed the Cassville (Georgia) *Standard* in November, "to know that our beau ideal of a first rate editor, *Jonce* Hooper, is at his post again. The yellow fever may have frightened him pretty badly, but it hasn't *scared* all the fun out of him, by a jug full, for the last number of his paper is running over with good things. We have marked a 'lot of 'em' for speedy insertion."[12]

By mid-November the *Weekly Mail* and the *Tri-Weekly Mail* had so prospered as to encourage their publishers also to launch a *Daily Mail,* the first issue of which appeared on the sixteenth.[13] It too was an "Independent Paper"—". . . a beautiful sheet," announced the Macon *Republican* . . . "which we hope will fully remunerate the outlay which it must have cost. The 'Mail' promises to be an excellent business and commercial sheet, as well as a valuable news, literary, and miscellaneous paper."[14] "We see that the Mail is now published *daily* as well as weekly," the Cassville *Standard* added. "Well, we don't wonder at it, for we can't very well see how *Jonce's* subscribers could do without a *daily mail,* when he has the job of making it up."[15] Hooper was "Principal Editor" of the daily, the tri-weekly and the weekly and as such he plunged headlong into the task of keeping his readers informed and amused. At least one short "funny" story or sketch appeared daily,[16] though it was apparent that "the Junior's" time was being more and more consumed by politics, Montgomery theatricals, literary societies and other local news items and hack-work, and that by contrast the standard of his humor was far below that of former days.[17]

To contemporary journalists it must have been apparent that, so recently a strong Whig editorialist, Hooper was now purposely avoiding an alignment with any party, though certainly they could not have doubted his political bent. Always a "zealous unionist . . . brought to the love of the Union, and to revere the wisdom which founded it," he foresaw only doom for the South at the hands of the "Northern States." He repeatedly called on his readers to stand as one man, "not on this or that palliative measure . . . but on the amplest recognition of every right to which we are entitled." Any other action simply invited defeat. "That we have suffered wrong for many years forms no reason that we should suffer it longer—especially at the hands of those who rate negroes higher than white people. The only hope of peace—of salvation—to the South, is to insist with the most determined earnestness on terms of perfect equality." "We need fresh, vigorous, determined minds, free from all aspirations beyond those they breathe for the safety of the South, and perfectly unclogged by past events and associations," he declared. "We speak thus of the duty of Southern Whigs, being members of no party ourselves, because we believe we indicate the true course for the good of the country. If the Southern Whig party should so act, it will drive their opponents . . . in that direction, to a similar course. The result would be a Southern phalanx . . . of both parties, that would work harmoniously on the slavery question, and in whose custody our section might safely leave the direction of its destiny." Two weeks later this was followed by a forthright and frank essay on the freedom of the press, entitled "Against Gagging." And two days following he repeated that the *Mail* was an "INDEPENDENT PAPER," adding that "its editors" had not supported Whig Winfield Scott in the 1852 presidential election and now see "precious little in the administration of [Franklin] Pierce on which to found a hope for the South." Moreover, he concluded, "[We] believe the best thing that could happen for the South would be a complete dissolution of both parties." Meanwhile, it was obvious that he was being slowly attracted to the "Know Nothing" party, though he most positively abhorred that body's attitudes toward religion: "As far as the feature of religious intolerance, charged against the order is concerned, we have regarded it, *if true*, as a very strong point of objection . . . If there be any religious test in this order of know-nothings, it ought to be abolished."[18]

Throughout these early months of the *Mail*, if Hooper failed to support a party, he was not reluctant to support his region. Everything "Southern" was of the best. The recently revived "Montgomery Literary Society" was beyond reproach. *Alone*, by Marion Harland, was reviewed flatteringly as a great "SOUTHERN NOVEL." "Mr. Crisp and his Talented Company" were making theatrical history in Montgomery's "Concert Hall." Professor Michael Tuomey, the state geologist, was given full columns to explain in detail the possibilities of "Copper in Alabama."[19] Nothing Southern was second rate. He advocated more manufactories, exports, educational institutions and railroads for Alabama, adding prophetically that the state's "imbedded minerals" alone would pay for the last.[20] Keenly aware of the need for a peaceful solution of the problems facing the South, Hooper nevertheless saw clearly the dangers that lay ahead—but at all costs, he wrote, "*peace we must have.*" As he had been for years he was yet a firm advocate of the Union. "The Masses of abolition are moving forward to attack us," he declared. "It is weakness and childish folly to talk longer of any hope outside ourselves. Upon this earth *there is none.* We must meet the foe. We must conquer a peace .... By firmness, by union, by preparation, we shall defend ourselves from utter ruin; and in them, is the only hope of preserving this Union. Vacillation, division, apathy, cowardice, will make it more difficult to preserve ourselves—they shall not add a year to the existence of the Union."[21] And then, wearily and as a bitter after-thought: "Whether we shall see a better state of things we know not; but our present dependence on the North is most degrading."[22]

In January, 1855, Hooper, no longer able to pursue his fence-straddling political policy, removed the words "Independent Paper" from the *Mail's* masthead and publicly announced his support of Robert A. Baker, "State Aid" Democrat from Mobile, for governor of Alabama, against John A. Winston, candidate of the Union Democrats, and for Thomas H. Watts, of Montgomery, for congressman from the Third District.[23] Watts "*is the man for the times,*" the editor wrote. Within ten days, however, he was off for Mobile to attend the first state convention of the American or "Know Nothing" party, reporting to his paper on varied political activities as well as on the theatre, commerce, and civic matters in the seaport city.[24] Evidently impressed by the "Know Nothing" platform,[25] but still vacillating, he returned home, made a "flying visit" to Atlanta ("ten years hence," he predicted, "it will be the great city of Georgia; no man need doubt that"),[26] spent his energies largely on non-political matters (such as, the fostering of Professor F. A. P. Barnard for presidency of the University of Alabama),[27] and in acknowledging the favorable reception being tendered his editorial efforts by a grateful public.[28] Meanwhile, his enthusiasm for Democrat Baker waned, and on June 7, even though the candidate's name still streamed from the *Daily Mail's* editorial page, Hooper penned a long, highly favorable sketch of "Know Nothing" George D. Shortridge, of Shelby, saying that he "is perhaps the more spoken of, now, than anyone else . . . The Judge is pretty well known as a *State Aid* man . . ." A week later the "Know Nothings" assembled for another convention in Montgomery—one hundred and fifty delegates, two-thirds of whom were known to have been former Whigs,[29] meeting behind closed doors—and nominated Shortridge as the American candidate for governor.

At last Hooper had unaffectedly made up his mind. The day the "Know Nothings" convened he came forth with a second strong editorial favoring Shortridge, declaring him a "State Aid and a strong Temperance man." The next day he printed the entire "American" platform in the *Daily Mail* and ran down the name of Robert A. Baker, whom he had been supporting for more than a half-year. It was not until June 22, however, that the name of Shortridge was "run up" on the paper: "We think *on the whole* [Shortridge] is a little more liberal in his views in regard State Aid, than his opponent," Hooper cautiously declared. "If we cannot get a whole loaf, we will e'en try to get a half one!" Three days later he added, "We have not hoisted the name of Shortridge as readily as we would have done, had his ideas of *State Aid* been less restricted . . . . He does not go *far* enough to suit our ideas; but we believe that he is more likely to do *something* for progress, than Governor Winston."[30] Shortridge and Watts, both "Know Nothing" candidates, were from that day "Hooper's men."[31]

However, avowedly a "Know Nothing," at heart Hooper was during the mid-1850's merely what he had always been—a "Southern Rights" advocate. From "our youth up," as he put it, he had supported Union organizations, but "Southern Patriotism" was the core of his philosophy. Thus did the *Mail* slowly become the state's most prominent newspaper of the Southern Rights wing of the "Know Nothing" party and as such was a powerful anti-Democratic influence from 1855 to the Civil War.

Regardless of party terminology, however, Hooper's political affiliations were weighed principally in terms of "saving" the South. That philosophy he clung to tenaciously. Whatever candidate he supported, all extraneous principles were sloughed off to clear the view of his region's betterment. As he himself wrote, "Everything in Subordination to the Rights of the South."[32] Although the *Mail* was only a year old, it had but one chief political idea behind it: unity of action in the South. Time had strengthened this conviction. "We must look abolitionism in the face. We want people to curse, in their hearts, all those party combinations for spoils, which in turn, *practically* whatever may be their theories, have contributed to lessen the power and degrade the political condition of the South. The South must throw *Whig* and *Democratic* views and politics to the winds, and ask themselves what are *their rights* boldly, and maintain them."[33] Hooper saw no hope for the South in the "Bogus Democrats."[34] In the "Know Nothing" party there was, he believed, not the whole answer to the South's problems, to be sure, but a partial one which, as he wrote, was better than none at all. Thus, in July, after the political conventions of 1855 were over, he could safely write, "The whig masses, as well as the democratic masses, have responded nobly to the call to form the *people's party.* Of the young, active, States'-Rights democracy, the order in Alabama has the very flower. [The American Party] is *the Only True Southern Party in Alabama.*"[35]

Had the elections been held in June or July, Hooper's party might possibly have won. As it was, throughout the heat of the summer and the campaign, the Democratic presses, especially Brittan's *Advertiser,* gave wide publicity to the alleged "oath-bound, dark-lantern, clap-trap, hypocritical, truth-sketching, abolition-hatched" policies of the "Know Nothings," stressed their secrecy and spying, and their anti-Catholicism, attacked their candiate, Shortridge, for illegal use of State Bank money, and in general so confused the issues as almost completely to put the American papers on the defensive. Much space was spent by them in denying that their new party was not merely the "Old Whig party in disguise." In Mobile a secret society called the "Sag Nichts" was organized to oppose the "secret Know Nothings," rioting broke out, and on election day the Americans of that city carefully stationed "watchers" at every polling place. The Democrats, not to be out-done, organized the "red Warriors" for the same purpose. It was a vicious campaign and the *Mail* was in the thick of things from first to last, Hooper and the *Advertiser's* Brittan attacking each other with bitter editorials.

Despite all, early in August the election went off peacefully. A decisive victory it was for Governor Winston, the Democrat, by a vote of 42,000 to 30,000 for Shortridge. The latter, indeed, carried only fifteen of the state's counties, twelve of which were in the Black Belt, the Whigs' old stronghold. To the *Mail's* credit, however, it must be added that Montgomery County, as well as the adjoining counties of Lowndes and Macon, voted "Know Nothing" by comfortable majorities.[36] Although Hooper had not anticipated so marked a defeat of his party, he was neveretheless not dejected. "If, in its very first *trial of strength* in Alabama, the new party had carried the State, it would have been . . . the most remarkable achievement of modern times," he wrote shortly after the elections. "It entered the field single-handed, against all old parties. It defied old party arrangements. It shocked all the fogyism of the times." And as a grand finale to the *Mail's* first political battle he added these too-eloquent words: "Defeated, indeed, are we—but not discouraged. The field is yet open to our energies, the mists and murkiness of prejudices will yet dissipate, before the glowing love of home and country . . . Every American heart vibrates to the glorious sentiment that *American liberties are safest in American hands*."[37] Ample forewarning was that from a strong "party man." His forces had been temporarily halted, to be true, but they were realigning, gathering strength, planning for greater forays. Soon the "Know Nothings" were to return, stronger than ever.

During the closing days of the campaign, Hooper had been quite unwell. In mid-July he had been forced to remain in his room at the Exchange Hotel, where he was then living, for three or four days. Early in August he went down again, this time for more than two weeks. "'[The editor] is advised," he wrote, "that his health requires some days, perhaps weeks, of mental and physical repose in the quiet of the country." Doubtless, he retired to La Fayette, where his wife and sons were living, but on the twentieth he felt better and resumed his duties on the *Mail*.[38] Inasmuch as there were no pressing political issues at the moment, his editorials were once again turned toward local matters, particularly yellow fever, which many believed was again this year reaching an epidemic stage in Montgomery. On September 3 he penned a prophetic essay on the future prospects of coal in Alabama, and three weeks later he begged "such of our patrons as approve the [American Party] principles of this paper . . . to give us the benefit of their personal exertions in increasing our list of subscribers."

Meanwhile, the number of cases of yellow fever in the city steadily increased—three of the *Mail's* "hands" going down in one day. Hooper acknowledged "the panic," but pled with his subscribers to bear with him. "It may be that hereafter we may only be able to get out a column or two—even less—or we may possibly have to suspend 'til a different condition of things is brought about. If, however ,we can keep a hand or two, we shall issue some sort of sheet, every day." The next day he editorially squelched a rumor that there were "several cases" of the fever at the Exchange Hotel, but in less than a week he himself again fell a victim to the dread disease. John C. Bates, his old friend and rival on the *Alabama Journal*, rushed to his aid and after "some days confinement" Hooper was back at his post. "Grateful are we," he wrote on October 8, "for the kindness of friends which kept the *Mail* going, and its editor doctored, nursed, and tended, during a very dull, unpleasant time. . . Nor can we omit to speak our gratification at the evidences of sympathy from our old and valued friend, Bates, of the *Journal*. There are some natures which do not change or grow cold by any lapse of time or alteration of circumstances; and the Major is one of them."

The epidemic continued throughout November—and so did the *Mail*, but with great difficulty. Employees were frequently absent and, worse, the publishers were in temporary financial difficulties. "There is no use mincing matters; we cannot publish, if we cannot get money," Hooper stated. "We have been fighting for eighteen months, against an unbroken series of adverse circumstances; and now, with greatly enfeebled health, our sole reliance is on the punctuality of our patrons . . . our weekly circulation is the second in town, and ought alone to suffice nearly to pay our expenses. And yet we are pressed beyond endurance!" But the *Mail* held on, missing no issues, and Hooper personally continued to grow in the esteem of his fellow-citizens, both his political friends and enemies.[39]

On November 12 the new legislature—consisting of a two-to-one Democratic majority—assembled in "Estelle Hall" for the opening caucus of its 1855-1856 session. Besides reporting to his patrons of the *Mail* on the passing political parade, Hooper attended as many daily meetings as was possible, and in December issued a humorously-tinged summary of the affairs in a sixteen-page pamphlet, entitled *Read and Circulate: Proceedings of the Democratic and Anti-Know-Nothing Party, in Caucus; or the Guillotine at Work, at the Capital, during the Session of 1855-'56.* Signed "By an Eye-Witness," the document clearly evidenced Hooper's antagonism toward the Democratic "'caucus method" that so obviously rejected any idea or man even remotely suspected of "Know-Nothing" tendencies.[40] His opponents, he claimed, were obviously playing politics, posing as champions, and putting party success far above the real issue—saving the South. As for the "Caw-kus secrecy," well:

> Old King Caw is a jolly old cuss,
> And he gets his friends out of many a muss;
> He hasn't a "lodge" but a sly old Hole,
> And it's there the old King calls his roll!
> King Caw! King Caw!
> Caw! Caw! Caw! Caw!
> Is the jolly old cock that makes the law.[41]

Then in a final gesture of good-humored bantering, he concluded, "We have met the enemy, and—*we are theirs!*"[42]

As might be supposed, Hooper's interest in politics, including his eternal fight for an "independent Southern press" and "the advancement of Southern interests" and against the "Thrice accursed 'compromise'" on slavery, had noticeably curtailed his time for creative journalism. Except for occasional anecdotes and an infrequent brief yarn, the quality of which, though clever, was far below that of his *Simon Suggs* and *Kit Kuncker* era, he wrote nothing to add lustre to his fame as a humorist.[43] Meanwhile, as a political essayist he grew in stature. This was in all probability exactly as Hooper desired, for by 1856 he is believed to have regretted sorely the identification of his name with that of "Simon, the shifty man" and wished that he had never published the humorous biography.[44] Now that he was a powerful, grave and thoughtful influence in the political life of the South, his reputation as a "funny man" was a hazard, a difficult obstacle in every way to his personal advancement and, consequently, he deduced, to the advancement of his beloved region.

His name, of course, was still loudly heralded across the nation as a humorist, and in the presses he was yet often referred to as "the funny man," "the ugly man," "the great wit of the Southwest," "the author of 'Simon Suggs' " and not infrequently as "Simon," himself. It is not surprising, therefore, to discover that from its beginning the *Mail* consistently made no reference to the fact that its editor was a nationally-known humorist and that, even on occasions when *Simon Suggs* could ethically have been publicized, the subject was gracefully ignored. After a fashion Hooper maintained his journalistic friendship with Porter of the *Spirit*, nevertheless, the latter now and then reprinting short excerpts from the *Mail*, such as "A Sharper Meeting One Keener" and "Matched to a Hair," in late 1854, and "A Great Speech," "Fish Breeding in Alabama," "Mike and the Kicking Horse," "Old Charlie," and "A Thing Unheard Before" in 1855.[45] The two men also called on each other for editorial tid-bits.[46] Porter occasionally picked up *Mail* items indirectly—"Sloshin' About," for instance, having been copied from *Harper's Magazine*—[47] and Hooper continued to rely on the *Spirit* for "quotes" and, as will be seen later, on Porter for "attention and kindness" in the preparation of a new non-humorous book, *Dog and Gun,* upon which he was then working. But that care-free editorial comraderie, which for a decade had characterized the friendly relationship between the metropolitan journalist and his once-remote, small-town colleague of the press, was no longer apparent. Much water had passed over the dam since that September morning of 1843, when Porter had so willingly placed "Taking the Census" on the breakfast tables of the nation.

As 1855 came to a close and Hooper looked out of the *Mail's* office window on Montgomery's many-angled Court Square,[48] he was one whose political philosophy had been slowly but at long last crystalized. His ideas were clear, well defined, firm, and neither friends nor enemies doubted his convictions. He was an "American," yes; but deeper by far he was of the South and for the South, ready to "hold all party obligations in subordination to the very Highest requisitions which Southern Patriotism can make." Abolitionsm he recognized as the one salient, ultimate issue yet to be looked "full in the face" for the "salvation, and independence" of the South. Early he prophesized "the impending contest." "At last . . .," he advocated "*pro-slavery* and *no-slavery* are at length to have an honest, fair and open fight . . ." and the South, "like an unhooded falcon, shall be able to take a proud, steady, upward flight in the fullness of her courage, strength and beauty."[49]

Few men, regardless of party affiliations, could have doubted that Hooper of the *Mail* was even now bespeaking the mind of the South.

CHAPTER SIX

"If Mr. Suggs is present . . ."

DESPITE Hooper's continued but not unusual plea for more subscribers, by 1856 the *Mail* was an already successful, expanding, though youthful concern. Barrett and Wimbish, publishers of Hooper's *Read and Circulate,* had moved into the establishment a few months before, greatly increasing its facilities for job printing. The *Daily, Tri-Weekly,* and *Weekly* were steadily growing in popularity, and in January became the "Official Journal" of the City of Montgomery.[1] In January, also, Joel Riggs, formerly employed by Alabama as "state comptroller of public accounts," purchased Knight's interest, entering the Company as an occasional editorial writer and business manager.[2] But the combination of Holifield, Hooper and Riggs lasted less than three months. On March 6 Hooper bought Holifield's share, his "Know Nothing" friends Thomas H. Watts and Thomas J. Judge securing his notes for $2300.[3] Thereafter, for nine months, the *Mail* was successfully published by "Riggs & Hooper, Editors and Proprietors." On November 5, however, Riggs' name was removed from the masthead, that of Henry E. Coyne, a former foreman on the rival *Alabama Journal,* substituted, and the firm changed to "Hooper and Coyne."[4] After this, Hooper was referred to as "the Senior Editor" and Coyne, who did most of the editorial writing during Hooper's many absences, as "the Junior."[5]

Flushed by the success of their new party in its first show of strength in state politics, the "Know Nothings" entered the field in 1856 with renewed vigor and determination, and this time for bigger game: the presidential election. The "native Americans," so-called, had supplanted the Whigs and at last the South was once more to have a strong two-party system, "Know Nothings" *versus* Democrats. But to those who followed politics intently it must have been obvious that the "Know Nothings," even before 1856, had already begun slowly to disintegrate, and that the day of that short-lived party as a powerful element was rapidly passing.[6]

In Alabama the first sign of collapse had come in late 1855, when the Americans in convention assembled had voted to abolish all secrecy, pass-words, ceremonials, and other "claptrap," standing finally on a solid platform of religious freedom and strict interpretation of the Constitution. These decisions at once rendered conciliation with the national American party impossible. However, in February, 1856, the State Council of the organization, led by Hooper of the *Mail*, Thomas H. Watts, Daniel Pratt, A. F. Hopkins and a half dozen others, met in Montgomery to adopt resolutions and select electors to represent Alabama at the national party convention in Philadelphia.[7] All of these men were former Whigs and all were fully aware of their political dilemma. But they went courageously ahead, appointing delegates pledged to support former President Fillmore and adopting a firm resolution on the extension of slavery in the territories—a resolution so firm, indeed, that those who read it believed it smacked strongly of the renowned "Alabama Platform" which had been advocated by the fire-eating William Lowndes Yancey at the Democratic state convention of 1848.[8]

At Philadelphia matters took yet a different turn. The Alabama delegates refused to approve the national platform, chiefly on account of its unsatisfactory attitude towards slavery, and the party became a house divided. One-time prominent Alabama "Know Nothings"—ex-Whigs, such as Luke Pryor, Mayor Jones M. Withers of Mobile, and others—refused to support the American nominees, some of them, Judge A. F. Hopkins and B. F. Porter, for examples, actually taking to the stump for the Democrats.

Hooper and the *Mail*, however, stood passively by the national party, giving Fillmore only mild, reluctant support. By June the editor was spending his efforts detailing the demands of "Southern Rights," opposing emigration from the South to Kansas and congratulating Preston Brooks of South Carolina for caning Charles Sumner because of his "Bleeding Kansas" speech.[9] The names of Millard Fillmore for president and Andrew J. Donelson for vice-president continued, nevertheless, to fly from the *Mail's* masthead,[10] and Hooper himself throughout the summer participated in party affairs, serving now and then as a member of the "American Executive Committee" and permitting the *Mail* office to be used as party "headquarters."[11]

When the rival Democratic party announced James Buchanan as its presidential candidate in the summer of 1856, honest Hooper was quick to praise him as "the only statesman before the Convention . . ., a *statesman* who has given eminent services to the country, and, in all moral, intellectual and political points, is *vastly* superior to his competitors, Pierce and Douglas." However, he quickly added, "he is objectionable, very objectionable, to the South, on political grounds." Buchanan, he believed, was not an "incendiary" on the "Slavery question," but "a decided Free Soiler"—and that was bad enough. Yet the Democratic party could have done so much worse "in either the squatty giant of Illinois, or the double-dealing *Hard-icicle* of New Hampshire" that Hooper was ready to tender his opponents "hearty congratulations *in achieving* a respectable nomination."[12]

With only mild enthusiasm for the "Know Nothing" Fillmore and no enthusiasm for the Democratic Buchanan, it is not difficult to understand why Hooper gave all his employees a holiday on July 4, saying, "Perhaps this is the last Fourth of July the American people will ever celebrate *as one nation.* Let us all, therefore, 'take a chance at it.'" Then, his party loyalty getting the best of him, he added as an afterthought: "It's a 'great old day,' any how, and if Fillmore is elected we believe it will continue to be observed for long years to come!"[18]

The campaign of 1856 was a bitter one. The Democrats fell in behind William Lowndes Yancey, who had waited six long years for the party to accept his "Alabama Platform" (he was yet to wait four more before Alabama would follow him into secession from the Union); and the "Know Nothings" rallied around Jeremiah Clemens and Henry W. Hilliard, who toured the state, defending "Southern Rights" and lambasting "Black Republicanism." Conditions in Kansas, the speeches of various abolitionists in Congress, the expenditures of the Federal government and many other issues were dragged out and displayed before countless mass meetings, picnics, barbecues, and political rallies to which special railroad excursions brought thousands of adherents of both parties. Ministers throughout the state, claiming that the American party stood for reform and morality, in general rallied around the "Know Nothings" and the Democrats retaliated by shouting that their opponents preached "Douglas and him damned" instead of "Christ and him crucified." But undergirding all the petty party bickerings there stood one common denominator of mutual understanding: preserving the rights of the South. That, in essence, was the one solid plank in both platforms, the first duty of both parties. Whether the rescue could best be accomplished by the Democrats or by the Americans remained the prime issue, the arguable uncertainty until the bitter end.

By an almost two-to-one majority the Democrats carried Alabama, winning in forty-four out of fifty-two counties. Great was their rejoicing. Throughout the state meetings were held to celebrate the victory, cannon were fired, and Democratic newspapers displayed large cuts of roosters crowing. The overjoyed Wetumpka *Dispatch,* for instance, shouted, "No North, No South, No East, No where, *Know Nothing,*"[14] and Hooper, politically squelched, received as a personal gift from an anonymous Democratic donor "a *Fillmourner* Hat . . . for 'distinguished service in the late campign,' " an antique mourning bonnet of blackest black. "These delicate little attentions of our Democratic friends," he replied, "have multiplied on us recently. Last week, we were made *Barber* on a Salt River Steamer and *Engineer* on another." It was his abiding wish, he added, that friends of Buchanan would find "it as easy to arrange the distribution of offices and gifts among their own partisans."[15] About all the chiding he was good-natured, conceding the rewards of victory while taunting his enemies with their fickleness, their "radiance" of heart and "beaming countenances." Some of the "happy faces," he added, had but "a few weeks, or a few months ago" managed to get over on the "*strong side*"—"they feel it is 'we' who . . . beat the Know-Nothings—and who have the right of admission into 'good society' in Montgomery. Ah, these fellows are happy—nobody happier, barring the Dutch!"[16]

Regardless of the bantering, Hooper realized that after the 1856 elections the Americans in Alabama, now irregularly organized, were doomed. True enough, he clung to the party loyally and for months to come, but as many of his fellow-travellers, both "Know Nothings" and "Southern Rights Whigs," turned gradually to the Buchanan Democrats as the only hope of the South, his loyalty waned, too. Out of the dubious battle came yet another advance toward secession: by 1860 the Americans were no more. And the South, at last united on an unwavering platform of "Southern Independence," marched on into the "irrepressible conflict . . ."

Throughout the "era of good feelings," as the years immediately before 1860 have been somewhat facetiously called, Hooper's pen was a sword for his section.[17] Now and then his humor came to the surface,[18] and in late 1856 when Porter, "My Dear Old Fellow," resigned as editor of the *Spirit* to start a magazine of his own, *Porter's Spirit of the Times*,[19] he wrote Hooper a personal letter inviting him to contribute.[20] Hooper wished him "the best of luck and lots of it," promising, "I shall be with you, *sure!*"[21] But nothing followed (except a brief sketch about Bird H. Young, signed "K"),[22] and in less than twenty-four months his editorial friend of thirteen years standing, the man who had contributed far more than anyone else to his literary reputation, was dead.[23] Hooper, too involved with fighting the South's battles, sang no requiem for his Yankee benefactor, wrote him no eulogy. At best he could only quote a short notice from the New Orleans *Picayune* and a long essay from the old *Spirit of the Times.* He himself remained silent.[24]

On December 8, 1856, there opened in Savannah, Georgia, the eleventh of fourteen famous Southern Commercial Conventions held between 1837 and 1859.[25] Five hundred and sixty-four delegates from ten states were present, including fifty Alabamians who had been officially appointed by the governor and furnished free round-trip tickets by the Montgomery & West Point Railroad. Among them, as secretary of the Alabama delegation, was Johnson J. Hooper, editor of the Montgomery *Mail.*[26]

Hooper had long realized the importance of the conventions, and was particularly hopeful that the one in Savannah would "effect something substantial." "The time *has come!*," he declared. "We have *talked* the South into a belief . . . that all the elements of progress, social, moral and commercial, abound in our people; and it remains only to cause, in some way, a practical development of the theory to such an extent as will convince not only *our own doubters, but the world.*" Long before the convention assembled, he had drawn up for the *Mail* an outline of the subjects which in his opinion needed first consideration at Savannah, and in general had given wide coverage to the benefits the conclave might afford "enterprises and capital of the South."[27] Indeed, so strongly had he publicized the prospects that he personally was heralded by the press as a sort of convention vanguard. Even the rival *Alabama Journal* recognized his activities,[28] while his own paper, of course, recorded his every move. Over in Savannah the editor of the *Republican* hailed his coming with apparent glee. " 'It is our misfortune never to have visited Savannah, but we propose to visit that 'comely maiden' of a city, on or about the 8th prox.,' " the *Republican* quoted Hooper, and added: "The 'comely maiden' we doubt not, will please our *Mail* friend, and mayhaps 'fascinate' him even to idolatry—particularly as he is a good *Hooper.*"[29]

When Hooper and the other delegates left Montgomery on December 8, Coyne, "the Junior," proclaimed, "Jonce has gone! He left us yesterday for Savannah, as a delegate to the Commercial Convention, which assembles next Monday . . . readers of the *Mail* must excuse its shortness for the next week." The next day he added that the paper had received its first "telegraphic dispatch" from Hooper, and that day-by-day, eye-witness descriptions of the convention, direct from "the Senior," would be available to *Mail* readers.[30] And upon his arrival in the Georgia seaport, Hooper was singled out for an interview by a Savannah *News* reporter who wrote, "Among the members of the pen and scissors fraternity, whom we have had the pleasure of greeting as delegates to the Convention, is Johnson J. Hooper, of the Montgomery *Mail.* We only mention the fact by way of correcting a gross slander against him . . . Like the old gentleman of whom we read, he ain't half as ugly as he's painted."[31]

Unfortunately for Hooper, who now wished more than any thing else to be known as a serious political journalist and an ardent advocate of the South, "Simon Suggs" had got to Savannah first . . .

At noon, December 8, 1856, in the city's Atheneum the Southern Commercial Convention was called to order by Temporary Chairman J. P. Scriven, mayor of Savannah. Immediately, a resolution was passed authorizing the appointment of a Joint Committee, composed of one delegate from each state, which would in turn "report permanent officers for this Convention, and also rules for its government."[32] While Mayor Scriven was yet in the chair, awaiting the Committee's report, Judge John A. Jones, a delegate from Georgia "formally moved in the presence of the six or eight hundred delegates" that Mr. Simon Suggs of Alabama be called upon "to give an account of himself for the last two years." The Chairman, evidently unfamiliar with the gentleman from Alabama, "arose with great dignity and said, 'If Mr. Suggs is present we should be glad to have him comply with the expressed wish of the convention by coming to the platform.'" At this moment "more than a thousand persons, in the galleries and elsewhere," craned their necks, looking here and there "on the tiptoe of expectations at hearing 'Simon Suggs' deliver his convulsive jokes," for he was "supposed by everybody to be always ripe for a frolic, and for a roar of merriment, and that he was as good at telling stories as in writing his droll descriptions, and thankful for the privilege."

But "Mr. Suggs" did not rise. Seated in the pit next to General Albert Pike of Arkansas and half-buried in a long, green blanket-coat, Hooper shrank "with embarrassment," and, overwhelmed by the pressure of the "unexpected demonstration . . ., stirred not an inch." At that precise instant the committee returned to the hall and, amid the excitement of the procedures, an end was put "to the embarrassment of Mr. Hooper." Within a few moments the convention heard the name of "Colonel Johnson J. Hooper" honored as Alabama's representative on the ten-man Joint Committee,[33] and the "Simon Suggs" incident had become history . . . or legend.

That night at the hotel the scene was referred to in Hooper's presence, not tauntingly but as sincere "evidence of [his] popularity, even out of his own State." Hooper vigorously objected, declaring that "a liberty had been taken with his name which was really offensive" and that he was glad he had "had the good sense to keep quiet." Evidently greatly chagrined by the experience, he was afraid that his renown as a "*chronic* story-teller" had overshadowed his efforts "in quite a different channel, to enjoy the respect of men." Wherever he went or whenever he tried to rise above this "depressing influence" of *Simon Suggs,* he found only that he "had unfortunately obtained a reputation which cut off all such hopes." Unhappily, however, the blunder had been made and he must suffer the consequences, knowing that "depreciation rather than exhaltation was his." "For once in his life," declared one crusading commentator, "Mr. Hooper appeared in earnest while deploring his *notoriety* . . . Let him stand as a beacon light, to give warning of the rock on which the manly ambition and hopes of his youth perished."[34]

For his *Mail* Hooper described the spirited convention in detail, devoting many dispatches to the discussions of direct trade with Europe, the proposed Pacific Coast railroad, the re-opening of the slave trade, and other matters. He made no reference to the "Simon Suggs" incident, of course; but upon his return to Montgomery he graciously thanked his "brethren of the Press" in Savannah for "their marked courtesy" during his week's sojourn in their city.[35]

At the year's end the rapidly-expanding *Mail* with but one

exception claimed "the largest circulation of any political paper in the interior of the State, by six or seven hundred copies" and, among "Know Nothing" sheets it was an acknowledged leader. As the editor carefully indicated, in distribution the *Mail* was "not equalled by more than one Democratic paper."[36] Party politics, however, received less and less attention as the months went along,[37] and, although the *Mail* flew a screaming eagle inscribed "American and Whig" as late as mid-1859, the editor's true and mounting sentiment was revealed on the paper's seventh anniversary, when he declared, "With but one political pledge—that we shall stand by the South, her interests and her honor, come what will . . . ."[38]

As for party affiliation, a secondary consideration now, in January, 1857, Hooper broke precedent by recommending the appointment of Yancey to the post in Democratic Buchanan's cabinet. "We are an opponent politically of Mr. Yancey's and personally a mere acquaintance," he editorialized, "but we will concede him his rights, and speak our opinion of his talents, in spite of those ominous growls which proceed from the [George S.] Houston faction."[39] Within three short years this candid but simple recognition of his opponent's capability, nurtured in their mutual love of the South, was to ripen into a deep and abiding loyalty. "Stand by Yancey!" was to be Hooper's cry in 1860, "*Stand by Yancey!*"[40] As one historian has suggested, "Hooper's serious responsibility for the political fortunes of William Lowndes Yancey is a fact which has been too frequently overlooked."[41]

That Hooper was in 1857 still "Know Nothing" as well as an apostle of good fun is evidenced by his "interest" in the proposed Democratic candidacy of Bird H. Young (oh! shades of "Simon Suggs") for the governor of Alabama. It all began, innocently enough, in March when the Camden (Alabama) *Republic* (with doubtful seriousness) advocated Young as a proper man for the high office. The *Mail* noted the announcement, added simply, "Capt. Young lives in Tallapoosa, and is a Democrat of the old sort," and let the matter drop. But some of Hooper's friends—"one of each party," he stated—wanted more: so ten days later the *Mail* re-printed the *Republic's* entire column, which contained such praise of the subject as "Bird was a 'broth of a boy' in his youth, as all may know who have read of the youthful exploits of 'Simon Suggs'" and "he has . . . been regarded as the purest of the 'Simon Pures.'" To the article Hooper cautiously affixed a comment, emphatically indicating that he was quoting the story by request, and that so far as he knew "Captain Young" was and had always been a Democrat opposed to State Aid and "things of the sort generally." "He is bold, energetic and resolute," Hooper continued, and with stinging "Know Nothing" sarcasm concluded, "if we *must* say it, we think [Young] would make an admirable representative, in the gubernatorial field of the anti-State Aid Democracy."[42] Beside the joviality evident in this brief episode, Hooper's failure to offer even a casual reference to Bird H. Young as the prototype of his famous *Simon Suggs* stands out clearly.[43] Perhaps, indeed, he had grown to feel that in "Simon's" shiftless company he could not longer enjoy "the respect of men."

Hooper's next publication, a serious little book upon which he had been working for more than two years, appeared in New York late in 1856. Entitled *Dog and Gun; A Few Loose Chapters on Shooting,*[44] and dedicated to Henry William Herbert ("Frank Forester"),[45] the volume contained thirteen brief chapters on various phases of hunting, guns, powder, and the selection and training of dogs, all of which had previously appeared in the *Southern Military Gazette* of Montgomery and Atlanta.[46] A goodly portion of the book Hooper himself had written, but he had also drawn heavily from the works of Herbert, C. W. Gooter and others, including William T. Stockton, who, as "Cor de Chasse," was well known to thousands of *Spirit* readers.[47] To his friend Porter Hooper paid respects by recommending him as the best authority on guns "out of the trade" and his magazine as an abundant source of "facts, feats, and general information in the sporting line." Copies of *Dog and Gun,* which the author referred to as his "A, B, C, of Shooting," did not reach Montgomery until February, 1857. "We note its arrival," Hooper modestly stated in the *Mail,* "in order to say that though nominally by the editor of this paper, its more valuable papers were contributed by Henry William Herbert, Esq., Doct. E[gbert] B. J[ohnston], of Tuskegee, and Colonel Wm. Stockton, of Florida . . . For the lack of a better opportunity to do so, we here express our obligations to our friend, W. T. Porter, Esq., of Porter's 'Spirit of the Times,' for his valuable attention and kindness in reading the proof sheets of our bantling."[48]

That the little volume met with favor in the sporting world is best attested by the fact that, in addition to the first printing (1856) by C. M. Saxton & Co., it was also issued in the same year (perhaps simultaneously) by A. O. Moore, New York, and again, by C. M. Saxton, Barker & Co., in 1860.[49] Meanwhile in 1858, A. O. Moore included the book, along with Mrs. L. G. Abell's *The Skillful Housewife's Book*, Browne's *Memoirs of Indian Corn* and other volumes in the Fourth Series of *Moore's Rural Hand Books.* In 1863 Saxton re-issued the volume, and in 1871, nine years after Hooper's death, Orange, Judd brought out yet another edition.[50] Interesting though *Dog and Gun* must have been to Hooper's contemporaries, it did not achieve the purpose, if indeed it was so intended, of erasing from their memories the convulsive adventures of a certain Captain of the Tallapoosa Volunteers. Like it or not, until his death—and, if he dared ponder the matter, long afterwards—Johnson J. Hooper was destined to be but a synonym for the immortal comedian—forever *alias Simon Suggs* . . .

After 1856, with the publication of *Dog and Gun* behind him and the *Mail* functioning smoothly under Coyne's able management, Hooper felt freer than ever to take life more leisurely. He now and then absented himself from the office,[51] resting and depending on his partner for editorials. Or, not infrequently, he would fill his columns with contributions from such celebrities as A. J. Pickett, the historian,[52] Sol Smith, the comedian,[53] Stephen Massett ("Col. Jeems Pipes of Pipeville"), the popular entertainer who addressed Hooper as "My Dear 'Simon' "[54] and General Thomas S. Woodward, an Alabamian then living in Vernon Parish, Louisiana.[55] At this time, too, Hooper travelled quite widely for his paper—to Tuskegee, Opelika, Mobile and Columbus (Georgia), and other places, largely for the purpose of reporting events, usually sporting or political.[56] Coyne jollied him about "lounging about . . . enjoying the good things of life" and attributed the Mobile trip of May, 1857, to a desire for "luxuriating . . . in the salt water baths and breezes, inhaling the perfume of magnolia and orange groves—and eating pompano!"[57] On this particular occasion Hooper was away only a few days, however, for in early June he hurried back, eager to settle a personal matter with Dr. N. B. Cloud, who had succeeded Brittan of the *Advertiser*, with pistols at ten paces on the field of honor. Little or nothing came of Hooper's challenge, however—except a hot, threat-filled, political editorial duel, all of which highly pleased the newspaper's subscribers and caused unending gossip on Court Square.[58]

Hooper's interest in Masonry, keen for a decade (he had joined the fraternity March 20, 1847),[59] was never greater than during these comparatively prosperous and leisurely days of the mid-1850's. When the Grand Lodge of Alabama met in 1857, he spent a happy week in the fellowship of his brothers and was instrumental in organizing the "University of Comus," a group of thirteen "choice spirits" within the fraternity, a *tredecim* composed of some of the best-known humorists in American literature. It was agreed that each of the participants would furnish a comic essay, "a spoke to the wheel" of a *Magnum Opus,* a satire upon the Masonic rituals and a "Monitorial Guide to the Workings of the Fellowship." Hooper was elected "Zenon, the Grand Secretary of the University" and his chapter, the ninth essay, was entitled "Thirteen Sages of Antiquity Caricatured."

Although he never lived to see its publication—the unique and bizarre volume, filled with grotesque drawings and incongruous ceremonials, did not make its appearance until twenty-eight years after his death—he doubtless would have been pleased that his contribution shared honors with those of A. B. Longstreet, Charles F. Browne ("Artemus Ward"), Edwin Forrest, the tragedian, George H. Derby ("John Phenix") and a host of other renowned wits. Wrote the editor of *Magnum Opus,* who had known Hooper personally, ". . . [his] satire was exquisite. His conversation sparkled with keen points. Conventional platitudes and pretentious and sentimental claims were ruthlessly plowed under by the share of his sarcasm. If his wit at time was coarse, it, at least, was not circus wit, operatic wit, or what passed thirty years since as newspaper wit, but glowed with originality. His *bon mots* are yet the local currency around Montgomery, as are those of [George D.] Prentice around Louisville, and [Thomas] Corwin around Lebanon, and, with all the other pupils in the School of Comedy of whom we are writing, 'they being dead, yet speak.' In the brilliant coterie of southern humorists . . . Hooper will ever rank among the foremost."[60]

Amid the fun of travel and the frolic of good fellowship, however, the *Mail* presses continued to roll, taking "the starch out of" Hooper and condemning him, who has "designed by nature to be the comic historian of Alabama . . . , to the setting up and knocking down of partisan politicans."[61]

In the 1857 state elections, for the first time since 1851, the Democratic party had no organized opposition from "Know Nothings" or Whigs, and the local campaigns turned out, in essence, to be a family affair: Union *versus* "Southern Rights" Democrats.[62] As various newspapers pointed out, the Democrats ruled the field (no doubt of that, for the Americans were unable even to organize sufficiently to nominate a candidate for governor) but cleavage within the old party rendered it virtually a house divided. The degree to which "Southern Rights" should be sponsored was still the chief campaign issue. All Democrats talked Democratic beliefs, but party *loyalty* rather than party *principles* held the divergent wings together. Hooper, on the outside looking in, as it were, described the national party's "loathsome, discordant ingredients" of the moment as:

> Eyes of Toombs, toe of Van
> Heart of fogy Buchanan,
> Foot of Cobb, nose of Cass,
> Ears of Old Virginia's Ass.[63]

It was this division of viewpoints, increasingly evident after the mid-1850's, which led to the ultimate split in 1860 and secession.

Five candidates, representing varying degrees of sectionalism, entered the state gubernatorial race, and it was not until the twenty-sixth ballot of the June convention, that "conservative" Judge A. B. Moore was able to defeat "radical" William F. Samford, an "uncompromising Southern Rights" man.

But the real threat to the Democrats centered around President Buchanan: would he protect "Southern Rights," in spite of his appointment of R. J. Walker as governor of Kansas? Was there collusion between the two? Would the President support the South? Public meetings were held throughout Alabama to debate the question. Hilliard, only lately a conservative Whig-American, but now actively consorting with the Democrats (a "democratic yearling . . . a year old, still at the breast," Yancey called him), made a speech before the Democratic convention. Yancey, the fierce "States Righter" called for party harmony, reluctantly urging "undiminished confidence" in Buchanan, at least until it could be *proved* that between the President and Governor Walker there was actual connivance. Hooper, his enthusiasm for Yancey mounting, refused to believe the orator sincere. "Everybody," he declared, "that knows Mr. Yancey politically must feel that his loathing of Mr. Buchanan cannot be much less potent than his contempt for Governor Walker."[64] As election day neared, Hooper became less cautious, throwing the *Mail's* weight against the "perpetrators of the Kansas Swindle." "Let every citizen of Alabama, who would not bow in quiet submission to the tyrannical yoke a Freesoil Administration is trying to put upon the South . . . rebuke the tyrants . . . If we endorse this Kansian outrage upon the South, by our votes, it throws the doors wide open for further aggressions upon our rights. Southerners! *do your duty.*[65] But, alas, once again, as he had always been, Hooper was on the losing side.

Moore's defeat of Samford in 1857 indicated the state's trend toward conservatism, but there were yet strong, isolated American pockets which, in the congressional elections, gave no quarter to the Democrats. One of these was Hooper's Montgomery, a county which had voted "Know Nothing" in the elections of 1855 and 1856. To the *Mail,* the only "Know Nothing" paper in the area, and hence to Hooper, its editor, must be attributed a measure of this minority party loyalty. Strongest opposition to the Democrats in the county was evident in the race between Thomas J. Judge, a "State Right Whig," against James F. McDowdell. The former pulled every political stop in his vigorous attempt to win, and he had Hooper's *Mail* solidly behind him,[66] but the assets of the Democrats, who imported Robert Toombs to stump the district, were too great.[67] Hooper tried to stem the tide by describing the Georgian's visit as "the Philistines are coming on," and begging for "the Ass with the best jawbone" with which to smite him.[68] On August 3, election day, the editor delivered one last significant and predictive thrust: "To endorse Buchanan is to endorse Walker! Is the South in a trance? Is it possible that she will submit to the great wrong, *done in the name of Democracy,* to resist which she was ready to spill her best blood, when attempted in the name of *Black Republicanism? This day* settles the question in Alabama. The man whose vote is given to those who stand by the Administration, repudiates our rights in the Territories and consents to the 'restriction of slavery.' If a majority of the State so vote, Alabama can never again be called a Southern Rights State. If you would take 'high ground,' *ever,* take it now!"

In spite of all, however, the "Free Soil Northern Democratic Party," as Hooper bitterly called it, carried every district in the state and every county except four: the combination of Yancey and Toombs and Hilliard, whose alliance with the Democrats caused many a "Know Nothing" groan,[69] had been too formidable. Now, the *Southern Advocate* of Huntsville, for instance, which up to 1855 had been the leading Whig journal in North Alabama, hopefully saw in the Democratic victory an "undivided front" and much promise for protection of the rights of the South. "With occasional errors and departures from the true lines of duty," the paper stated, "the Democratic party is and has been, true to the Constitution, the Union, and the rights of States."[70] But Hooper of the *Mail* could grant his opponents no such grace. For him the basic principles remained unaltered: the South had sold its birthright for a mess of Yankee pottage. "The result of the recent elections in the South indicates that the people . . . throw themselves willingly and with utmost confidence upon the tender mercies of the Freesoilers, for all time to come . . . ," he declared. "The voice of the South just expressed very cordially invites the extinction of her most important institution, and the consequent reduction in the production of her staple commodities, and her people may rest assured that the invitation will be readily accepted."[71] As for Hooper himself, he remained "steadfast to the end" a staunch "Southern Rights American." The editors of the *Mail,* he wrote, "have been in minorities during all their political lives; they therefore are not likely to shrink from opposing majorities." And as his bitterness toward the Union increased, he more and more deplored the measuring of party principles against the "absolute *rights*" of his region. "If . . . the Union is worth more than the institution of slavery . . . ," he shouted, "Lord forbid that we should be Union men. And to remain in the Union, with ceaseless aggression and insult from the North, is a little too much, we should think, for any man who has Southern blood in his veins."[72]

Thus did the rebellious senior editor speak in 1858, while yet the *Mail's* motto was "American Principles and Southern Rights." Not until 1860, when the people had caught up with their prophet, was Hooper to convert that slogan into the simpler, but caustic *"State Rights, Without Abatement."*

CHAPTER SEVEN

". . . then, where shall we be?"

THE YEAR 1858 was a quiet one in Alabama politics, enlivened only by William Lowndes Yancey's continual fight to gain active leadership of the Democratic party.[1] Simply, his plan was age-old: to divide and conquer. Withdrawal from the national party was to be the first move. Then, in order were to follow the creation of a separate "Southern Rights" party, the election of himself as United States senator, and, lastly, secession from the Union.[2] As a means to these ends he actively sponsored the organization of the "Leagues of United Southerners," the purpose of which was obviously to mold voters into a party to enforce without compromise the rights of the South. Although the idea met stern opposition from die-hard Democrats, it received the encouragement of such "States Rights" stalwarts as William F. Samford (who believed the Leagues would "unite all those who are willing to fight for the South [which] will then be the League!") and Johnson J. Hooper, whose *Mail* adherred rigidly to the principles of the Leagues.[3]

Meanwhile, Yancey was using his genius of oratory in support of General William Walker's Nicaraguan filibuster. Again Hooper supported him. Indeed, the editor was elected secretary of the "Nicaraguan Meeting," held in Montgomery's Commercial Hall, January 23, 1858.[4] But when the Nicaraguan scheme fell by the wayside and Yancey finally abandoned the short-lived organization,[5] Hooper retired momentarily from active politics and devoted his attention to the constant promotion of "things Southern," to rest and travel, and to the improvement and enlargement of his paper.[6]

Between August and November, 1857, Hooper and Coyne, obviously prospering, installed complete fonts of new type for the *Mail,* and "dressed it up" as "the handsomest paper in two States." They believed it compared "favorably with any paper in all this region of the country." Brittan, Hooper's old rival of the *Advertiser,* who now was editing a small Montgomery paper, the *Daily Messenger,* complimented the *Mail* on its "brand new suit of type" and the editors for their ability at "money making." "Go on, brothers Hooper & Coyne," he added, "for in the bright lexicon of the *Mail* there is no such word as a small circulation—there are thousands of names in its bright lexicon of an address book."[7]

At this time also Hooper and Coyne began negotiation with John F. Whitfield, who was interested in buying an interest in the *Mail*—a deal which was finally consummated early in 1858.[8] Whitfield served the paper as news and local editor, relieving Hooper of much of the writing. The additional leisure was doubtless appreciated, for Mrs. Hooper and the boys had now moved to Montgomery and the family, after several years' separation, was at long last together again.[9]

Into the new *Mail* these prosperous days Hooper put much more local news, especially theatrical, and passed up no opportunity to pay tribute to the South: Alabama books, women, cigars, and wines were the finest; Southern magazines, horse-races, boats, guns, dogs, newspapers, and foods were the choicest. Even "Southern Cordial" was best for "persons afflicted with Bowel diseases."[10] Significantly enough, Hooper also began in October to publish a series of historical though nostalgic essays about "Old Times in Alabama," by General

Thomas S. Woodward, a Georgian who had settled in Alabama about 1810, fought in the Seminole War under Andrew Jackson, and as a "Brigadier General of Militia" had conducted La Fayette from Fort Mitchell to Montgomery on his famous tour of 1824.[11] The first two "letters," addressed to Edward ("Horseshoe Ned") Hanrick, of Montgomery, a mutual friend whom Hooper had described in *A Ride with Old Kit Kuncker*,[12] were dated May 2 and December 9, 1857, from Wheeling, Louisiana, where Woodward was then living. Evidently enthralled by the old Indian fighter's descriptions of early Alabama, Hooper engaged him to furnish the *Mail* a series of such reminiscences, and on February 12, 1858, "Number 1" appeared. Thereafter, at infrequent intervals throughout the year the essays continued,[13] Hooper declaring that they were read "with more avidity than any contribution ever given in the *Mail.*" Soon he indicated his personal interest in collecting, editing, and publishing them in book form. Within three months the job was under way: "the very interesting and valuable letters . . . will make a neat little volume of about 125 pages and will be retailed at half a dollar each," he wrote, "[and] will be issued from the press in this city."[14]

When the volume appeared in January, 1859,[15] under the title *Woodward's Reminiscences of the Creek, or Muscogee Indians, Contained in Letters to Friends in Georgia and Alabama*,[16] it contained twenty-six letters—two to Hanrick, seventeen to Hooper (or "Eds. *Mail*"), three to A. J. Pickett, one each to F. A. Rutherford and John Banks, one from Pickett to Woodward, and one which had appeared earlier in the Columbus (Georgia) *Sun.* Besides copyrighting the volume in his own name, Hooper also supplied a lengthy introduction in which he stated that twenty years earlier in East Alabama he had known Woodward and that he was well remembered "as a brave, rough, warm-hearted man, of fine intellectual endowments, a most sagacious judge of character, extensive knowledge of Creek Indian history, manners and character." Confident that the volume was historically valuable to Alabamians, Hooper proffered free copies to all "Literary Institutions in the State" and to all state newspapers which would "notice" the work, placed the edition on sale through Montgomery bookstores and by mail, and then, a month later, sold all remaining copies to G. A. Cushing of Montgomery.

By mid-February three-fourths of the stock had been disposed of ("those who want had better apply early") and by mid-March practically sold out ("the Reminiscences have been eagerly sought for and only a few copies remain on sale.") And in April General Woodward, who had meanwhile moved to Texas, sent Hooper "two centipedes and a tarantula" by mail—in grateful appreciation! The insects were almost dead upon arrival, Hooper stated, and he pitifully drowned their sorrows in a bottle of "the best alcohol."[17] As for the *Reminiscences,* it not only received highly favorable contemporary reviews,[18] but also soon became a collectors' item of the rarest sort and was not re-issued in any form until seventy-seven years after Hooper's death, in 1939.[19]

While the Woodward letters (and, it will be remembered, those of Pickett, Massett, and Sol Smith) were filling the *Mail's* columns and Whitfield, the new partner, was writing the local news, Hooper had more leisure time than ever before. His health was not too good either and now and again he was "absent for a few days, to recuperate."[20] On March 9, 1858, Coyne recorded, he "abruptly broke from the ranks of the Can't-Get-Away Club" on the longest trip he had made since the horseback jaunt westward across the Mississippi into Louisiana with Joseph A. Johnson twenty years before. This time, Coyne wrote, he was "heading eastward and northward [to] Old North Carolina, in which he originated, and Washington City, where there are many originals *[sic]* . . . to whose care we confidently consign our associate."[21]

Hooper's sojourn in North Carolina must have been short (if, indeed, he stopped there at all), for on April 2 the *Mail* contained the first of three letters entitled "Some Things We Saw at Washington," in which "the Senior" stated that he had arrived in the Capitol City on March 15.[22] He had been met by "Horseshoe Ned" Hanrick, who walked him about twenty miles the first day, "pointing out the lions." Hanrick ("he knows everybody in Washington") secured for his visitor audiences with General Lewis Cass, Buchanan's secretary of state, and Senator Sam Houston and in general escorted him everywhere. They talked with various members of the Alabama delegation, sat in the Senate gallery, ate in several finely-appointed establishments, and "trotted at an awful pace through all parts of the city." Hooper noted many details for his readers, including "the large number of ladies loose on the streets, without escorts," but apparently he was not at all favorably impressed by the political scene. He complained of the inaccessibility of officials in high places, the generals who "pocket visitors in ante-chambers," the incivility of Southerners towards "anti-slavery men," and the coldness of the "aristocracy of office . . . , an outrage under our republican form of government." But the aristocracy was thoroughly established, he believed, "and will no doubt grow more and more exacting, until the present metropolis shall hold the capitol of neither the North or South." Then, prophetically, he concluded, "How long it shall be before the consummation is reached, is for the South to say."

Hooper returned to Montgomery suffering from rheumatism,[23] but he felt well enough to go to Benton, Alabama, in mid-July for one of Yancey's many political rallies. The speech lasted two hours "amid breathless silence," he reported to the *Mail*, "and the occasional cheerings which he received were at points where the argument culminated in the ultimate idea of Southern Independence."[24] Afterwards, Hooper travelled to Talladega, a fashionable resort, seeking a cure for his pains: "He will not . . . be able to participate in the pleasures of the ball-room with his accustomed ease and gracefulness," Coyne kidded, "but a little exercise in that way will no doubt benefit him materially." Finding little relief in Talladega's mineral waters, Hooper moved on to Shelby Springs and on July 30 returned home. Two weeks later, still unwell,[25] he again went to Talladega for ten days, returning earlier than he had wished in order to permit "the Junior" to make a business trip into North Alabama.[26] Trying earnestly to carry his share of the editorial load in spite of his ailment, Hooper wrote humorously about a burglar who had robbed him of a pair of pants and a gold pen-and-case given him by N. A. Ramsey,[27] and sadly about the death of his "accomplished friend," John G. Barr of Tuscaloosa, who, as "Omega," had, like himself, in the "old days" contributed many humorous sketches to the *Spirit of the Times* and other journals.[28]

But the strain was too great and on September 13 Coyne notified the *Mail* readers that "the Senior editor—whose general health, we regret to say, has been in the decline for some time—has gone to the country [Tuskegee] to recruit his health and regain his strength, which were sadly shattered by the arduous labors which he undertook and performed during the last session of the legislature, and from which he has not yet fully recovered."[29] Two weeks later Hooper was home again, however, obviously feeling better and able to report the Montgomery Fall Races for the *Spirit* over his old signature, "Number Eight."[30] "We are obliged to our neighbor, the *Advertiser*," he quipped, "for correcting the mistake of the Richmond [Virginia] *Dispatch*, to the effect that we (the Senior Editor) had retired from the editorship of the *Mail*. Our only chance, we suspect, of 'retiring' will be in a box about six feet long!"[31]

In the same good-humored vein Hooper wrote T. B. Thorpe,

who had recently joined Edward E. Jones as co-editor of the *Spirit*, that he would again act as regular correspondent for the "dear 'Old Spirit'" by contributing original material as well as horse-racing news. "To many of us here in the South," Hooper declared, "we have been accustomed to regard the 'Old Spirit' as the single remaining link which bound us in kindly feeling and sympathy to New York . . . Mr. Thorpe is the well-known 'Tom Owen, the Bee Hunter,' a writer in his line of literature, unsurpassed in this country . . . For the love of the 'old times,' and for the memory of old friends, let us rally to the aid of the glorious old 'Spirit.'" Thorpe, not displeased, listed "Number Eight" as one of his active correspondents and editorially proclaimed his joy by reminding readers that "our old friend 'Simon Suggs' [will come] to the rescue, with saddle-bags full of specie, and a heartful of sympathetic offerings." He further predicted that "'Simon's' experience, and 'Suggs'' hopes" would lend renewed prestige to the *Spirit*.[32] As events unfolded, however, in the months that followed "friend Hooper" contributed only scattered reports on various horse-races in Mobile, New Orleans and Montgomery but, regretfully, no original stories. And Thorpe, foreseeing the failure of the "old" *Spirit*, in March, 1861, sold his share of the magazine to Jones, who in less than three months was forced to bring the thirty-year old weekly to a close.[33]

From October through Christmas of 1858 Hooper did no travelling, but as the year ended he "took a little trip towards the mountains of Tennessee, through the hills of Georgia," stopping *en route* for a day and a night's rest in the "terribly-switched and railway-mangled city of Atlanta." As he had written three years before on a previous visit, he still believed Atlanta "destined to become one of the first inland cities . . . , the railroad city of the South." Passing through Marietta and Dalton, Georgia, ("whose depot smelt intolerably of hogs, whereof hundreds squealed in trains on the side-tracks"), he arrived in Cleveland, Tennessee, "the depot" of the great Ducktown Copper Mines, forty miles to the east. Two days later, silent as a grave about what he had seen at Ducktown, he boarded the cars for the return trip to Montgomery. So far as readers of the *Mail* knew, the journey to the mountains had been but another recuperative jaunt. The next month he made a second visit to Cleveland and on March 5th the *Mail* contained an article describing in detail the Ducktown mines, copied from the Charleston (S. C.) *Mercury*, to which Hooper added: "We hope not to be considered extravagant, when we say that the writer does not tell therein the half that might [be said] in support of the immense value of those mines."

Within a week the reason for the editor's visits and enthusiasm became apparent: the Alleghany Mining Company was organized in a meeting at the Exchange Hotel in Montgomery, March 12, "to purchase and work certain mines and mining properties in Ducktown, Polk County, Tennessee." Doctor L. H. Anderson was elected president, C. G. Gunter, treasurer, and Johnson J. Hooper, secretary. And one of the prominent subscribers to the venture was none other than William Lowndes Yancey. Lieutenant [M. F.?] Maury and Doctor [Richard O.?] Currey, it was stated, had surveyed the prospective holdings of the new company, whose members considered "Ducktown undoubtedly . . . the great copper deposit of the world . . . [and] the Alleghany Properties to be the very cream of Ducktown."[34]

Meanwhile, Hooper and Coyne, enjoying the fruits of these turbulently prosperous pre-war days,[35] purchased a 80′ x 100′ city lot on the corner of Montgomery and Wilkerson streets for $1500,[36] and advertised for a "permanent office on Commerce street . . . the whole of a third story to be built according to a plan dictated by us, and ready for occupation by the

1st of October next."[37] Besides greatly increased circulation, the *Mail* was now official "Printers for the City and Post Office," facts which doubtless necessitated expanding quarters for new machinery and additional employees. More new type was installed and the paper "enlarged and improved," rendering it, according to the Pensacola (Florida) *Gazette*, "one of the best printed and edited papers in the South. In fact, the *Mail* is really an 'institution' of Montgomery, and will be, as long as friend Hooper has anything to do with it . . . That's right! Follow the *Mail*—adopt all its views; and you'll be certain never to *fall into the ditch* (of Democracy, or Black Republicanism)."[38] And Stephen Massett, the travelling comedian who had earlier contributed to Hooper's paper, notified the *Spirit* that he had personally been entertained in Montgomery by "'Simon Suggs,' the genial and kind-hearted" and would never forget his kindness and the "pleasant hours" spent in his company.[39]

After securing "a friend . . . to occupy his place and furnish . . . political articles," in March Hooper embarked on the *St. Nicholas* for a trip down the Alabama River to attend the Mobile horseraces. Among the two hundred passengers on board was John W. Audubon, son of the famous naturalist, who was seeking subscribers for "his father's great work." Hooper immediately struck up an acquaintance and made a deal with the salesman, not only to buy *Birds of America*, but also to become "agent" for the expensive volumes in the state of Alabama. (Upon his return to Montgomery, he proudly displayed the specimen plates at Pfister & White's Book Store and announced that, whereas the first edition of Audubon had sold for $1000, "this may be had for $440.")[40]

At Mobile's Magnolia Racing Course Hooper the sportsman was in his glory. He wrote Coyne in great detail about each race, described the horses, the turf, and the people he saw, and sent long stories to the "old" *Spirit*, signed "Number

Eight,"[41] and to *Porter's Spirit,* reporting his "delightful week."[42] A Mr. Mason was there, he wrote, writing for the Charleston *Mercury,* and Hooper advised Coyne to copy him in the *Mail.* "He wears spectacles *and* a lorgnette, and, therefore, is bound to give particulars more accurately than yours truly . . ." From Mobile Hooper, thoroughly enjoying himself, travelled on to New Orleans to attend another racing carnival. "If my protracted stay here surprises and annoys you, *amigo mio,*" he declared, "just imagine the attractions which New Orleans presents . . . to a man fond of witnessing the powers of steeds of glorious name and noble blood." There he met "Col. [D. J.] Kenner . . . the idol of New Orleans," the owner of "Planet" and "Fannie Washington," attended the St. Charles Theatre and enjoyed the fine sea-foods. But he heartily disliked the St. Charles Hotel, finding it far inferior to Mobile's Battle House: the "flunkeys" were haughty, the comforts were "by no means such as the costiliness and pretentiousness of the establishment lead one to expect" and he thoroughly despised the "unfiltered Mississippi water."[43]

Not until April 9, after an absence of three restful weeks, did he return to Alabama—time enough, however, to report the Montgomery Spring Races for the "old" *Spirit,*[44] and once more to pit the influence of the eagle-bedecked "Southern Rights Whig-American" *Mail* against the onslaught of the national Democrats in the state elections of 1859.[45]

Not quite yet, however, were Alabamians ready to follow Yancey and Samford, the Southern Rights Democrats' gubernatorial candidates, into a new "States Rights" party.[46] The Conservative Democrats, under Governor A. B. Moore's cautious leadership, still looked to the national party to defeat the Republicans in 1860 and thus save the South. It was the *duty* of the Federal government, they reasoned, to protect slaves in the territories, just as it was to protect all other property, and their ballots confirmed their beliefs. Moore was returned to the governor's chair by an overwhelming vote, Samford carrying only two counties. In the congressional elections the old-line Democrats were equally successful in every district of the state.[47]

Thus, outwardly, did the majority of Alabamians demonstrate their unreadiness to divorce the Union, even in late 1859. But in spite of all the jubilant torch-light processions, bon-fires, bands, sky-rockets, and cannon shots of enthusiasm,[48] fear hung over the state like an oppressive cloud in the heavens. Even the preponderantly Democratic legislature, as it assembled in November,[49] was nervously apprehensive. Acts were passed authorizing expenditures of $200,000 to equip an 8,000-man volunteer state militia, the University of Alabama was appropriated funds with which to introduce military training, and the Southern Fire Arms Company was chartered to manufacture munitions for Alabama's army. Most significant of all was the passage (by the House 75 to 2 and by the Senate 28 to 0) of a joint resolution authorizing Governor Moore, in the event "a sectional party calling itself Republicans" should be successful in the approaching presidential election, to call a state convention, "to determine and do whatever . . . the rights, interest and honor of the State of Alabama requires to be done for their protection."[50]

Hooper, doubtless weary of it all and in poor health, took time out to follow the fascinating legal disputes that had arisen in New York City between the "old" *Spirit, Porter's Spirit,* and *Wilkes' Spirit,* to report the Montgomery Fall Races (in which an Albion colt named *Jonce Hooper,* owned by Major Thomas G. Bacon of South Carolina, ran), the Montgomery Jockey Club (of which he was secretary) and the Montgomery Trotting Club for the *Spirit,*[51] and to take a trip to New York. Early in October he wrote Thorpe that he was heading North,[52] and by the fifteenth was comfortably housed in the Fifth Avenue Hotel. Thorpe editorialized his arrival as "Col.

Simon Suggs, or rather our friend, Johnson J. Hooper, Esq., of the 'Montgomery (Ala.) Mail' . . . [whom] our friends generally know as the efficient Secretary of the Montgomery, Ala., Jockey Club, and is, besides, an honor to the press, of which he is a distinguished member." Evidently not "at home" in Yankee New York, however, Hooper cut his stay short, hurried down to Virginia to attend the Petersburg Races, and by the end of the month was back in Montgomery.[53]

He, as did many of his associates, believed that secession was just around the corner.[54]

By January, 1860, the South had put the Union on probation. For twenty years, long before the trying days of the Wilmot Proviso and of Yancey's "Alabama Platform" and throughout the passive later period of "non-intervention," many Southern Democratic leaders, sucking at the breast of the national party, had been filled with the pap of partisan politics, disillusioned, and nurtured on ambiguities. Malnutrition had resulted and strife within strife. The time for a show-down was at hand: everything hinged on the coming national election in November and everybody knew it.

In Alabama the situation was particularly acute.[55] The Democratic party had finally been split asunder, the "Squatters" of Stephen A. Douglas *versus* the "State Rights Men" of John C. Breckinridge. Each wing claimed priority and each contended that its candidate only could defeat the Republican Lincoln and thus rescue the South from Freesoil oblivion. A third party, the "Constitutional Unionists," claiming that neither of the "Democracies" could win both Southern and Northern votes, arose to support John Bell. And, as if the confusion were not already great enough, a fourth party, the Southern Rights Oppositionists, whose members bitterly declared they "would never join any party called 'Democrats'" and heartily distrusted the Douglasites, the Breckinridgers and the "Bell Ringers," sprang full-born into being in the Spring of 1860.[56] All were agreed, however, in varying degrees on the fundamental issue of protecting slavery in the territories. Not which party but, rather, which party would follow its principles farther or faster down the road to secession—that was the searing question.

Hooper of the *Mail* and his colleagues among the short-lived Southern Rights Oppositionists would go all the way. To them everything Democratic now stank to high heaven. Even the name "Democracy" was insulting. "Who knows . . . how many weeks will elapse before the two sections of this same 'Democracy' may find some common ground—then, where shall *we be?*," Hooper asked. "Hundreds of good men and true—State Rights to the core—who have never called themselves 'Democratic'—*will not* join any association bearing that designation." On the contrary, the Opposition Party meant absolute freedom from entangling affiliations: it was the one "organization broad enough in name to furnish us all a resting-place for the sole of our political feet." As the *Mail* proclaimed, the Oppositionists stood firmly for "State Rights, Without Abatement," and "bound by no ties to any National Party." They had high hope, however, that "a great Southern Party [would] speedily arise; but, whether it shall prove so or not, *we* shall be found battling for *States Rights* and *Southern Rights*—for protection in the Territories—and the maintenance of every other Constitutional right."

Among the leaders of the new party were Thomas H. Watts, Samuel F. Rice, Thomas J. Judge and William H. Rives, all former Whigs or "Know Nothings," and, again, Hooper was their spokesman. The platform upon which they now stood was that of "the American (Alabama) Platform of 1856," a document Hooper himself had written in part.[57] Thus, between April and August, 1860, the *Mail* spent its strength building up the Oppositionists and attempting to tear down the several "Democracies." Neither plan worked, however, for during the Southern Rights Opposition convention, held in Montgomery, July 2, the new party split itself asunder over a resolution upholding certain views held by the "Bell Ringers," the Watts minority bolted, and the majority, including Hooper, swung once more to the ubiquitous leadership of Yancey in his support of John C. Breckinridge against the "Black Republican" Lincoln.[58]

Meanwhile, for the rejuvenated *Mail* ("now printed on new and beautiful type [and] the largest paper printed in Alabama, and if not the best, at least equal to any") all was not politics.[59] For years Hooper's interest in the South had included the publicizing of the assets of the region, industrial, commercial, theatrical, literary, oratorical, agricultural (the *Weekly Mail* now carried a column entitled "Southern Husbandman"), military, educational and otherwise, and, if possible, these features were accentuated in 1860.[60] Behind the idea was the owners' candid belief that "*Industrial Independence* [is] the best preparation for *Political Independence*." For example, in January Hooper "Viewed" the University of the South (Sewanee) "in connection with Southern Independence," contributed long essays on Montgomery's new theatre and Dr. John B. Irving's lectures and was himself elected secretary of the newly-chartered "Montgomery Racing Association."[61] And the *Mail,* evidencing the editor's strong partisanship, flew from its masthead a large engraving of the state capitol, done by an Alabamian, H. Bosse of Montgomery.[62]

Two months later Hooper was off on another one of his "Southern rambles," this time "with a view to improve his health and finances," but principally to report upon the region's railroads, "'finished' and unfinished, and all other works of improvement and development."[63] Primarily a reporter for the *Mail,* he had also agreed on this trip to furnish feature articles for the Charleston *Mercury,* the Augusta (Georgia)

Field and Fireside, and the *Spirit of the Times*, the editor of which publicly begged that "'Col. Suggs'" be extended "all the honors he deserves as a gentleman, and all that he could or should have accorded to him as the representative of the 'Old Spirit.'"[64]

He arrived in Mobile in mid-March (having stopped over in Selma, Alabama, to record for his paper the Constitutional Union Convention), and was heartily greeted by the Mobile *Mercury* as the "inimitable Jonce Hooper of the Montgomery *Mail* . . . one of the largest and most readable papers in the South. Aside from his ability as a writer, the world does not contain a better nor a braver heart than throbs in the bosom of J. J. Hooper."[65] At once Hooper began to report his activities in "editorial letters." The "trip down," the horseraces (which, as a wearer of a "white badge," he witnessed from the "judges' stand"), the Battle House, recent fires in the city and other events were described in great detail, both for his own paper and for the *Spirit* (under his old penname, "Number Eight").[66] After a week in the seaport he went north to Columbus, Mississippi, "where by chance [his] eyes fell upon a paragraph . . . copied from the Charleston *Mercury* into the Columbus *Democrat*." The South Carolina paper had "dubbed" him "a Major," and his "kind friends [had] adopted the title instanter—so I am a Major of Mississippi Militia to the end of the chapter, or until the next war . . ."[67] April 1 found him in New Orleans where he was graciously received by the *Cresent* as "the Southern author and humorist, the immortal chronicler of the sayings and doings of 'Simon Suggs' and the editor of the Montgomery *Mail*. 'Jonce Hooper,' as his friends call him, has a taste for horseflesh . . . but meantime is on hand for business as a proprietor and representative of the best, largest and widest circulated paper in Central Alabama. He also represents the old New York *Spirit of the Times* and the Charleston *Mercury* . . . For these sterling publications he will receive subscriptions and transact other business for their account."[68] And with keen enthusiasm the Alabamian again wrote about the theatres, horseraces, and hotels— except that this time it was the City Hotel and not the St. Charles with its piped-in, foul-tasting Mississippi River water.[69]

Wherever he journeyed, however, above the roar of the turf and the laughter of sightseers he heard the ominous rumble of war clouds gathering. People talked of little else but the impending crisis, especially to Hooper, for by now he was known widely over the South not only as the humorist and sportsman,[70] but as the fiery advocate of independence, the spokesman for secession. A Florida paper, the Pensacola *Gazette,* described him as a man of "great ingenuity in bringing folks around to his opinion of things, no matter how long they have raved an opposite doctrine." Over in South Carolina the Charleston *Courier,* one of the South's oldest and best dailies, agreed, adding that Hooper's "high toned abilities and spirited patriotism . . . deserves and appreciates support." And in Atlanta the *Confederacy* avowed that "the *Mail* has won an enviable reputation, in the noble cause of Southern rights, and we cannot but admire the bold stand which . . . J. J. Hooper, Esq., has taken in behalf of the South. Pinning his faith on no party, or politician, Hooper has entered the arena, determined to do battle, to the bitter end, in defence of the South."[71]

Everywhere people nervously asked Hooper, Will there be war? Will South Carolina go out? What about Charleston? Yet, they all knew that the coming Democratic National Convention, scheduled for April 23, held "in its yet unspoken councils," as Hooper had told them, "the fate of the Slave States," for that "convention is the only body carrying with it sufficient moral power to commit any party or section to a proper defence of the constitutional rights of slavery."[72]

Few, indeed, doubted the ultimate outcome.[73]

CHAPTER EIGHT

". . . at liberty, is this our birth month . . ."

DESPITE the separating wedges of internal strife, in April, 1860, Alabama's delegation, led by Yancey, entrained for the national convention with great hopes, *positively instructed* to take their stand against any encroachment on the rights of slavery in the territories.[1] Hooper, who was destined not to attend this momentous session in Charleston's Institute Hall,[2] sent his old friend "Horseshoe Ned" Hanrick as correspondent for the *Mail.* On the eve of the meeting, however, Hooper, his heart in Carolina, could not restrain himself:

The South

Men of the South! look up,
  There are omens in the sky;
The murky clouds are gathering,
  Red meteors flash on high;
And there are moans and mutterings
  Sent up by heaving waves;
Our eagle poises on his wings
  And shrieks o'er patriots' graves.

Men of the South! the brand
  Hath flared upon the heath;
Its flame hath tinged the leaden clouds,
  And hissed its song of death.

The rifle and the murderous knife
Have seen the light of day,
And ruffian men, prepared for strife,
Stood up in bold array.

Men of the South! your homes,
Where peace and plenty smiled,
Have been assailed by thieving bands,
And by their tread defiled.
The canting traitors of the North
With lying tongues declaim,
And spit at you their slime and froth,
Their venom and their flame.

Men of the South! take heed—
Be watchful and be firm;
Ye have to smite the giant's head
And crush the poisonous worm.
Arrayed around your chartered right,
Strong in your holy cause,
Be this your cry in valor's fight:
Our State—Our Rights—Our Laws![3]

Hanrick's daily, almost hourly, communications from Charleston were the spiciest the usually sedate *Mail* had ever published, and Hooper conspiciously embellished each with a cut of a horseshoe, inscribed "Ned." In addition to the news Hanrick, a clever reporter, frequently permitted his pen to run off onto personalities, oddities and personal opinions. But the editor deleted not a word. "I don't like Douglas much now . . . he's a dead cock," Ned wrote the first day. "We are all here from Alabama. We have things our own way . . . . We Alabamians have been making speeches, and we make good speeches; d----d if we don't." Hour by hour, as the tension mounted, Ned became more disturbed, however. Even in his jolly, devil-may-care attitude he foresaw trouble and his stories were rife with expressions like "astounding news!" and "immense excitement" and "more d----d uncertainty!" On the twenty-sixth he deplored, "Nobody knows anything. The pot is boiling, I tell you, and it's devilish hard to sift the scum on the top! . . . The responsibility (and bad whiskey) is breaking me down." When the convention at last adopted the "Squatter Sovereignty Platform" and the Alabama delegation, accompanied by those of Mississippi, South Carolina, Louisiana, Florida, Georgia, Texas, and Arkansas, walked out in defiance, Ned exclaimed: "*Night.* All gone to the devil! No use talking . . . The Douglas devils would put the Squatter doctrine in. Where will a patriot go now? . . . I weep—d----d if I don't—for the death of the old Democracy. Bu'sted up with sudden fit of *Squatter Morbus,* she pegged out—d-----d if didn't—like an old horse with the colic, dashing out her hind legs in the last agonies, and breaking the shins of her best friends!"[4]

As a thousand men gathered about the telegraph office on Montgomery's Court Square (the very same office from which Confederate Secretary of War Leroy Pope Walker was a short year later to wire General Beauregard to fire on Fort Sumter), nervously interpreting the preliminary dispatches from Charleston, Hooper wondered if the South had grown "comatose." "She sees the weapon at her throat," he forewarned, "but like a man in a dream has no power to raise an arm to dash it aside . . . . Will the South stand Douglas? Take Douglas?" And then, emphatically, with all his venom: "By no means! . . . We are Southern to the core . . .but if the Convention fail to discharge its [duty to the South] fully—if it hesitate, equivocate or dodge . . . , we shall be found opposing it to the bitter end." His section, not the party, was all that mattered now: if the "rights of the South be ignored, the Democratic party is gone forever."

On April 30 the fatal news came. It was a brief message, only a few words. Alabama, led by Yancey, had bolted the convention and the "seceding Southern delegates" were to meet independently "at St. Andrews Hall, this evening." From the Potomac to the Brazos men sighed: at long last the issue had been joined "between the enemies and friends of the institution of African Slavery," Hooper declared in the *Daily Mail,* May 1. To him the brief dispatch was "one of the most important passages in History . . . Aye! even the old hoary Democracy is shaken from its granite foundations, by the undermining of a miserable destructive fanaticism." In his estimation the patriotic actions in Charleston would "probably be the most important which have taken place since the Revolution of 1776." Editorially, he shouted, "Stand by Yancey!" "*Stand by Yancey!*" And then, more soberly, "with but one political pledge—that we shall stand by the South, her interests and her honor, *come what will!*—we go on our way, trusting that all our friends will consider themselves at liberty, in this our birth month . . . ."[5]

Yancey's thundering speech at Charleston had turned the tide.[6] Enthusiastically, Hooper bought hundreds of copies of the famous address and sent one free to each of the *Mail's* subscribers. And on May 10, when Yancey and his fellow delegates returned to Montgomery, he was "conveyed from the depot in an elegant phaeton drawn by four horses" as thousands upon thousands of cheering men and women lined the streets and bands of music filled the air with "stirring pieces."

Two days later the great man, his hour at hand, addressed the citizens. Since Estelle Hall proved much too small for the immense crowd, the meeting was adjourned to Market Street, in front of the Montgomery Hall, "where a stand was erected and bonfires kindled." For two hours he spoke, "blistering and peeling all the skin off the political backs of certain outsiders at Charleston, hailing from Alabama, who made themselves very busy among the Northern delegates." His account of the convention precisely explained why the hated North had behaved as it had and why Alabama could not "in justice to her own self-respect and honor" send delegates to the next National Democratic Convention (which had been scheduled at Baltimore in June). Magnetized by his oratory, the vast audience listened "with profound attention." Never in Montgomery's history had there been such a moving meeting, such an impressive scene as Yancey in the firelight of his fame . . .[7]

For twelve years the Arch Secessionist had fought the fight of State Rights, with his back to the wall and through frequent defeats. Now, as victory loomed into sight, he was triumphant, invincible. Neither the press nor oratory nor political stratagems could stop him, and "his enemies, more dead than alive, crept away . . . moping about the streets." For weeks he carried his battle about the state, winning new friends and adherents. Then, in response to urgent requests of the Breckinridge Democrats, in mid-summer he left Alabama on "the most remarkable oratorical tour in American history." For seven weeks he travelled throughout New York, Ohio and other Northern states, advocating the justice of the South's cause in twenty remarkable addresses. Never had the nation seen the like of his courage and reasoning, his respectful arguments and sauve urbanity.[8] Alabama and the South were proud of their Demosthenes who, on the eve of his ultimate victory, realized that he held the South in the palm of his hand, finally.

Would it now be Richmond or Baltimore—Douglas, Breckinridge or Bell?[9] Throughout the summer Alabama's four parties fought it out on the platform, in the press, in conventions, on street corners. On June 4 the Conservative Democrats met in Montgomery to appoint their delegates to the Baltimore convention—they were Douglasites. Across town on the same day Yancey's Seceders assembled and instructed their delegates to Richmond to support no cause which failed to embody the "Alabama Platform"—they were Breckinridgers.[10] On June 27 the Constitutional Unionists convened in Selma and, claiming protection for slavery under the Dred Scott decisions, appointed electors to support their party—they were "Bell Ringers." And a week later the weakening State Rights Oppositionists gathered in Montgomery, passed powerful resolutions advocating secession in the event of Lincoln's election, organized "Minute Men" clubs "for the purpose of declaring to the *world* that we *will not* submit to the control of a Black Republican as President of the United States"—and, then, with anti-climactic suddeness split over a resolution introduced by Thomas J. Watts. In the ensuing quarrel over Bell or Breckinridge they witnessed their infant but belligerent party crumble into nothingness, yet their "Minute Men," with the editorial support of Hooper's *Mail,* lived on to make brief but inconsequential history in Alabama's Black Belt.

Hooper's pen could now write of nothing save the gallant and rightful South or the evil and usurping North. Daily he appealed to "all the people of the South opposed to Squatter Sovereignty" to stand firm, to "*stand to principle.*" He told "The Way the Wind Blows," balanced Breckinridge against Lincoln, argued against "The Rising Tide, North," declared "The Independence of the South," described "The Perfidious Douglas," and "Black Republicans" and flatteringly depicted the "Condition of the South." "Shall Southern Rights Men Give Up?" he asked, and "Intervention—What Is It?" Letter after letter, speech after speech and poem after poem he printed in the *Mail* to keep his readers informed on public opinion. He ran supplements and at his own expense distributed throughout Alabama hundreds of "Minute Men" pamphlets, such as the resounding *The South Should Govern the South and African Slavery Should Be Controlled by Those*

Only Who Are Friendly to It, by John Townsend of South Carolina.[11] Yet, over all his enthusiasm there seemed to lurk a feeling of disturbing uneasiness akin to sadness, which made him doubt the past and question the future. "And now the South stands alone—," he wrote, "behind her, broken pledges, useless surrenders, disappointed hopes and sacrifices, and before her, a united North, banded together against her rights and interests, threatening dangers . . . In what way the South will secure her protection time alone can show. Events are in the hands of God—we can only do our duty in the present."[12]

The attraction of two national Democratic conventions meeting in the same vicinity simultaneously was too strong for Hooper to ignore, although he had previously engaged "Horseshoe Ned" again to report the sessions for the *Mail.* Besides, his "neuralgic affection" *[sic]* made a "change of climate for a few days, desirable." Instructing Coyne that it was his "intention . . . to be at Richmond during the Convention . . . [and] possibly at Baltimore, also," he left on June 8, travelling by train as far as Savannah and thence to New York on the steamship *Montgomery.*[13] (Promptly, several Alabama "Squatter journals" circulated reports that he had gone North to "enrich the Yankees!," but Coyne squelched the rumor by writing that "Mr. Hooper never goes to New York for pleasure, nor purchases anything the South can supply . . . .")

Upon his arrival, he notified Coyne by wire of his "good health," and promised a letter for publication in a day or two. From the Fifth Avenue Hotel, which he found "the finest in the world . . . patronized largely by Southerners,"[14] he went as he pleased throughout the metropolis, visiting the great steamships (the *Prince of Wales* and the *Great Eastern* were in port), viewing the "immense and indescribable Japanese [Embassy] Reception" as it paraded down Broadway,[15] and otherwise amused himself in the company of W. M. Fleming "of the Savannah, Wilmington [North Carolina] and Macon [Georgia] theatres," and Doctor J. Marion Sims.[16] His friends on the *Spirit* greeted him as the "distinguished visitor . . . J. J. Hooper, Esq., ('Colonel Simon Suggs' of Alabama)," hoping that he would enjoy "the Japanese, the Great Eastern, and the fair weather."[17] He did not neglect business, however, for on June 12 the New York *Herald* ran the following advertisement:

> *Alabama Trade*: The Editor of the Montgomery Daily Mail, (J. J. Hooper) a well established journal, circulating largely among Southern business men, is now in the city, and will receive advertisements for his paper from houses friendly to the South. No Abolition or Republican patronage desired or received . . .

Meantime, "Horseshoe Ned" had made his way to the Baltimore convention and was preparing to feed his "d----d if I don't" dispatches to the *Mail.* As the delegates assembled, however, he found that Yancey and the Seceders were on hand, too: after having assembled in Richmond June 9-12, last-minute strategy had forced them to test the national party once more ("the Richmond gathering," stated the New York *Times,* "was designed simply as a sort of screw for coercing Baltimore").[18] This situation was most bewildering, especially to Ned. "Things have got into such a confusion," he wrote on June 19, "d----d if they haven't . . . too devilish much pulling and hauling here to suit me." The Douglasites refused to seat the delegates from the states which had walked out at Charleston two months earlier—"haven't even let [them] come in yet," Ned added on the twenty-third, and "things are getting desperate . . . and about coming to a focus." But Yancey would not be throttled. As "the whole hall reverberated with cries of 'Yancey!' 'Yancey!'," he made a speech out of doors and "it looked like everybody in Baltimore got around him, and such hollering as the crowd made you never heard in all your life."[19] The excitement was great. "Things have got into such confusion," Ned repeated.

Then, finally, the inevitable happened, just as it had happened two months earlier: the Seceders walked out again. "[They've] given up the Convention," "Horseshoe" wired the *Mail,* "and are going to organize on *their own hook* . . . We'll all have to support Richmond now, or we're busted, and blown a devilish sight higher than the Baltimore Convention is. Douglas might have known he stood no more chance with Yancey against him than the 'cook when Capt. Scott drew a bead on him. . . .' "[20]

By now Hooper had concluded that his New York business was not so important, after all. He boarded the train for Baltimore, arriving in time to hear Breckinridge accept the nomination of the "Richmond Seceders."[21] And from that moment Breckinridge was his candidate—Breckinridge and Lane "without equivocation." No longer did Whig or "Know Nothing" or State Rights Opposition matter, these issues of yesterday. Only Breckinridge, "the great and calm soul of Breckinridge" and Hooper's beloved South. "All had ended harmoniously and well for [us]," he later wrote, "and we have now only to meet the great issues involved, and compel them to contribute to our deliverance and liberty." Under the leadership of his candidates there could be no evasion of principles and no ambiguities. "Look at the platform," he pleaded. "There is the palladium of your rights—all your rights under the Constitution . . . Can any true and loyal Southern man hesitate a moment to decide that Breckinridge and Lane are the ticket that demands his support?" To Hooper they and they alone presented the united front which could defeat "Black Republican" Lincoln.[22]

If Yancey was the orator of secession, Hooper was its journalist.[23]

Upon his return to Montgomery the editor plunged deeper than ever into the fight for "Separate State Action," mustering all force at his command.[24] Editorially, he stabbed Douglas with every available political stiletto,[25] accusing him unmercifully of campaigning in the South to "give the 'nigger' his share" and calling his visit to Montgomery "proof of the consciousness of want of strength in the opposition to Mr. Breckinridge."[26] He attacked parties or persons boldly in print as "traitors to the South,"[27] devoted column upon column of the *Mail* to the activities of the gallant "Minute Men" who had sworn never "to submit to the control of a Black Republican as President,"[28] he bitterly denounced Lincoln and "rampant abolitionism," and he served as a member of the Executive Committee of the "Montgomery Breckinridge and Lane Club."[29] As the election neared, he gave increasing space to southern literature and southern products and to such articles as "Warlike Preparations in Virginia."[30]

Meanwhile, of course, the *Mail* followed Yancey up and down Alabama and into the North as he preached the doctrine of State Rights.[31] As mass meetings were held throughout the state for "Separate State Action," Hooper recorded them in detail; and when Robert Toombs visited Montgomery in late October to take the stump for Breckinridge and Lane, he received from the editor of the *Mail* a far different reception than that which had been accorded the Georgian in the campaign of 1857.[32] On September 2 Hooper's enthusiasm for Breckinridge carried him so far as Ashland, Kentucky, several hundred miles away, simply to hear one of the candidate's addresses. For three hours Breckinridge spoke, and Hooper, one man of 15,000 in the audience, noted "the great speech" intently. The orator's characteristics, he reported to the *Mail*, were "calmness, candor, lucidity, and elevation of thought. We could not have wished it to differ, in any respect, from what it was; and it will go far to convince the people at large that its author possesses the great and calm soul which befits the Presidential chair." Upon his return to Montgomery,[33] Hooper implored his fellow citizens to "organize, *organize*" and defeat the "Perfidious Douglas." We "labor for the Independence of the South . . . Friends, stand by us, as we intend to stand by you and 'sink or swim' *with the South!*"[34] If Lincoln were elected, he added, "the only hope for Slave States, is *instant secession* . . . Out with your banners, men of the South! . . . In the struggle for maintaining the ascendancy of our race in the South—our home—we see no chance for victory but in withdrawing from the Union. To remain in the Union is to lose all that white men hold dear in Government. We vote to *go out!*"[35]

Yancey returned from his "political missionary tour among the Black Republican heathen of the North" on the eve of the fateful election and, again, as upon his return from the Charleston convention, "never before, in the history of Montgomery, was such a welcome tendered to any man." In describing the "torches, transparencies and fireworks" and the "splendid phaeton with four fine horses" in which Yancey threaded his way through the crowded streets, Hooper was enraptured. He described "the waving handkerchiefs of the ladies [on] the balconies, verandahs and sidewalks," the "shouts and huzzas of the people," the mad rush for seats for "the Grand Rally" in New theatre (which proved to be too small) and the adjournment of the crowd to the open air of Market street. Yancey again was superb. The man and the moment had met.

"To the Polls ! To the Polls," Hooper proclaimed the next day: "Friends of the South . . . friends of Breckinridge and Lane, prepare your tickets for election! Watch every voter, that none may vote illegally, and there is no fear that unconditional Unionism, and Douglasism, and Lincolnism will not be crushed out *at once*. . . ."[36]

But such was not the case. As incomplete election returns were reported in the *Mail*, Hooper wrote dejectedly, "Lincoln Undoubtedly Elected."[37] The climax had come. Details were not worth publishing. "It is enough for the present to know that the North is determined, if we submit, *to wipe us from the face of the earth.* The details by telegraph would cost us a sum of money which we cannot conveniently lavish for such news."[38] And then, proudly: "Now there is but one party . . . the Southern Party, the Anti-Lincoln Party!!" "Minute Men" of Alabama, Mississippi, the Carolinas—stand guard! "The first and highest duty of the citizen is that which he owes his State."

As a reminder to the state legislature (and, ironically, set next to an article entitled, "Federal Troops in the South") Hooper now inserted into the *Mail* the complete text of the "Joint Resolution Calling for a Convention in a Certain Contingency, in the Election of a President of the United States," which, as everyone knew, had been approved by Governor Moore the previous February. When would the Governor act? Hadn't South Carolina already laid its "Declaration of Independence . . . before President Buchanan?" Mass meetings for secession were being held in every county in the state.[39] A new flag of Alabama had been made by "the maids and matrons of Montgomery." The Governor himself had already declared separate action the "reserved right" of each state. Senator Toombs had resigned his seat and left Washington. The "Wetumpka Light Guards" and scores of other military companies had written to the Governor, offering their services "in any emergency that may arise growing out of the recent election of a Black Republican President and Vice-President of the United States." Even the Baptist churches of Alabama, under the leadership of Dr. Basil Manly, former president of the University of Alabama, had "*heartily, deliberately, unanimously and solemnly united*" to defend the sovereignty and independence of the state, and the members of the Methodist conference, endorsing "African Slavery," had voted "to place their lives and fortunes upon the altar of their state."[40] Whatever was the Governor waiting on?

On the fourteenth the Governor replied: he had been uselessly but legally biding his time till all electoral votes had been counted, he wrote. But now he was ready to act. December 24 would be the day for election of delegates and January 7, 1861, the date of "the Convention of the people of our State."[41]

Immediately Hooper ran up the names of William L. Yancey and Thomas H. Watts as the *Mail's* "Secession Nominees." That night (why wait until December 24?) in a "great secession meeting at the Capitol" the citizens of Montgomery County confirmed his choices by acclamation, and adopted a resolution: "whatever course our sister States of the South may see fit to follow, Alabama shall never, by our voice, remain a member of the government of Abraham Lincoln." And the omnipresent Yancey added, "[our decision] means *certain and speedy State action, on the part of Alabama, as soon after 'consultation' with sister States, as possible*. It means—*The Flag with the Blue Field and Single Star*."

To Hooper it meant more. The *Mail* for the first time carried small cuts of crossed rifles atop its news columns, and from the pen of its editor startling essays on "What the South Must Expect from Lincoln," "Virginia Made Arms," and "Getting Used to Weapons." Jubilantly, the latter began: "One marked advantage which the South possesses, in the event of a collision between the two sections, is that every man and boy among us, is accustomed to the use of firearms. . . ."

When South Carolina seceded, December 20, Hooper printed that state's "Declaration of Independence" widely across the *Mail's* first page, exclaiming, "The Palmetto is in front—*let it stay there!* There is but one road to Southern safety and we rely on the great heart of South Carolina to *lead the way!* If she does, all will be well; if she falters, all is lost. Wherever the Palmetto floats, *we will follow*." And the day after, as the Montgomery "True Blues" were called up in full military regalia "to honor the independence" of the "noble" Pepperbox State with a one-hundred-gun salute on Capitol Hill, Hooper removed the engravings of small rifles from the *Mail* and substituted an enormous cut of a cannon firing and a flag with but a single star—the "glorious Republic of Alabama."[42] Still somewhat doubtful whether the Alabama State Convention would take the final step to secession, however, Hooper did his active best to bring it about by working for the "Central Committee of Safety," the primary object of which was "to induce the State of Alabama to exercise her indisputable right to secede from the Union of the United States, in every contingency, freely consulting and advising with, but not controlled by the action of the other Southern States, or any of them; and to do all that is just and honorable to effect this object, 'we pledge our lives, our fortunes and our sacred honor.'" Of this body William L. Yancey, Samuel F. Rice, and Thomas H. Watts were members, W. C. Bibb was president, and Hooper himself one of five men who composed the "Committee of Correspondence."[43]

Amid such patriotic excitement and "great anxiety" as the City of Montgomery had never before experienced, the one hundred delegates to the Alabama State Convention assembled in the Capitol on January 7, 1861.[44] Long before the hour enthusiastic crowds had gathered in the galleries, in the rotunda and out on the sloping sides of Goat Hill. From top to bottom the stone building was filled. Hundreds of men, women and children pushed and jammed in the corridors, each fighting for a glimpse of the great men assembled. Uniformed cadets and Capitol caretakers strove in vain to keep the celebrants quiet—even the peanut peddlers and vendors of refreshments were forced, according to one eye-witness, "to beat a hasty retreat for the safety of themselves and their valuables."[45] Telegraph messengers raced back and forth, "keeping up the animation." Men shouted and women waved handkerchiefs. Impossible was it to describe "the great excitement that prevailed in the Convention, and the deep interest that every member felt in passing events."[46]

Montgomery newspapers of course enjoyed an editorial field day—and none more so than Hooper's *Mail.* For days ahead the editor had concentrated on the assembly, giving names of delegates and commenting on their past records. He had spared no words in predicting that the convention would vote for secession, and quickly. He had added journalistic color to the event by printing full accounts of the retreat of the U. S. S. *Star of the West* out of Charleston harbor, letter after letter from eager citizens like himself, and communications from sundry organizations and individuals who proudly offered their services to the state in case of ultimate crisis. On the eve of the convention he listed the personnel of military companies—the "True Blues," "Metropolitan Guards," "Independent Rifles," "Tuskegee Light Infantry," and the "Wetumpka Light Guards"—which had only the day before entrained for Fort Barrancas (Pensacola) to bolster the defenses of West Florida. (The fact that one of his partners, twenty-four year old Whitfield, had gone with the "True Blues" as a second corporal was not overlooked.) Warlike articles, such as "Southern Arms—That Factory," urging the establishment of a cannon and other weapons manufactories in Alabama, were prominently displayed, and much space was devoted to telegraphic dispatches from Mississippi, Georgia, the Carolinas and other Southern states, all belligerent, or, to say the least, of doubtfully peaceful tone. When word finally came that the Charleston military had "answered a Federal Pirate" off the harbor, Hooper gleefully heralded the event: "*Glad Tidings of Great Joy!* This is the best news we have heard lately."

And when the historic convention was opened with a prayer by the Reverend Dr. Basil Manly, Hooper, serious now and never more solemn, declared, "Patriotism, wisdom, humanity, point to but one course, *instant and unconditional secession!*"[47] For one so ardent there could scarcely have been another road . . .

On the morning of the seventh, as one by one the hundred delegates to the Alabama State Convention were called forward to sign their names, the crammed galleries and lobby shook with cheering. So great, indeed, was the demonstration when Montgomery's own Yancey and Watts approached the desk that temporary President William S. Phillips was obliged to stop procedures to chastise the audience. On the second day matters were worse—and the convention, now presided over by President William M. Brooks, resolved, after lengthy debate from the floor, to hold their sessions in secret. Whereupon, the unhappy throngs sulked from the legislative chambers and hall to mill about the Capitol grounds, awaiting the joyful news in the chilly out-of-doors.[48] From somewhere they obtained "Little Texas," a twelve-pound cannon, loaded and ready to fire in celebration—but for three long days they and all Alabama waited.[49]

Not until weeks afterwards, when the history of the secret sessions became available, did the people actually know how debateful and thrilling the fight had been between the "Cooperationists" (led by Robert Jemison, Jr. and William R. Smith, of Tuscaloosa) and the "Straight-outs" (led by Yancey and Watts.)[50] All they knew now was rumor, false and fanciful rumor that swept Goat Hill like the wind and appeared in the newspapers as reports and allegations, for even the press was excluded. But the crowds hung on.

Among the anxious thousands disgusted by the delay was Hooper of the *Mail.* Tired of waiting on the "cautious movements of the Sovereign Convention of Alabama," on the eleventh he hoisted his own flag, a borrowed one, from the parapet of his office—"a flag eighteen feet long, by twelve, broad: a deep blue field, with a six foot, silver star, having in its center the letter A, in red."[51]

Nor did the people know the heated words that were flung back and forth across the convention floor, the threats and accusations and political conniving that passed between the conservatives of North Alabama and the separatists of the Black Belt.[52] Not even did they know, when at last the final vote came on the afternoon of the fifth day, that it was far from unanimous: 61 *ayes*, 39 *noes*.[53] "At this writing," Hooper stated early that fateful morning, "we have not heard the report of the cannon, on Capitol Hill . . . but before we go to press, we *shall* hear the joyful sound. The Ordinance, we believe, will be adopted, this afternoon, without serious objection, and under a sentiment of patriotic conciliation, which is the happiest omen of the day."[54]

At twenty-five minutes past two o'clock on the eleventh the doors of the convention hall were thrown open—the Ordinance of Secession had been adopted! Alabama was "a free, sovereign and independent State." At once a mad, vast crowd "thronged the porticoes, windows and parapets . . . and men, women and children rushed into the hall amid scenes of wildest excitement." Someone signalled from a third-story window to Mrs. A. G. Walker, wife of the chief justice of the Supreme Court, and instantly she pulled "Little Texas'" lanyard—the first salute to the new Republic of Alabama. Quickly the twelve-pounder was thrice reloaded, and thrice fired again, for the "gallant honor of South Carolina, Florida, and Mississippi."[55] Inside the Senate chamber "wild shouts and rounds of rapturous applause . . . greeted the speakers in impromptu assembly . . . the lobby and galleries were filled to suffocation [and] ladies were there in crowds, with visible eagerness to participate." It would have been impossible, declared an eyewitness, "to describe with accuracy the scenes that presented themselves in and around the Capitol during this day." Suddenly, out of nowhere a flag appeared, a large flag, so large that "gentlemen mounted tables and desks, held up the floating end, the better thus to display its figures. The cheering was now deafening . . . It seemed really there would be no end to the raptures." In less than an hour the flag, bearing a large cotton plant on one side and a coiled rattlesnake on the other, had been accepted by Yancey, apostrophised by William R. Smith, received officially by Alpheus Baker and flung in Alabama's breeze from the top-most roof of the Capitol.[56]

Throughout the afternoon and until the early hours of the next morning Montgomery was mad. Roar of cannon thundered forth the people's joy. Small boys shot fire-crackers. Replicas of the new flag appeared mysteriously in windows of stores and houses and eager hundreds thronging the streets met, wept and embraced. As night closed in, bon-fires lighted every principal street and orators addressed the shouting multitudes. Political parties which had so lately been standing in sullen antagonism were forgotten—there was but one party now, and one cause. Up and down Dexter Avenue and on Artesian Square decorated "illuminations" of Montgomery Hall, the theatre, the telegraph office, the *Mail*, the *Advertiser* and many other business firms flashed and the people yelled. Only the "one universal glow of fervent patriotism," wrote an observer, shone brighter than the torches and the fire-works, kindling "the enraptured community."

It was a great day, indeed, replete with scenes "indelibly impressed upon our memories," solemn and imperishable. As President Brooks believed, so did everyone, "Looking back at the many grievous wrongs under which we have so long suffered at the hands of our Northern *brethren*, and reflecting upon the threatened perils from which we have escaped by withdrawing from the Union, I cannot but rejoice at our deliverance; and this joy is increased by an abiding conviction that come what may, sink or swim, live or die, survive or perish, Alabama will never again enter its ill-fated portals; no, never—never—never!"[57]

And in the dark hours of the night, as the tumult and shouting floated down the rivers and plains south and over the hills north, carrying the message of state sovereignty to Alabamians everywhere, Johnson J. Hooper of the *Mail*, once Whig, once "Know Nothing," but always a "States Right Southerner," had at last won his long-sought victory over Black Republicanism. Proudly he wrote for the *Mail* of the twelfth: "*Te Deum Laudamus!* And so, all hail! to the glorious, free and independent Flag of the Sovereign Republic of Alabama! Forever may it wave in honor over a happy, chivalrous, united people. And to that sentiment, we know, that all our 'people say Amen!' "[58]

CHAPTER NINE

"If it be agreeable to the Convention . . ."

THE PROBLEMS instantly befalling Alabama after the passage of the Ordinance of Secession were vexatious and many. First, the state had somehow to be converted rapidly but gracefully into a new "free and independent Republic." Most surely this was a colossal undertaking. Matters previously unthought of pressed for immediate action: problems judicial, legal, military, postal, civil, social, economic, and many more. Overnight, officials of every conceivable type and authority were needed. And myriad other perplexing and crisis-ridden difficulties cried out for solution. Added to these was the grave political uncertainty of the day and of the morrow. Unnoticed amid the sound and fury of jubilation a civilization was crumbling at a people's feet . . .[1]

Already disharmony had reared its ugly head in Alabama: old political feuds die slowly and in their death throes agonize. Many North Alabamians, far from enthusiastic over the Ordinance of Secession, felt that the hot-headed "Separatists" of the Low Country, led by fire-eating "Bill" Yancey, had acted unwisely in quitting the Union without benefit of popular poll—in short, the South had usurped the North *within* Alabama! Bitterness ran rife. In Huntsville men declared they would spend their "last dollar" to preserve the Union. Others threatened to lead the northern counties into secession from the state and join with counties of South and East Tennessee in the formation of a new "State of Nickajack." Citizens of other localities burned Yancey in effigy and otherwise indulged in "violent manifestations of resentment" over what they considered the unfair, incautious and precipitant decisions of the convention. "Separatists" and "Cooperationists" fought it out in the press and on the stump in every corner of Alabama. The former joyfully boasted that "they would drink every drop of blood" shed because of the state's withdrawal from the Union; their opponents foresaw only doom and destruction: one man actually kept his home in complete darkness during all the celebrations, prophesying that every house "would be in mourning before the end of twelve months."[2]

Nevertheless, amid such confusion, misunderstanding, and feuding Alabama continued its preparations for a called meeting, February 4 in Montgomery, of the "Southern Congress," to which all seceded states had been invited to send representatives for the purpose of forming a new national government.

Newspapers squeezed every conceivable drop of publicity out of the proposed assemblage as well as out of even merest rumors. The organization of "Home Guards," military companies, the movement of men, the speeches of politicians, the hour-by-hour events in Charleston Harbor, the designing of flags, the election of delegates, the size and strength of forts and arsenals, the perfection of new-type rifles or artillery—anything was grist for the journalistic mill. Poems, letters, essays, speeches appeared in the press day after day from burning, praiseful Southern pens, and scissors-and-paste were freely used to extract from Yankee journals articles reflecting even the slightest weakness, fallacy or naivete of that teeming and likewise turbulent region.

Down at the Montgomery *Mail* Johnson J. Hooper was swamped. Second Corporal Whitfield, his youngest partner, had "to the wars gone" with the "True Blues" and was now stationed near Pensacola, Florida. Coyne, "the Junior," had been forced on account of ill health to take leave of absence, departing January 23 for Mobile and New Orleans. Thus did the unusually heavy responsibility of publishing the paper single-handedly fall on "the Senior" who, himself, was far from robust. "*All alone!*" he cried late in January. "When one man is called on to pass on all correspondence . . . , to correct . . . the crudities of manuscripts which *must* go to the printers—and, (least of all,) to write the hasty paragraphs which appear . . ., it is an occupation not much more pleasant than that of a man on a tread-mill, with only about equal honor and emolument."[3] Whitfield did his best to help, however, by writing long letters to the *Mail*, describing his tour of duty at Fort Barrancas, and Hooper eagerly printed them in full.[4] Then, as always, letters from soldiers made good copy. One in particular, from an anonymous member of the "Montgomery Rifles," explained the naming of their cannon at Fort Morgan: "Number 5" they had dubbed the *William L. Yancey*, "that pet and pride of Alabama, the political prophet of the South. You can have no idea of [his] popularity here; at the bare mention of his name," the writer added, "the wildest *huzzas* are rapturously sent up to the Heavens."[5]

Hooper himself wrote piece after piece for the *Mail*, short fiery essays on the South and its rights, articles that crushed Lincoln and Black Republicanism in his inkwell. He raised high "The Duty of Alabama," editorialized at length on the favorable reaction of the London *Times* to the proposed new confederacy, and gave ample space to the invention of revolutionary "Minnie Muskets" and other weapons. But mostly the *Mail* was filled with advertisements, copied material, such as "The Reduction of Fort Sumter" from the *Mercury*, and terse telegraphic dispatches.[6] On February 1 the spectacular visit to Montgomery of the University of Alabama cadets, accompanied by President Landon C. Garland, was given wide coverage: "We already have a *Military Academy,* at the University, more than half formed," Hooper announced. In the same issue he printed a letter to himself from Mrs. Winston Hunter, who had presented him with a flag of Alabama "as a *slight tribute,* for many gallant and meritorious services, in the cause of Southern Rights and Southern Independence . . . And for the certainty now existing of *Liberty* and *Independence,* happiness and prosperity under such a ["Cotton"] 'Republic,' much is due to *you,* and the magic influence of *your* pen."[7]

Meantime, on January 21 the state legislature had assembled and the Alabama State Convention was in session—both for the primary purpose of attempting harmoniously to settle difficulties which had risen out of the secession and of electing state deputies to the "Southern Congress." Would the people of Alabama once again look to Yancey and Watts and their colleagues, their most able and prominent citizens, those who for so long now had directed the state's destiny? Certainly, it would have seemed reasonable to assume such action. Here now, if ever, as a new nation was in the offing, Alabama would need to call upon its most talented and experienced statesmen to guide the people through the "impending crisis." Surely, the men who had so courageously taken the state out of the Union would now be drafted to guide the state into the new "Confederacy."

But such was not the case. As one historian has written, "with unwarranted self-abnegation, the convention passed over its own members, with two exceptions, and also the members of the legislature, in selecting the State's representative to the forthcoming congress."[8] Mounting dissension and strife between the "Separatists" and the "Cooperationists" had led to distrust and antagonism. Neither group believed in the other; both were afraid. And so, seeking harmony above all things, the two bodies passed Yancey by and Watts and the rest, selecting from their own two-hundred-thirty-three men, only two experienced statesmen, Jabez L. M. Curry and William P. Chilton. The other seven delegates were relatively obscure men of doubtful talent and achievement. Thus the nine, two "Deputies at Large" and seven who were selected from the state's several districts, were sent to represent Alabama in the "Southern Congress," a body charged with making the most vital decisions in the state's forty-two-year-old history.[9]

"As far as we know," Hooper declared, voicing the opinion of many citizens, "The deputies selected are men of ability and personal worth. Some were *not* elected whom we should have been glad to have seen thus honored." But he, like the others, accepted the verdict, hoping that the task of forming the confederacy would be done well and quickly. "If we delay and fail to act, *the Border States have an excuse for remaining in the Old Wreck,*" he wrote. Since Yancey, for obvious political reasons had not been appointed a deputy, perhaps there was yet a chance for him to get the larger, more responsible post of president of the Congress. Hooper did not overlook the possibility. Several letters suggesting that course appeared in the *Mail* during the days immediately preceding the assemblage, but they did no good. Robert W. Barnwell of South Carolina and Howell Cobb of Georgia were the names most prominently mentioned, and Hooper, realizing the stigma attached to any member of the so-called "Montgomery Regency" and desiring peace and cooperation for the good of all, failed to press Yancey's candidacy beyond a few suggestive editorials.[10]

On February 4 "at 12½ o'clock in the Senate Chamber of the Capitol" the first session of the Southern Convention was called to order by W. P. Chilton, of Alabama. South Carolina's Barnwell was elected temporary chairman, Dr. Manly prayed, and the deputies from Alabama, Florida, Georgia, Louisiana, Mississippi, and South Carolina filed forward to present their credentials and sign their names in the official record.[11] The first item of business was the election of a permanent president, an honor which fell to Cobb of Georgia. The second, was the election of a permanent secretary. President Cobb immediately recognized Deputy Chilton.

"If it be agreeable to the Convention," said Chilton, "I will nominate Johnson J. Hooper, Esq., of Alabama, for that office. He is a gentlemen too well and favorably known, to render it necessary for me to say anything about his ability and qualifications, for the proper discharge of the duties of that office."

"I move that the nomination of J. J. Hooper, for Secretary, be made by acclamation," shouted Robert Toombs of Georgia, seconding the nomination.

Promptly the motion was agreed to and from the galleries there broke forth round after round of enthusiastic applause and shouts. So much, in fact, that President Cobb demanded that "all manifestations of approbation should be, for the future, discontinued."[12] And Hooper, in the new and proud role of secretary of the Southern Congress, a body which within a few days was to become the Provisional Congress of the Confederate States of America, walked to the platform to begin the arduous duties of office.[13]

Even now, at this, his supreme moment, as the eyes of the South were upon him, the farcical "Shifty Man" stalked Johnson Hooper. "The Southern Congress has met," wrote an eyewitness in all seriousness, "Howell Cobb of Georgia presiding and Simon Suggs of Montgomery clerk."[14] And a correspondent of the *Spirit,* describing events "down here in the 'Sunny South' while the 'big crisis' was 'gyne on,'" compared Hooper's "personal pulchritude" with that of the "rail-splitting and replusive Abraham Lincoln," and described him as "author of the 'sides-shaking Simon Suggs,' which everybody *ought* to read, Senior Editor of the 'Montgomery Mail,' which everybody *does* read, undisputed owner—in fact, monopolist of one of the ugliest phizes which everybody forewarned, tried hard not to see." But continued the reporter, Hooper "bore the honor of his appointment with becoming modesty and dignity, and promises, that is, bids fair, after getting the 'quid' out of his mouth, and the 'quid pro quo' fairly into it, to discharge the duties of his post with credit to himself and satisfaction to the honorable Congress."[15] Thus, eighteen years after the creation of his famous character and during this solemn hour, as he accepted the highest responsibility of his life, Hooper was not Hooper—but still *alias Simon Suggs.*[16]

Hooper's election to the secretaryship could scarcely have been a surprise, either to Alabamians or to himself. No one doubted his rabid secession tendencies and, as Chilton had said, his ability and qualifications were beyond reproach. For at least a week rumors indicating his possible election to the position had been rife. The Montgomery *Advertiser* had already, a week before, declared him "in every way well qualified for that important office, and such a position would be proper testimonial of his gallant service in the cause of a Southern Confederacy."[17] Hooper himself, through his various friendships, might somehow have been assured of the appointment. Be that as it may, the day of his election the *Mail* carried this short editorial: "From this date, the senior editor will probably have little to do, for some weeks, with the *Mail.* Correspondents and others who generally communicate with him personally, will please remember this."[18]

As was to be expected, the Southern Congress, like the Alabama State Convention before it, deemed it prudent to conduct its transactions in secret, and day after day behind closed doors the solons went meticulously about their business of forming "a Provisional and Permanent Government between the seceding States." Within a week Secretary Hooper, overwhelmed by his new job, realized that active service for the *Mail* was at least temporarily an impossibility. Indeed, he had no time even to read the paper. When at last he found time to go over the issues of a week, he unhappily noted several articles which he heartily disapproved and the publication of which he regretted. One was an essay about the Congress, dated February 7 (Coyne did not return from New Orleans until the fifteenth), another a letter from Corporal Whitfield at Fort Barrancas, and a third, an extract from the Eufaula (Alabama) *Spirit of the South.* "Without indicating any opinion as to any one of the matters discussed in the several articles," Hooper editorialized, "I simply state that I disapprove of their publication and that I would, if they had passed under my eye, have excluded them."[19] Obviously, the Congress was consuming almost all of Hooper's time. Although he perhaps did not recognize the fact at the moment, only a few weeks were to pass before he would be forced to terminate completely his services on the *Mail* and, entering wholly into the new career, thus to put journalism forever behind him.

Throughout February and on until its adjournment, March 16, many vitally important matters were slowly brought to solution by Congress. On February 8 the "Constitution of the Provisional Government of the Confederate States of America" was unanimously adopted, the next day Jefferson Davis and Alexander H. Stephens were elected president and vice-president,[20] and afterwards, Robert Toombs, C. G. Memminger, Leroy Pope Walker and S. R. Mallory were speedily appointed to the secretariats of state, the treasury, war, and the navy. Henry T. Ellett and Judah P. Benjamin were unanimously elected postmaster- and attorney-general. Committees on finance, foreign affairs, the judiciary, military and naval affairs, public lands, rules, postal affairs and many other areas of government were set in operation. Three "Commissioners to Europe" (one of whom was the ubiquitous William L. Yancey) were nominated and charged with the heavy responsibility of winning the allegiance of foreign countries. especially England and France.[21] Every day Secretary Hooper sat through long proceedings, laboriously recording motions, nominations, and speeches, attesting and signing credentials and documents, and reading messages from the President and others to the Congress.[22] Less than two weeks after the opening, he was assigned the duty of arranging "for the publication the Provisional Constitution for the Government of the Confederate States of America, with the Autograph Signatures of the Members of Congress," and before the month was out he had also been charged with preparing for publication "fair copies of all acts passed by Congress," the public journal of proceedings and "a full index for the same."[23]

On February 21, the sixteenth day of the session, Leroy Pope Walker was elected secretary of war, and immediately, he employed Hooper as his "Private Secretary."[24] Thus, Hooper became a "staff officer of the Confederate States Army," a post which he filled temporarily in addition to his position as secretary of Congress.[25] With all his responsibility, not until March 15, the next to last day of the first session, did he learn that his salary was to be fixed at $2500 annually.[26]

Work on the *Mail* progressed well enough under the circumstances, meanwhile. Coyne and Whitfield were now back in Montgomery and, although Hooper had had precious little to do with the paper since early February, his partners were maintaining fairly high editorial standards. Luckily, there was no dearth of news. The Congress was "front page" always, and, of course, the inauguration of Lincoln, the "Peace Convention" in Virginia, the adoption of the Confederate Constitution, the bombardment of Fort Sumter by Beauregard's Carolinians, the anticipated secession of Arkansas, North Carolina, Virginia, and Tennessee, the mobilization and movements of troops and a thousand other crises daily, indeed hourly, made news of the rarest types. Rumors were plentiful, too, about the possibility of transferring the capital of the Confederacy from Montgomery—would it be Selma, Tuscaloosa, Mobile, Columbus, Atlanta, Huntsville, Richmond? (After all, what was wrong with Montgomery?)[27]

Amid all this confusion and already over-taxed with the double duties of secretary of Congress and secretary to the Secretary of War, Hooper decided to quit the *Mail.* On March 14, therefore, only six weeks after his election, he ceased writing. The announcement was a simple one: "*Special Notice*—Mr. Hooper, senior editor of the *Mail,* is not now engaged in furnishing copy for the paper.[28]

As the work of Congress had grown heavier, he had progressively realized the futility of even a nominal affiliation with the paper. War with the North was a surety now, only a matter of time. The seat of government would in all probability be moved shortly from Montgomery, anyhow, and if it went, wherever it went, he would go with it. Faced with the ultimate decision of relinquishing his career Hooper began quietly and no doubt remorsefully to seek a purchaser for his interest in the prospering firm.[29] Soon he found one in the person of Robert Frasier, a young man of Jackson County, who for a year had been editing the Bellefont *Era,* and the deal was quickly consummated. In the same issue of the *Mail* which contained news of the bombardment of Fort Sumter and Lincoln's hasty call for 75,000 volunteers for the Union Army Hooper announced his sale to "a most worthy and competent gentleman of North Alabama," adding that he would soon take a more formal leave of his friends and subscribers who for so many years had sustained him in his editorial career.[30] Thus, abruptly and without fanfare, Johnson Hooper left the profession he had followed for almost twenty years—since 1842, when he had edited J. F. Gilbert's Whig weekly, the little *East Alabamian,* in the remote frontier village of La Fayette. Regretfully noting his departure from the press, the Montgomery *Confederation* bade him fond farewell: "Johnson J. Hooper, Esq., . . . was a witty, spicey writer, and will be very much missed by the readers of the Mail."[31]

Heralded by political and military victories, the second session of the Provisional Congress was called to order on April 29.[32] Two weeks before Virginia had voted to cast her lot with the Confederacy, soon to be followed by Arkansas, North Carolina, and Tennessee. Rumor had it that Delaware, Maryland, Kentucky, and Missouri would also leave the Union.[33] Southern troops had begun rapidly to mobilize, Fort Sumter had been evacuated by the Federals, and Lincoln had declared a blockade (which of course could only prove ineffectual) of all Confederate ports.[34] Throughout the South military activity was accompanied by cheerful anticipation of a short war, one that would be quick to win and easy. In Congress routine work went forward slowly. General Beauregard was thanked for his conduct "in the affair of Fort Sumter," military forces were strengthened, mail service was extended, appropriations for the Navy were approved, and various other acts and regulations passed. Among them was one which granted Secretary Hooper authority to employ "additional clerical force . . . at six dollars per day each" to take care of an accumulating arrearage of copying.[35] Simultaneously, he was given yet another duty—the librarianship of the Confederate Congress,[36] a post which he was destined to occupy for almost a year, until the reorganization of the government in February, 1862.[37]

But the most disconcerting news of the moment, at least as far as Alabamians were concerned, was the threatened move of the Confederate capital from Montgomery to Richmond. Everyone "began to wail," wrote one citizen, for the transfer would most certainly "ruin the trade, the morals and the reputation of the town."[38] The *Daily Advertiser* bitterly denounced the proposal as "so preposterous, so utterly at variance with the dictates of prudence and sound policy, that heretofore we have not deemed the subject worthy of the slightest consideration." If hot weather were the reason, or the belief that Montgomery were "subject to contagious diseases," the ideas were "ridiculous in the extreme."[39] All Alabama newspapers joined in the fight—of course—but to no avail. On May 21, 1861, the act was passed, declaring that the "several departments, with the archives thereof" should be transferred to Richmond before July 20, at which time the Congress would reconvene for a third session.[40]

Immediately, the move began.[41] More than a thousand government employees, after packing their personal belongings and office records, started on the circuitous trek to Richmond, via Atlanta, Augusta, Wilmington and Petersburg, over railroads already crowded with troops, supplies, and munitions. Of necessity, among the first to leave was Hooper.[42] Hastily had he seen after his few remaining business affairs, gathered up for passage his personal effects and bade his friends goodbye. Only yesterday he had made this same trip, as humorist, as journalist, as sportsman, as businessman—it was no novelty, certainly. But now things were different. In each hamlet along the route through Georgia and the Carolinas he saw a new flag flying, a strange but excitingly handsome flag, and young men marching and women with moistened kerchiefs waving. Yes, things were different. And he knew that he was different, too. No longer newspaperman nor leisurely traveler, he was an official of a great new empire, one that but lately had risen to show the world how free men think and, in God's own time, would show how free men act. Behind him were the milestones of a long and checkered career, the law, his presses, and his politics, all of another age. And away back in the dim recesses of the Tallapoosa piney-woods he was leaving yet another marker, an illiterate rascal etched by his pen, one that oft had brought him regret but which now, in new and unjointed times like these, would happily have no place . . .

Late in May he arrived in the new capital to find that the transfer of government had served but to increase his obligations tenfold. Much of the responsibility of establishing new offices, securing equipment and the like fell upon the Secretary, and he was sought for many duties, even that of locating displaced persons.[43] So busy was he that letters piled up unanswered on his desk and his mail lay uncalled for in the local postoffice.[44] But he personally was not overlooked by the press. "Among the strangers now in our city, we have been most happy to meet Johnson J. Hooper, Esq., of Montgomery, the brilliant orator and wit," declared the editor of the Richmond *Daily Dispatch.* "Mr. Hooper is Secretary of the Southern Congress and is equally admired for his genius and humor, and for the sterling qualities of the high-toned gentleman. 'Simon Suggs,' if Mr. Hooper had never produced anything else, would alone immortalize him."[45]

Once more, alas, the Shifty Man had got there first . . .

CHAPTER TEN

". . . through spits of rain and snow . . ."

BY JUNE, 1861, Confederate Richmond, whose pre-war population of 40,000 new-comers found swelled to almost three times that number by the sudden pressure of soldiers, politicians, businessmen, and hangers-on, had quickly gone mad.[1] Wretched hotel accommodations or rooms in cheap boarding-houses, which had sprung up like mushrooms in every block, were virtually impossible to secure, even at greatly inflated rates "of flagrant bribery."[2] Rowdyism was rampant, so bad in fact that the *Daily Dispatch* and other papers frequently editorialized against it, and the Mayor's and Husting's courts were daily filled with every type of law-breaker. Arrests for stealing, drunkenness, assault and housebreaking were common, and with consistent regularity keepers of "disorderly houses" were apprehended, fined, and as "frail sisters" turned away to renew their solicitation, particularly of soldiers.[3] And to make matters worse, recruits by the thousands were being mobilized, drilled, and rushed off "on the cars" for a great battle-to-be somewhere in the vicinity of a little, out-of-the-way creek called, no one knew why, Bull's Run. Richmond was "absolutely overwhelmed . . . [as] the whole dense population settled down," wedged into every conceivable nook and corner of the cobble-streeted and beleaguered city.[4]

With government help high dignitaries fared better, of

course.[5] President Davis and his Cabinet were comfortably settled in suites at the Spotswood Hotel, but lesser officials had to fend the best possible in the wild and frenzied new capital. Luckily, Secretary Hooper obtained permanent quarters for himself, his wife and young Adolph in the Richmond House, a respectable hotel where many of the other officers of Congress were staying.[6] The older son, seventeen-year-old William, now a second lieutenant in the Confederate Army, had been left behind in Montgomery.[7]

On July 20 the third session of the Provisional Congress convened as scheduled,[8] but the actions of this important body were temporarily forgotten as citizens of Richmond and the South read screaming headlines of the "Glorious Victory at Manassas! Federals Routed with Awful Slaughter! Great Distress in Washington City!"[9] Routine congressional work continued in many open, secret, and executive sessions, however: acts and resolutions providing for the care of supplies for sick and wounded soldiers, respecting alien enemies, appointing surgeons for the Army and commissioners to Europe, and acts appropriating funds for hospitals, construction of gunboats—the list was long and far more direful than those of earlier sessions.[10] Secretary Hooper and his assistants labored day and night to keep up with recordings, correspondence and the balancing of accounts.[11] Now and again, as custom dictated, Hooper himself was called upon to read messages to Congress or to write letters to President Davis, informing him of congressional recommendations or actions.[12]

Throughout this session, which ended August 31, the special session of September 3, and into the fourth, which convened November 16, Hooper's obviously monotonous duties with the Provisional Congress continued. On February 15, 1862, as the fourth session drew to a close, he read to Congress two acts, already approved by the President, one of which "provided for preservation and future publication of the Journals of the

Provisional Congress and the proceedings of the convention which framed the provisional and permanent Constitutions."[13] Although at the moment he doubtless did not know it, the passage of this act, sponsored by his friend Howell Cobb of Georgia, was within a few days to prove a financial Godsend to Hooper and his family as he faced a jobless future in wartime Richmond.[14]

All was not work for the Secretary, however. Off duty he enjoyed the companionship of his wife and son as they sat chatting in the gas-lit lobby of the Richmond House or strolled about Capitol Square and up and down Ross and Governor streets. William, now stationed at Fort Morgan (Mobile), was a favorite topic of conversation and his letters home were "anxiously awaited." If they did not arrive on schedule, Hooper would telegraph inquiries. "You don't know," the father wrote in October, 1861, "how solicitous I am about you; not about your personal safety, for that a soldier must risk, but about yr *[sic]* habits, moral and intellectual. There was never a true soldier to whom his honor was not dearer than his life; there was never a great one, who was not a student . . ."[15]

War news Hooper followed daily, as did everyone, although throughout the fall and winter of '61 not much in the way of real fighting was occurring, only brief engagements, skirmishes, occupations—and waiting. Mobilization and training were proceeding rapidly North and South, however, and there were men on both sides—though by no means all men—who believed large scale maneuvers lay just ahead. Times were getting harder. In Richmond prices had doubled and were still rising and simple, everyday commodities were becoming scarcer. Even the Montgomery *Mail*, which Hooper now subscribed for and read avidly, had "been forced, by hard times, scarcity of paper and neglect of patrons to pay, to suspend its daily and tri-weekly issues," and now came but once a week.[16] Too bad that Whitfield, Coyne and Frazier were facing difficulties, but they were of another time now, another world. . . . In Richmond, too, war though actually near seemed so far away—Manassas had proved that. To be true, there were wounded men still lying about in hospitals, but they were comparatively few and well cared for by the ladies.[17] Troops were coming and going at all hours of the day and night, some southward to establish themselves in seaport cities and along the outposts of the far-off Mississippi, and some northward to the nearby Potomac. Young men were scurrying around trying to find uniforms, fearful lest the war should suddenly cease before they had their chance to be heroic. After all, it was common knowledge that the North wouldn't fight, or couldn't, and everyone knew that the South was "full of fighting men, every man of whom is more than a match for three invaders" and could "hold out fourteen years, forty years, four hundred years, before our native land should be subdued."[18]

All was not well in government circles, however. Davis was having troubles with his Cabinet and, especially, with his generals. He and Beauregard and Joseph Johnston and Gustavus Smith and L. B. Northrup, who was in charge of supplies, were known to have quarrelled already: Richmond newspapers had aired their misunderstandings. Ever since Manassas Confederate outposts had been in sight of the enemy Capitol and "Stonewall" Jackson had said to the President: "Give me five thousand fresh men and I will be in Washington tomorrow morning." But Davis, a military man himself, had other plans. And throughout the long winter of discontent officers and men lolled about in camps along the Potomac, oiling and polishing their weapons and waiting, or riotously celebrated their furloughs in Richmond, still waiting.

Ladies of the city were not happy either. They had openly opposed the new "society" swept into Richmond by the war, complaining that "the Washington atmosphere" was detrimental to the comfortable old aristocracy, and that professional politicans, office-seekers and other unwanted parasites should expect and would certainly receive no nods from *their* aristocratic bonnets. And in the brilliant social season of 1861-1862, which was as gay and expensive as ever one had been before the war, only the choicest "new families" were recognized—those belonging to the learned professions and high government or military ranks. The rest didn't count.

Commercially, Richmond was booming. New stores and shops were springing up almost daily, and three theatres were nightly jammed with capacity crowds.[19] Newspapers were filled with advertisements of every conceivable new article or gadget, from French china and perfume and Chinese toilet soap to pianos, plows and billiard tables, and steamers were reported unloading fresh stocks from Europe on schedule. Everyday commodities, however, such as corn, potatoes, beans, sugar and molasses were becoming ever scarcer, and already women were trying out honey for sugar, willow leaves for tea and various substitutes, including dandelions, for coffee. Prices were mounting. By early 1862 coffee ("supply nearly exhausted") had jumped to $2 a pound and butter was selling for $1.25. Wood had risen to $10 a cord, bacon to 65c a pound, and flour $15 a barrel. There was no salt and no molasses for sale, and the "small supply" of lard was offered at 45c per pound.[20] Few people cared to admit it, but times were getting "hard." Had the Federal blockade become so highly effective so quickly? Or was it merely the age-old story of greed and inflation?

But nobody seemed to be worried. Business was excellent. Foundries and forges, machine shops and manufactories filled the air with fumes. The Tredegar Iron Works was blacking the sky with smoke, making armor plate, shot, shells and heavy artillery.[21] Real estate was booming—everybody had lots for sale at prices ten times their value. Hat makers were offering to buy 50,000 rabbits, muskrats, raccoon and mink skins "for the highest prices," private businesses as well as the military were advertising for laborers and teamsters, and slaves were being regularly auctioned on commission at Odd-Fellows Hall and other locations. Franklin Street stores were displaying the latest ladies' dresses, packets were coming and going between Lexington, Scottsville, Jamestown, and Richmond, and the Richmond & Petersburg, the Virginia Central, and the York River railroads were running on schedule. Work for everybody who wanted work was plentiful and wages high. Gaily dressed Zouaves, high-plumed cadets, dashing cavalrymen in broad-brimmed hats and brass-buttoned Confederates in grey swaggered around Capitol Square. And along Main Street bands played "Dixie" and "The Bonny Blue Flag." Why should anyone worry? Wouldn't the war be over in three months or sooner,[22] anyhow?

In blooming, beleagured Richmond Johnson J. Hooper, secretary and librarian of Congress, was accepted unquestionedly. His position as a Confederate official, a man close to Jefferson Davis and his Cabinet and a personal friend of Howell Cobb, Leroy Pope Walker and others of the heirarchy, would have guaranteed his entree into society's elite circles. But he needed not to rely upon them. Already his fame as a rock-firm secession journalist and as a rare *raconteur*, the author of *Simon Suggs*, had preceeded him. Upon his arrival in Richmond the old Powhatan Club on Main Street, a private institution numbering among its proud and limited membership only "gifted and accomplished men of letters, lawyers, doctors, clergymen and philosophers in every range of human thought," extended him the courtesy of their clubrooms. The Grattans, Henrys, Ayletts, Littlejohns, Tazwells and Harwells, old members all, welcomed the new-comers, such men as William Acker Cooke, Charles Cotesworth Pinckney, James F. DeBow,

William H. Prescott, Archibald Roan, Alexander Clitherall "and by no means least, J. J. Hooper of Alabama," with open arms. And during the long winter evenings of 1861-1862 this cultured, convivial group sat semi-circled about the club's broad fireplace motto, *focus Perrennis Esto,* discussing matters abstract and stimulating, but never financial, for the Powhatans "had nothing whatever to do with commerce."

Of the distinguished group Hooper soon became a prominent figure. A fast friend of all, he mingled his great fund of humor with the sparkling wisdom of a practical philosopher. As a yarn-spinner he was superior to anyone the Powhatans had ever heard, for his delightful stories flowed "with great ease of expression in apt and expressive language." Hours on end he thus intrigued his fellows with "much that was solid food for the mind, well prepared and served in such a manner as to insure the physical and intellectual being against the possibility of dyspepsia in any form."[23]

In war-worried Richmond, too, during these uncertain, imponderable days Hooper's attention turned, apparently for the first time, to a serious consideration of personal religion. Previously, as one acquaintance wrote with unpardonable harshness, the subject "seemed never to have entered his thought, or at least never had any perceptible influence on his conduct."[24] To be true, he had described himself a decade before as "not much of a church-goer, not very orthodox" in his religious opinions,[25] but it was equally well-known that the faith he nursed, however unsatisfactory in the eyes of his pious, psalm-singing critics, was of a sort abiding and sincere. In politics he had scorned religion as a platform, welcoming its abolishment as a "Know Nothing" plank in 1856, and, once at least he had insisted that an attempt to bring "any member of any church into contempt *because of his connection with it,* is a violation of all the rules which should govern" a political campaign.[26] An Episcopalian by education and association,[27] in his newspaper days he had frequently attended various other Montgomery churches, and often he had praised their pastors' sermons and the music of their choirs. "We are sure," he wrote in March, 1857, for instance, after having listened to the Reverend G. L. Petrie of the Presbyterian Church, "that there was not a hearer who was not instructed [by his] interesting and forcible sermon . . . simple, accurate, and luminous in point of style, and warm and catholic in its tone and spirit."[28] If he never signed the roll of the "Sons of Temperance," it was not because of that organization's articles, for he publicly proclaimed to be "a pretty fair friend to temperance." Rather, he abhorred intemperance, as he frankly stated, "as the great curse of the country." But he was no man to put "faith in moralising enactments."[29] To his "liberal, truly American mind . . . nothing [was] more abhorrent . . . than any attempt, through any mode of coercion, to dictate to us how we *shall worship [our] God!*"[30] Early and late in life he was known "as a scholar and a man of thought . . . of large and guileless heart, a vigorous and fertile intellect, an affable and genial disposition, and a most unpretending manner . . . . With these qualities it is not a wonder that he was popular and beloved" by both family and friends.[31]

Whatever the reason, after his arrival in Richmond Hooper became greatly concerned with religion and after "much discussion and thought," fostered by the guiding council of Father Robert Hayne Andrews of St. Peter's Cathedral, decided at last to join the Catholic Church.[32] Even his intimate friends and admirers—Albert R. Lamar, from Montgomery, for example, and the Powhatans—were bewilderingly impressed by his conversion, though none dared doubt his absolute seriousness and the tenacity with which he clung to his new-found faith. Afterwards, it was said, Hooper "always carried on his person a Catholic prayer book and was very fond, when with some appreciative friend, to recite the prayers in Latin, repeating several from memory, and especially with much force and elocutionary effect the prayer of Mary Queen of Scots before her execution." Throughout the lingering illness which soon was to strike him down and to his death he remained a loyal churchman and a fast friend of Father Andrews, who, when the need came, administered the last rites of his church and laid the frail and worn body away besides those of hundreds of Confederate compatriots in beautiful Shockhoe Hill Cemetery.[33]

By Spring, 1862, the war which was to have been won with pop-guns (except that the Federals wouldn't fight it that way) was becoming a stark reality, and President Davis had called for 40,000 additional troops from Virginia alone.[34] The Union lines were tediously closing in about the Confederacy and, although the South had won most of the major battles on the Eastern Front, the slow process of engulfment had begun. Richmond alone had half a hundred hospitals, loaded with wounded from Seven Pines and other battles.[35] Strategic Forts Henry and Donelson on the Tennessee had been seized by far-sighted Union generals in February and Nashville had been captured, thus depriving the South of most of Kentucky and Middle Tennessee. In March New Bern had fallen, and a few days later went Fort Pulaski, Fort Macon, and Pensacola. Port Royal had been beaten into submission before the end of the old year and already the Union had a strong fleet based on Hilton Head Island. Charleston was under siege and Admiral Farragut's gunboats were fast joining the upper-Mississippi fleet above Vicksburg. On all sides the South was being bottled up: the blockade was on. Early in April Albert Sidney Johnston, Braxton Bragg and Beauregard and their 40,000 Confederates had met serious defeat in a two-day battle, the deadliest thus far of the war, at a little log chapel in South Tennessee called Shiloh—a place of no importance and then unknown, but now forever to be remembered: General Johnston and 4,000 other Southern dead had been left on the field and 16,000 wounded and another 2,000 taken away to Federal prison camps.[36] Never again need it be said that the North wouldn't fight . . .

Richmond was electric with suspense. The *Examiner* had warned that the enemy was raising an army of a half million fresh men, and that 40,000 of them were arriving in Washington monthly. They were building a huge navy, too, and through its many rivers the South was vulnerable. The Charleston *Mercury,* as well as scores of other Confederate papers, were attacking President Davis and the Cabinet for their inactivity, their fumbling policies, their failures to stem the North's rising tide. (Vital information was leaking out to the enemy—were there spies in the Capitol, or traitors? Otherwise, how was it that the New York *Herald* had been able to publish, only two weeks after the Battle of Manassas, an accurate roster of Confederate camps, including the names and ranks of all officers?) At Bull Run and Bethel the Army had hurled back the invader, true enough, but that was months ago. Enlistments for the "short war" were running out in the Spring of '62 and men were going home to their farms and homes—why stagnate longer in camps? Would conscription be necessary, "enforced enlistments," the *Examiner* called it, "something like a conscript army." Would Southerners have to be *made* to fight for their homeland? "These," lamented the unoriginal *Daily Dispatch,* "are the times that try men's souls."[37]

During such gloom, grief and uncertainty the fourth session of the Confederate Congress had been in action since early Fall. In spite of the attacks levelled at him and his "do nothing" policies the President had been re-elected without opposition in November for a "permanent" six-year term. Frail little Alexander H. Stephens had likewise been retained, as vice-president, but in the Congress and Cabinet there were many new members. In the latter, besides Memminger, Mallory, and Reagan (who kept their old positions as secretaries of the treasury, navy, and postmaster-general) there were former Attorney-General Judah P. Benjamin, now secretary of war, succeeding Leroy Pope Walker, and Attorney-General Thomas Bragg, who had replaced Benjamin. The position of Secretary of State was still vacant, however, Toombs having resigned after a quarrel with the President, and his successor, Hunter, had been elected senator from Virginia.

Otherwise, too, all up and down the line from the highest to the lowest levels of authority the government of the Confederacy had undergone a reorganization from a "provisional" to a "permanent" basis.[38] As a consequence, many old familiar faces were to be seen no more in the congressional chambers. Among many changes, the unified Provisional Congress had been abolished and in its stead a separate House and Senate created. Overnight the position of Secretary of Congress, which had been filled faithfully and loyally for more than a year by Johnson Jones Hooper of Alabama, had gone with the wind of ruthless political patronage. In the election of February 18, 1862, he tried in vain to recuperate his standing by offering his services as secretary of the Senate—but four other men also sought the position and on the sixth ballot he was defeated by one vote by James H. Nash, of South Carolina. That day chagrin had worn a second face: Robert E. Dixon, of Georgia, Hooper's former assistant secretary of the Provisional Congress, was simultaneously elected clerk of the House of Representatives.[39]

Thus, as a fellow Powhatan lamented, on the cold, soggy Washington's Birthday, 1862, when President Davis and his inauguration coterie assembled to parade "in solemn procession from the Hall of Delegates of Virginia . . . through spits of rain and snow, across Capitol Park to the noble statue of Washington, Johnson Jones Hooper was a part of it no more."[40]

The Confederacy for which he had fought long and labored hard had passed him by at last—"God Save the President!"

Alone now, for the pressure of war had forced Mary and Adolph back to Montgomery,[41] in wretched health and doubly despairing for want of work, Hooper turned again to Howell Cobb, who only a few days before had been authorized by Congress to sponsor the editing and publishing of the proceedings of the Provisional Congress and the constitutions of the Confederate States of America.[42] As these important documents were already in possession of the former Secretary of Congress, he was the logical person to do the copying and correcting. Cobb immediately assigned his old friend to the task.[43]

As rumors were rife that the "Yankees have landed 17,000 men at Newport News,"[44] assiduously Hooper began the work. But he had scarcely skimmed the papers over before he went down with a debilitating illness,[45] probably tuberculosis, and for two months lay sick abed at the Richmond House, attended by kind friends who brought him mail from home and daily visited by loyal Father Andrews.[46] "Ah! Well do I remember our vigils at his bed-side," wrote one friend, "the sweet gentle words of love to those who were watching the death of the vital spark, the calm great sleep of his noble spirit . . ."[47] On Saturday, June 7, as General Robert E. Lee—"Evacuating Lee," the papers had dubbed him—assumed command of the Army of Northern Virginia and all Richmond talked of nothing but impending disaster and the casualty lists from Seven Pines,[48] Hooper slipped slowly away, a smile on his face and his friends about him. The time was twenty minutes to seven o'clock. Monday, the ninth, the day after the tomorrow, would have been his forty-seventh birthday.[49] Thus, quietly, lamented the editor of the Richmond *Enquirer*, "he gave up to God as noble a soul as beat in human breast. Peace be with him—his memory with us!"[50]

Two days later, as a pelting rain beat down upon the horse-drawn hearse and eight regiments of fresh Confederates hurried by it on the double to reinforce "Stonewall" Jackson on the Chickahominy and the *Enquirer* devoted a whole page to "Casualties in Battle Below Richmond," Hooper's friends bore his body high on Hollywood hill, overlooking the river, to a spot he had loved and admired, "where the murmuring waters of the James will sing for him a requiem while time shall endure."[51]

News of Hooper's death reached Montgomery belatedly, not until June 14. His friend, Henry E. Coyne, now editor of the *Mail*, draped the thin weekly in mourning and penned a long biographical sketch of his "late friend and colleague," concluding, "Few men have ever lived of more genial impulses and warmer affections . . . and he never stopped to consider the sacrifice to himself if he could serve a friend. The past year has deprived every community of some of its best loved, but of the many who have fallen in war or by diseases, few will be more severely regretted, or longer remembered, than Johnson J. Hooper."[52]

To those who loved him this generous tribute and those of four Richmond newspapers must surely in some measure have assuaged the anguish of their bereavement.[53] But none could have been more comforting to his friends in far-away Alabama than the thoughtful comment of the *Whig and Public Advertiser*: "It will be a satisfaction to his friends to learn that his many excellent qualities were appreciated here, and that Mr. Hooper received during his last illness, the sympathies and services due his character."[54]

Peace be with him—his memory with us . . .

EPILOGUE

AT THE TIME OF HIS DEATH in 1862 Johnson Jones Hooper was one of America's best-known literary comedians.[1] His *Adventures of Simon Suggs,* first issued by Carey & Hart of Philadelphia in late 1845, had gone into a second edition before the end of that year, a third by early 1846, a fourth in April, 1848, a fifth and sixth, published by A. Hart, successor to Carey & Hart, in 1850, a seventh, eighth, ninth and tenth in 1851-1852 (by Getz & Buck, T. B. Peterson, Philadelphia, and Stringer & Townsend, New York), and in 1856 an eleventh, as a volume in Peterson's Illustrated Uniform Edition of Humorous American Works. *A Ride With Old Kit Kuncker,* published initially by Slade of Tuscaloosa in 1849, had been reissued two years later by A. Hart as *The Widow Rugby's Husband,* again in 1853 by the same firm, and in 1856 in Peterson's Humorous series. At least five editions of *Dog and Gun* had appeared—two in 1856, two in 1858, and one in 1860, and another was to follow in 1863. And of *Read and Circulate* and *Woodward's Reminiscences* one edition each had been published, in 1855 and 1859, respectively.[2] In eighteen years, therefore, at least twenty-one editions of his five books had been placed in the hands of American readers.

Moreover, selections from his writings had been included in four editions of two of the nation's most popular humorous collections—the 1845, 1855, and 1858 editions of *The Big Bear of Arkansas,* edited by William T. Porter, and the 1851 edition of Thomas A. Burke's *Polly Peablossom's Wedding, and Other*

Tales, a volume which was also dedicated to Hooper. His fame had also been given impetus in 1853, 1854, and 1856 by Joseph G. Baldwin who, in four editions of *Flush Times of Alabama and Mississippi*, had devoted a lengthy chapter to a character, complete with pictures, called "Simon Suggs, Jr.," obviously based on Hooper's.[3] Earlier, John S. Robb, of St. Louis, known widely as "Solitaire," had paid special tribute to Hooper in his introduction to *Streaks of Squatter Life and Far Western Scenes* by declaring that his "amusing delineaations," along with those of Thorpe, Field, and Sol Smith, had given "assurance that the rivers and valleys of this western land will no longer be neglected."[4] Besides, Hooper had received the public praise of Sol Smith, Joseph M. Field, Stephen C. Massett, Thomas Bangs Thorpe and, most important, that of his long-time friend and benefactor, William T. Porter, editor of the *Spirit*.

In 1852 Thomas Chandler Haliburton, the Nova Scotian creator of "Sam Slick," had edited and published in London one of the most widely circulated early humorous anthologies, *Traits of American Humour, By Native Authors.* Included were three of Hooper's stories, "Widow Rugby's Husband," "A Ride with Old Kit Kuncker," and "Captain Stick and Toney."[5] A year later William Jerdan had issued, also in London, a volume called *Yankee Humour, and Uncle Sam's Fun,* which contained copious selections from *Simon Suggs.* To Jerdan, Suggs was "a vividly drawn character of hypocrisy and craft . . . [whose adventures embodied] the uttermost sharpness, not to say rascality, of the resolute go-a-head character in a new country, which would rather succeed by foul than fair means, and in which it is declared to be good to be shifty." Hooper's "sketches of manners, laws, and customs, are lively and droll, and taking the census [were considered] most truly and peculiarly American."[6]

Meanwhile, in the South plans were being made for publication of the first "Southern humorous anthology," *Southern and South-Western Sketches: Fun, Sentiment and Adventure.* "Edited by a Gentleman of Richmond," the book appeared in 1855 and included "The Hanimal Show," a modified version of "The Elephant in La Fayette," from *Widow Rugby's Husband.* The sketch, the editor declared, "is by the graphic feather of Johnson J. Hooper . . . we consider him, next to Longstreet, the best delineator of country life, manners, and customs." The Richmond *Dispatch,* commenting on the volume, added, "The book is a collection of Tales, which had their origins chiefly in the South and Southwest. We most heartily commend it to the attention of the public . . . it is particularly deserving [of] public encouragement."[7] Two years later Rufus N. Griswold, in the fourth edition of *Prose Writers of America,* praised Hooper's *Simon Suggs* as one of the "productions of the South and West which give abundant promise to the future," declaring that their "originality and riant boldness justify expectations of an original and indigenous literature of this kind from the cotton regions and the valley of the Mississippi."[8] And in 1858 when William E. Burton's three-volume *Cyclopedia of Wit and Humor* was issued, it contained four Hooper pieces, "Widow Rugby's Husband," "An Alligator Story," "Captain McSpadden," and "In Favor of the Hog," thus putting the Alabamian in company of "the most Eminent Humorists of America, Iceland, Scotland, and England."[9] Add to these the fact that for almost twenty years, since September 9, 1843, the day his first story had appeared in the *Spirit,* the droll outputs of Hooper's pen had been printed and reprinted in countless newspapers and magazines throughout the nation, and it was not difficult to believe that at the time of his death his name (or, better perhaps, the name of his chief character) was a household word in every section of the United States. Everywhere his rich joviality was "eagerly devoured by the public," and he was accorded "absolute ascendency" in the field of American wit and humor.[10]

But the Civil War and all that went with it forecast the end of the popularity of Hooper's *genre* of indigenous American humor, bending and twisting the chain of continuity in a thousand ways and ultimately rendering the "old" writers all but voiceless against the new and noisy "platform" wit of the years that followed. Hooper's simple homespun frontier yarns, like those of his brilliant ante-bellum contemporaries, were doomed for long to have no firm place in the enduring literature of America. Out of the West and out of the War came a new laughter, a new product, a new era of national literary humor, sponsored mostly by men who were yet unborn when *Simon Suggs* had sprung full-grown onto American bookstalls: David Ross Locke ("Petroleum V. Nasby"), Charles F. Browne ("Artemus Ward"), Robert Henry Newell ("Orpheus C. Kerr"), Thomas Nast, Edgar Wilson ("Bill") Nye, Henry Wheeler Shaw ("Josh Billings"), Samuel L. Clemens ("Mark Twain"), and others.[11] And, as they came, their predecessors, to whom they unwittingly owed much but paid little, were crowded slowly but surely from the field to become untimely, laughless, and in many cases difficult of reading by the new generation without benefit of footnotes.

The "old" humorists had striven hard, to be true, but they had fought for the most part singly and in local sectors only. Remarkably rich in mother wit, they had nevertheless been provincial, sporadic, independent. Thus widely deployed, their front had presented little unity—for them there had been no "school," no nation-wide, distinct pattern.[12] What they lacked (and in the period prior to the Civil War this is easily understandable) was a spirit of *nationalism*, a new nationalism that could have come only in the wake of the irrepressible conflict. Within a year after Appomattox a reviewer of *Artemus Ward: His Travels*, one of the first of the new humor books, shrewdly observed that the old, provincial product had waned. Let the "new" humorists, he wrote, "seek to embody the wit and humor of all parts of the country, not only of the one city where their paper is published. . . . Let them form a nucleus which will draw to itself all the waggery and wit of America."[13] In part his prophecy was fulfilled. For soon the "new" writers *belonged,* and, as another critic has observed, they quickly became a different but "understood and accepted" school that made fun of a *whole* society in its struggle for democracy, laughing "equally at idlers and idealists, at fools and poets, at unsuccessful sinners and unsuccessful saints." This broad, slurring attitude toward life they could take easily, for standing behind them, and they knew it, was "the great American majority . . ., hearty, kindly, fair-intentioned, but self-satisfied and unspeculative."[14]

But only in part was the reviewer correct. The chain of continuity, bent and twisted, had not indeed been broken: the new literary comedians were but a part of all they had met. They plowed the same old furrows as had their predecessors and whether they plowed them longer or deeper or straighter is purely a matter of opinion. In other words, as Walter Blair has written, "America by 1850 had discovered most of the things it was going to laugh at, and thereafter authors played variations on themes already announced."[15]

However, comparatively few social and literary historians have seen fit to delve critically and seriously into this treasury of early American humor, especially that of the South and Southwest. Perhaps they have been too proud. There is also a possibility that they have lived in ignorance of the field, unaware of its virgin and almost inexhaustible wealth. The few who have lifted the lid have discovered veritable mines of pertinent information concerning practically every phase of life, manners and customs during the nation's formative period. These graphic pictures of the South and Southwest, wrote a critic seventy-five years ago, "if purged of their grossness, and artistically inwoven with some genial purpose, would better represent our national idiosyncrasies, with their reckless heroism, quaint extravagances, and novel parlance, than any other portion of our literature."[16] The humor of them all, another has observed, "spontaneously bubbling forth from everyday life, dealt with *real* incidents and *real* characters."[17] Certainly, wrote a third, "America's boisterous nineteenth century literary comedians, writing honestly of the life about them, were significant pioneers in the development of realism in American fiction."[18]

No better proof of this is needed than the ever-increasing evidence of the dependence of Artemus Ward, Bret Harte and Mark Twain, to name but three of the outstanding postbellum humorists, on those literary comedians who had preceded them. "The humor of Bret Harte and Mark Twain," W. P. Trent wrote in 1901, "may not claim kin with that of Longstreet and Johnson J. Hooper, but this is mainly due to the fact that the family tree has not been drawn."[19] Stephen Leacock, believing likewise, stated in 1936 that they "made the mold in which our present thought is cast . . . [for their] influence was to help make the triumphant American Humor, applauded of all the world."[20] More recently it has been stated that "the germ of an American literary prose based upon the vernacular instead of upon a literary tradition" is to be found in the humorists of the frontier and that their contributions to a folk tradition was "destined to flower in Mark Twain."[21]

Nor were the biographies of the post-Civil War humorists greatly unlike those of the earlier men. They, too, were mostly printers or editors, planters or lawyers, or soldiers or traders who first turned to writing as an avocation. Browne, Locke, Nye, Finley P. Dunne ("Mr. Dooley"), and Robert H. Newell were journalists; Charles H. Smith ("Bill Arp") and Shaw were farmers, the former being also a lawyer and judge, the latter a steamboat captain and auctioneer; and Clemens, the greatest of them all, as is well known, was a combination of many things. In other respects they were blood brothers to their predecessors: in subject matter, style, and even in the use of anecdotes, aphorisms, letters, tall tales, and cacography. Indeed, a careful reading of the new writers reveals that they aped their ante-bellum predecessors of the Old Southwest and East in almost every conceivable way. "Plainly," as has been observed, they were sailing in an already well-dredged "main channel of American literature."[22] But they were also louder, less subtle, more plentiful and more productive, and for the first time they showed the world that a funny man could make a good living out of simply being funny, either in print or on a platform.

So, from the Civil War to the end of the century the presses of America rattled off more humor books than ever before—the new ones in amazing, fast-selling quantities and the old ones, the regional volumes, in ever-smaller editions, just enough to meet the declining popular demand. Beside Artemus Ward, Petroleum V. Nasby, Josh Billings, and Bill Arp on the bookshelves of the nation one therefore found new editions of Longstreet's *Georgia Scenes* in 1860, 1884, 1894, and 1897, of *Major Jones* in 1872, 1879, and 1880, of *Flush Times in Alabama and Mississippi* in 1876, 1879, 1887, 1899 (printed in San Francisco), and 1908, and of the *Sut Lovingood* yarns as late as 1937.[23]

By comparison, Johnson Jones Hooper's works may be said to have fared slightly less well. For *Dog and Gun* reached only one new edition after 1865, that in 1871 (it was in print as late as 1876), *Simon Suggs* two, one in 1881 and another more recently, in 1928, and *Woodward's Reminiscences* a second printing in 1939.[24] Perhaps the Alabamian died too soon—two years before the creator of "Ovid Bolus, Esq." and "Simon

Suggs, Jr.," five before "Sut Lovingood," eight before *Georgia Scenes,* sixteen before the "Big Bear," and twenty before "Major Jones." Perhaps he died at the wrong moment, in the second year of the Civil War. Or perhaps in his last years he wrote too little, feeling ashamed of his grotesque creatures, divorcing his art for politics, and then dying "poor and neglected at the tail-end of a lost cause."[25] Be that as it may, neither Hooper's name nor his works has been possible of omission in any serious history of American humor for a hundred years. From William Makepeace Thackeray, who loudly praised his art, and is reputed to have believed "Hooper to be the most promising writer of his day,"[26] and Mark Twain, who stole his thunder,[27] down to and including the more recent critics—Franklin J. Meine, Walter Blair, Bernard DeVoto, Jeanette Tandy, Arthur P. Hudson, Constance Rourke, James R. Aswell and others—the author of *Simon Suggs* has never failed to receive top or near-top billing.[28]

Hudson, for instance, called Hooper "one of the brilliant company of local-color humorists" and *Simon Suggs,* a well-known 'classic'."[29] Blair, following the lead of Frank W. Chandler, who earlier stated that *Simon Suggs* is "a notable contribution" to the literature of roguery,[30] found it impossible to believe that, without a knowledge of European picaresque fiction, "Hooper could have learned how to draw Simon Suggs."[31] Henry Clay Lukens described him as one of the "notable laugh-raisers" among the "many native literary comedians of rare talent."[32] Will Howe attributed to him "the most delicate touch of his time and section."[33] And Henry Watterson paid him glowing tribute in these words: "[Captain Simon Suggs] is to the humor of the South what Sam Weller is to the humor of England, and Sancho Panza to the humor of Spain. Of course, he is a sharper and a philosopher. But he stands out of the canvas whereon an obscure local Rubens has depicted him as lifelike and vivid as Gil Blas of Santillane."[34]

For twenty or more years after the Civil War Hooper's stories were freely printed in newspapers of the nation, especially those of the New South, as they had been before. "Rest assured," an eminent historian who recently made a study of hundreds of weekly Southern newspapers since 1870, has written, "Rest assured . . . that I have seen *The Adventures of Simon Suggs* many times."[35] Over and over again Hooper's stories were recopied and for years after his death his unrecorded anecdotes were remembered and sent in to various editors who were pleased not only to print them, but also to preface them with glowing tributes to his memory.[36] In 1894 a Montgomery judge recalled him as "the wittiest man I ever knew" and a minister, describing Hooper as a sensitive, chivalrous gentleman, declared that he "wrote with great freedom and accuracy, was wisely brief and to the point, and his first manuscript was used without correction or changes."[37] And three years later one of Hooper's personal friends, publicly expressing the wish that a publisher would bring out a new edition of *Simon Suggs,* declared that the "rich and rare" book abounded in "pithy sayings and striking situations, which charmed as much by their naturalness as by the fun and frolic with which they were attended . . . . It is worth a baker's dozen of most of the so-called works of humor that are annually thrown from the American press." Hooper himself, the speaker continued, was beloved of all who knew him, a man "frail in body and so mild and gentle in manner and so quiet and kind in face. But . . . in a rough and tumble political fight he always 'held his own'—could give and take hard knocks although he never violated the proprieties of his responsible post."[38]

In New York in 1869 James Wood Davidson issued the first post-Civil War anthology, *The Living Writers of the South.* As the title indicates, none of Hooper's stories was included, but the editor did not fail the opportunity to express his high regard for the Alabamian. *Georgia Scenes,* he wrote, "is Judge Longstreet's *magnum opus.* It compares favorably with most similar works, though I consider it less uniformly humorous than the *Adventures of Simon Suggs* . . ."[39] Thirteen years later Henry Watterson edited one of the better-known collections of Southern humorous yarns, *Oddities in Southern Life and Character,* devoting fifty-odd pages to *Simon Suggs.* Hooper he stated, "was a most genial and entertaining person, and the central figure of a brilliant coterie of writers and speakers. . . ." *Simon Suggs* he described as a "masterpiece," the subject as a "sharp and vulgar, sunny and venal swashbuckler . . . a representative character, the Sam Slick of the South; only, I should say, the Sam Slick of Judge Haliburton is not nearly so true to nature, so graphic, or so picturesque." In Watterson's mind there was obviously no doubt of Hooper's permanence: "At all events, Simon has survived the ephemeral creations of contemporary humor, and is as fresh and lively today as he was five and thirty years ago."[40] Samuel L. Clemens' *Mark Twain's Library of Humor,* published in 1888, contains "Simon Suggs Gets a 'Soft Snap' from His Daddy," embellished with three Kemble illustrations,[41] and James Barr's *The Humor of America,* an anthology published in London in 1893, places Hooper in the company of Mark Twain, Ward, Joel Chandler Harris and James Russell Lowell by including "Captain Stick and Toney." The editor briefly described Hooper's humor as "clever, but somewhat broad."[42] Ten years later Samuel Albert Link devoted a chapter of his *Pioneers of Southern Literature* to Hooper, quoting copiously from *Simon Suggs.* The character, he believed, would "live at least in tradition, if not in literature."[43] In 1906 Carl Holliday, reprinting a part of "Taking the Census" in *A History of Southern Literature,* saw in Hooper's humor "an element of pathos, but added that the purpose of *Simon Suggs* was "fun-making, and in that particular it is a decided success."[44] A year later

A Pocket Book of Early American Humorists appeared in Boston containing selections from the works of many authors, beginning with Washington Irving. Three of Hooper's yarns, "A Judgment for Costs," "An Alabama Sairey Gamp," and "The Bailiff that Stuck to His Oath," were included. "In his character of *Simon Suggs*," the editor stated, "[Hooper] satirically describes the career of an amusing rascal in the early Southwest . . . although little known today, Mr. Hooper's work deserves to be remembered among the best early humor of the South."[45]

In 1907 at least three anthologies contained Hooper's stories—*The Wit and Humor of America*, edited by Marshall P. Wilder ("Simon Starts in the World"),[46] Joel Chandler Harris' *American Wit and Humor by One Hundred of America's Leading Humorists* ("Taking the Census," Part II),[47] and the monumental *Library of Southern Literature* ("The Captain Is Arraigned Before a Jury" and "Taking the Census"). C. Alphonso Smith, briefly discussing Hooper's writings in the last-named volume, declared that his "reputation was national" and added, quoting Trent, that it would be "hard to assign the palm among these Southwestern humorists. 'Sut Lovingood,' 'Captain Simon Suggs,' 'Major Jones,' and 'Ned Brace' are all worthies whom it is well to have known at one time or another, provided one is not squeamish or puritanical."[48] More recently, Hooper's stories have been increasingly popular with editors and anthologists. Napier Wilt, for example, chose four sections of *Simon Suggs* for *Some American Humorists*,[49] Arthur Palmer Hudson included "The Elephant in La Fayette" and "A Night at the Ugly Man's" in his *Humor of the Old Deep South*,[50] and Blair selected "Simon Becomes Captain" and "Simon Suggs Attends a Camp-Meeting" for *Native American Humor* (1936).[51] Meine included "How Simon Raised Jack," "Simon Gets a 'Soft Snap' Out of His Daddy," "Simon Suggs Becomes Captain," "Colonel Hawkins and the Court,"

"Shifting the Responsibility," "Captain Suggs and Lieut. Snipes 'Court-Martial' Widow Haycock" and "Simon Suggs Attends a Camp-Meeting" in *Tall Tales of the Southwest*,[52] V. L. O. Chittick selected "Col. Hawkins and the Court," "The Captain Attends a Camp-Meeting," "The Muscadine Story" and "The Widow Ruby's Husband" for his *Ring-Tailed Roarers: Tall Tales of the American Frontier*, 1830-1860 (1946),[53] and James R. Aswell chose "Taking the Census" and "Up to the Lord" for *Native American Humor* (1947).[54]

As has been stated, evidence of the dependence of the "new" or post-bellum American humorists on the writings of Longstreet, Harris, Baldwin, Hooper and others has never been carefully analyzed—but undeniably the evidence is plentiful and increasing. Certainly, there is no doubt, as Meine has clearly stated, that "Mark Twain's early writings marked the climax of a rich development [of humor in America], rather than the beginning of one," and that Mark Twain, himself "saturated" with the writings of his predecessors, fostered and wrought to perfection a *genre* whose roots reached back to the wild frontier of the Old Southwest.[55] Blair has strongly reaffirmed this belief by declaring that the early humor furnished Mark Twain "his materials, his methods, and his inspiration."[56] And Bernard DeVoto has observed that "the direct line of [Mark Twain's] inheritance" goes back to Field, Thompson, Sol Smith, Hooper and others of the ante-bellum days: "Their accomplishment was considerable; and it may be intelligently argued that Tom Sawyer and Huck Finn could not have existed if Sut Lovingood had not been born, that the perceptions of Longstreet pointed the way to much that is fruitful in the commonwealths of 'The Gilded Age' and its successors, and that Hooper staked out much land that Mark Twain came to occupy."[57] Specifically, as DeVoto has pointed out, Mark Twain's "most important reproduction" of his predecessors occurs in the twentieth chapter of *Huckleberry Finn*, the description of the camp-meeting into which Huck and his cohorts so naively wander. It is "all but identical," according to DeVoto, with *The Adventures of Captain Simon Suggs* (Chapter X) and "provides an instance of Mark Twain's literary judgment betrayed into error." In the scene Twain "falls below his predecessor . . . Hooper lacks the Olympian detachment of Mark Twain and his sketch therefore exists on a lower level, but its realism is sharper, its intelligence quite as great, and its conviction considerably greater. Simon Suggs repents his life of sin and deception quite naturally. His conviction and conversion are set in the experiences of his audience and his swindling is therefore credible. A high moment in 'Huckleberry Finn' would have been better if Mark Twain had adhered to the scene that unquestionably produced it. The instance is memorable as the only one in which the literature to which he belonged surpassed him in a subject of his choice."[58]

One who is familiar with Hooper does not read Mark Twain without a thought reminiscent, without an intuitive feeling, as it were, that somewhere, somehow the paths of the humorists might well have crossed and recrossed. (It is indeed amusing, but it is also a strangely significant fact, for instance, that "Bull" Harbison, the dog in *Tom Sawyer,* bears the same name as "Bull" Wilkerson, Aunt Hetty's dog in "Taking the Census.")[59] If Mark Twain was reluctant to memorialize individually his literary antecedents, he did after a fashion acknowledge his debt to the *genre* of ante-bellum humor. The whole problem of the "influence" of certain "old," pre-Civil War humorists on his works, however, as well as on the works of his contemporaries, invites serious investigation. Off-hand, it is safe to say that Mark Twain, genius though he was, could never have reached the pinnacle of American literary fame had he not been guided safely there by those stalwarts who went before him.

And not the least of them was Johnson Jones Hooper of Alabama, author of the immortal *Simon Suggs.*

* * *

For ninety years after Hooper's hasty burial in Richmond's Shockhoe Hill Cemetery his grave remained unmarked. Several efforts to interest the officials of the Virginia Conservation Commission in placing an appropriate marker on the spot failed. Late in 1950 eleven men, eight from Alabama and three from Illinois—three Yankees and eight Rebels!—all ardent admirers of one of America's greatest humorists and appreciative of his work, contributed funds for the purchase and erection of an appropriate memorial.[60] The stone is inscribed:

JOHNSON JONES HOOPER
of Alabama
June 9, 1815 - July 7, 1862
Author-Editor-Lawyer
Secretary, Provisional Congress
of the
Confederate States of America
1861 - 1862
Erected by His Friends Dec. 1950

NOTES

PROLOGUE

1. J. G. Burr, "A Fragmentary History of Johnson Hooper," in James Sprunt, *Chronicles of the Cape Fear River* (Raleigh, 1914), pp. 212-215. In the *Cape-Fear Recorder*, April 18, 1832, Anthony Milan [Meilan] served notice that he was Wilmington agent "for the London Phoenix Fire Office."

2. Facts concerning the Hooper family have been gathered from various sources. Especially helpful were Archibald Maclaine Hooper, "Life of William Hooper, Signer of the Declaration of Independence," Hillsboro (N. C.) *Recorder*, November 13, 20, 27, December 4, 1822, reprinted with a supplement, "The Hooper Family," by Fanny Hooper Whitaker, in *The North Carolina Booklet*, V, 39-71 (July, 1905); Griffith J. McRee, "The Late Archibald Maclaine Hooper," *University of North Carolina Magazine*, IV, 57-62 (March, 1855); Edwin A. Alderman, "Address . . . on the life of William Hooper, 'The Prophet of American Independence'" (Chapel Hill, 1894); John H. Wheeler, *Historical Sketches of North Carolina, from 1584 to 1851* (Philadelphia, 1851), II, 282-290; *Dictionary of American Biography* (New York, 1923-1936), IX, 202, 204-205; *Twentieth Century Biographical Dictionary of Notable Americans*, (Boston, 1904), V, n.p.; and John Howard Brown, *Biographical Sketches* [reprinted from *ibid.*] (Boston, 1915), *passim*.

3. William I was the son of Robert and Mary Jaffray Hooper (married August 2, 1692) who, in 1704, the year William was born, were living on their farm near Kelso, Ednan Parish, in South Scotland. William received his A. M. degree from Edinburgh University in 1723, and in 1737 came to Boston as pastor of the West Congregational Church. He held this position for nine years, becoming an Episcopalian in 1746. His wife was Mary Dennie, daughter of John Dennie, a Boston merchant. To them were born five children: William II ("the Signer"), George (Johnson's grandfather), Thomas, John, who died in infancy, and Mary, who married John Russell Spencer. William Hooper died in 1767.

4. William II, "the Signer," (1742-1790) married Anne Clark, daughter of Wilmington's High-Sheriff Thomas Clark, and sired three children, Thomas, Elizabeth, and William III, father of William IV (1792-1876),

who was for many years a professor at the University of North Carolina and from 1846 to 1849 president of Wake Forest College (for photograph see Whitaker, *op. cit.*, V, 68, July, 1905).

5. Archibald Maclaine was a member of the Hillsborough (N. C.) Congress (1775) and of the Wilmington District Committee for Safety (1776), a participant in the Hillsborough Convention which met to adopt the Federal Constitution (1789), and for many years represented the Wilmington District in the North Carolina state legislature.

6. Johnson Hooper's mother, Charlotte DeBerniere, was a descendant of "one of the most noble and ancient families in France," one which "in the reign of Louis XIV . . . had the right by royal license to bear the fleur-de-lys of France on their arms."

7. In the summer of 1832 Archibald Maclaine Hooper offered his weekly for sale and on August 2, 1832, his establishment was partially destroyed by fire (see *Cape-Fear Recorder*, June 13-August 7, 1832).

8. See, for instance, Archibald Maclaine Hooper, "Abridgement of the Memoirs of Maj. Gen. Robert Howe, of North Carolina," *The North-Carolina University Magazine*, II, 209-221 (June, 1853).

9. Their sisters were Mary (1819-1837) and Louisa (1816-1846), who married (1) the Reverend Daniel Coba, of South Carolina, and (2) the Reverend John J. Roberts. By the latter she had two children, John DeBerniere and Mary Charlotte.

10. In the Johnson Jones Hooper Collection, Evans Memorial Library, Aberdeen, Mississippi, is a copy of Rollins, *The Method of Teaching and Studying the Belles Lettres* (London, 1761), inscribed, "A. M. Hooper to Johnson J. Hooper."

11. Years later, when Hooper had attained national fame as a humorist, he was chided about the "Muscat Club" by another of its former members and asked to put their escapades in print. Hooper refused by saying that he understood "a reward of $200 was offered for the perpetrator of their principal exploit!!" See *The Spirit of the Times, A Chronicle of the Turf, Literature, and the Stage*, XV, 9, 57 (March 8, April 5, 1845); XVI, 102 (April 25, 1846). Hereinafter referred to as *Spirit*.

12. *Dictionary of American Biography*, IX, 202. Johnson is said to have followed him and obtained work on a Charleston newspaper, but this is difficult to believe. He was only fifteen in 1830 and his father, editor of the *Recorder* at the time, was doubtless able to support him. However, see Willis Brewer, *Alabama: Her History and Resources, and Public Men, from 1540* to *1872* (Montgomery, 1872), p. 465. Examination of the Charleston (S. C.) *Courier*, 1830-1835, failed to reveal any mention of either George or Johnson Hooper, although there is a reference to a Miss Hooper who arrived from Wilmington (December 17, 1835) and a Mr. Hooper who arrived from Augusta (January 29,

1834). Neither is listed in the city directories from 1828-1829, 1831, or 1837-1838.

13. *Tallapoosa* (Alabama) *County Record Book, 1834-1839*, A, 1, indicates that George Hooper produced his license to practice there, a neighboring county, in the spring of 1834.

CHAPTER ONE

1. *Op. cit.*, p. 465.

2. Peter A. Brannon, "Jons Hooper's Influence in Early State Literature," Montgomery *Advertiser*, Centennial Edition, March 15, 1928, p. 52.

3. *Dictionary of American Biography*, IX, 202.

4. Ulrich B. Phillips, *A History of Transportation in the Eastern Cotton Belt to 1860* (New York, 1908), p. 129.

5. *Ibid.*, p. 167. Only eleven hours were spent in travel, although passengers were required to spend the night in Aiken, S. C., sixteen miles out of Hamburg. The fare was 5c a mile, or $6.75 for the entire length of the road.

6. *An Accompaniment of Mitchell's Reference and Distance Map of the United States . . . together with . . . an Account of the Actual and Perspective Internal Improvements throughout the Union . . .* (Philadelphia, 1834), p. 274

7. Thomas P. Abernethy, *The Formative Period in Alabama, 1815-1828* (Montgomery, 1922), pp. 30, 163.

8. Tyrone Power, *Impressions of America during the Years 1833, 1834 and 1835*, II, 123 (London, 1836), estimated that 10,000 families left Carolina and Georgia for Alabama in one season alone in 1835.

9. *United States Census* (Sixth), 1840 [Original MSS. Returns], Alabama, I, 169-230, and *Sixth Census or Enumeration of the Inhabitants of the United States, as Corrected at the Department of State, in 1840* (Washington, 1841), pp. 244-245. Of the 17,333, 7,141 were slaves and 4 free colored persons. However, see also Clanton W. Williams, editor, "Presidential Election Returns and Related Data for Ante- Bellum Alabama," *The Alabama Review*, I, 279-293 (October, 1948).

10. *United States Census* (Seventh), 1850 [Original MSS. Returns], Alabama, II, 527-832, and *The Seventh Census of the United States: 1850* (Washington, 1853), pp. 414-421. The population of Chambers County was 23,960 in 1850, including 11,176 slaves. See also Williams, *op. cit.*, II, 63-73 (January, 1949).

11. *Some Adventures of Captain Simon Suggs, Late of the Tallapoosa Volunteers; Together with 'Taking the Census,' and Other Alabama Sketches.* By a Country Editor. (Philadelphia, 1845), p. 72. Hereinafter referred to as *Simon Suggs.*

12. *Ibid.*, p. 69.

13. Harriet Martineau, *Society in America* (New York, 1837), I, 217.

14. Early court records mention Indian misdemeanors with frequency (see, for example, "the State *vs* Eas-tar-char-co" for murder in October, 1835, in *Chambers County State Docket, 1834-1836*, item 38, n. p.).

15. *Simon Suggs*, p. 72.

16. Annie Mae Hollingsworth, "Johnson Jones Hooper, Alabama's Mark Twain, Champion of the Creeks," Montgomery *Advertiser*, March 23, 1931, p. 3.

17. *Simon Suggs*, p. 70.

18. See, for example, W. Stanley Hoole, editor, "Advice to an Overseer: Extracts from the 1840-1842 Plantation Journal of John Horry Dent," *The Alabama Review*, I, 50-63 (January, 1948), and Martineau, *op. cit.*, II, 216.

19. Of course, this was true of the American frontier everywhere. See Walter Blair and Franklin J. Meine, *Mike Fink: King of Mississippi Keelboatmen* (New York, 1933), pp. 36ff., for instance.

20. Quoted by Albert Burton Moore, *History of Alabama* (University, 1934), p. 156.

21. *Oddities in Southern Life and Character* (Boston, 1883), p. vii.

22. For excellent eyewitness descriptions of these so-called "Poor White Trash" see D. L. Hundley, *Social Relations in Our Southern States* (New York, 1860), pp. 250ff., and Walter B. Posey, "Alabama in the 1830's as Recorded by British Travellers," *Birmingham-Southern College Bulletin*, XXXI, 1-47 (December, 1938).

23. See Shields McIlwaine, *The Southern Poor-White from Lubberland to Tobacco Road* (Norman, 1939). Frank L. Owsley has more recently contributed largely to an understanding of the "poor whites" in "The Pattern of Migration and Settlement on the Southern Frontier," *The Journal of Southern History*, XI, 147-176 (May, 1945), and *Plain Folk of the Old South* (Baton Rouge, 1949).

24. Jeannette Tandy, *Crackerbox Philosophers in American Humor and Satire* (New York, 1925), pp. 65-66.

25. Paul H. Buck, "The Poor Whites of the Ante-Bellum South," *American Historical Review*, XXXI, 41-54 (October, 1925).

26. Thomas C. Haliburton, editor, *Traits of American Humor, By Native Authors* (London, 1852), II, 126.

27. Quoted by Ulrich B. Phillips, *Life and Labor in the Old South* (Boston, 1929), pp. 340-341.

28. H. E. Taliaferro ("Skitt"), *Fisher's River (North Carolina) Scenes and Characters* (New York, 1859), pp. 253-254.

29. The first is the unscrupulous rascal in Henry Junius Nott, *Novelettes of a Traveller* (New York, 1834) and the second, of course, the "hero" of Erskine Caldwell's *Tobacco Road* (New York, 1932).

30. Charles Meeker Kozlay, *The Lectures of Bret Harte* (Brooklyn, 1909), p. 22.

31. Bernard DeVoto, "Frontier America," *The Saturday Review of Literature,* V, 1067 (June 1, 1929).

32. *Tall Tales of the Southwest* (New York, 1937), p. xvi.

33. *The Big Bear of Arkansas, and Other Sketches, Illustrative of Character and Incidents in the South and South-West* (Philadelphia, 1845), pp. vii-xii.

34. James R. Aswell, editor, *Native American Humor* (New York, 1947), p. xii.

35. *Simon Suggs,* p. 3.

36. See, for examples, O. P. Fitzgerald, *Judge Longstreet: A Life Sketch* (Nashville, 1891), p. 88; John Donald Wade, *Augustus Baldwin Longstreet: A Study of the Development of Culture in the South* (New York, 1924), p. 318; Walter Blair, *Native American Humor (1800-1900),* (New York, 1937), pp. 108-109; and M. L. Rutherford, *The South in History and Literature* (Atlanta, 1907), pp. 6-7. Longstreet, after becoming a preacher and later a college president was "very anxious" to suppress his *Georgia Scenes,* calling the volume "mere bagatelle, the pastime of more youthful days." His efforts failed. Hooper is also reported to have been ashamed of "Simon Suggs" (*ibid.,* p. 378). See *supra,* pp. 102-103.

37. Bernard DeVoto, "The Matrix of Mark Twain's Humor," *The Bookman,* LXXIV, 172-178 (October, 1931).

38. *Op. cit.,* p. xxvi.

39. Besides the works of Meine, McIlwaine, Tandy, Aswell, Wade, and Blair, already mentioned, see, for examples, Walter Blair, *Tall Tale America* (New York, 1933); *Horse Sense in American Humor* (Chicago, 1942); B. A. Botkin, editor, *A Treasury of American Folklore* (New York, 1944); Bernard DeVoto, *Mark Twain's America* (Boston, 1932); Richard M. Dorson, *Jonathan Draws the Long Bow* (Cambridge, 1946); Arthur Palmer Hudson, *Humor of the Old Deep South* (New York, 1936); James R. Masterson, *Tall Tales of Arkansaw* (Boston, 1943); Constance Rourke, *American Humor: A Study of National Character* (New York, 1931), and others.

40. See Grace Warren Landrum, "Sir Walter Scott and His Literary Rivals in the Old South," *American Literature,* II, 256-276 (November, 1930) and "Notes on the Reading of the Old South," *ibid.,* III, 60-71 (March, 1931). See also Jay B. Hubbell "Cavalier and Indentured Servant in Virginia Fiction," *The South Atlantic Quarterly,* XXVI, 22-39 (January, 1927).

41. In the preparation of the background sections of this chapter the writer has leaned heavily on Moore, *op. cit.,* pp. 128-158, Tandy, *op. cit.,*

pp. 65-72, and, with the kind permission of the publishers, on his own *Sam Slick in Texas* (San Antonio, 1945), pp. 1-6. Moore's chapter on "Backwoods Times" is far and away the most interesting delineation of the subject he has seen.

CHAPTER TWO

1. In 1840 George D. Hooper and wife had a son under five, a daughter between five and ten and owned three slaves, according to *United States Census* (Sixth), 1840 [Original MSS. Returns], Alabama, I, 175.

2. *Chambers County Deed Record, February 8, 1833-July 7, 1837,* I, 429, lists him as purchaser of two acres in La Fayette from J. Henry Kellam, February 4, 1837; *Chambers County Deed Record, April 23-October 9, 1844,* VI, 322; *ibid., November 15, 1854-June 12, 1857,* XII, 30, 54, 291; and *ibid., July 15, 1857-October 3, 1860,* XIII, 529, list other land transactions of George Hooper.

3. *Chambers County Estray Book, 1833-1839,* pp. 8, 13-14 and *passim,* records Hooper's services as justice of peace. See also *Chambers County Bond Book of Public Officials, 1833-1841, passim.*

4. For examples of George Hooper's legal activities in La Fayette see *Chambers County Minutes of Circuit Court, 1833-1837,* I, 120; *ibid., October Term, 1844-Fall Term, 1849,* V, 21, 83, 103, and *passim; ibid., Spring Term, 1850-Fall Term, 1853,* VI, 8, 54, 110, 178, 217; *Chambers County Orphans Court Record, 1837-1838,* III, 3; *Chambers County Orphans Court Trial Docket, November Term, 1843-June Term, 1847, passim; Chambers County Bar Trial Docket, November Term, 1846-Fall Term, 1849, passim;* and *Chambers County Minutes of Chancery Court, 1842-1862,* p. 22.

5. *Tallapoosa County Deed Record Book, 1844-1846,* D, 34, 167, 179, 422; *ibid., 1848-1849,* F, 286; *Tallapoosa County Chancery Court Trial Docket, May Term, 1848-May Term, 1851,* pp. 94-159; *ibid., May Term, 1844-November Term, 1854,* p. 175; *ibid., May Term, 1852-November Term, 1853,* pp. 24, 74, 122-123; *Tallapoosa County Subpoena Docket, 1851-1859,* pp. 2, 25, 38, and *passim; Tallapoosa County Records Docket, 1854-1855,* pp. 16, 62; and *Tallapoosa County Trial Docket, 1839-1841, passim.*

6. *Index to the Map of the Town of Dadeville* [1838-1840], pp. 2-3, 5-6, 23, lists Young, Holly, Stone, and Perry as "original purchasers" of town lots. Brantley, later to become Johnson Hooper's father-in-law, was one of Dadeville's most prominent settlers, an attorney and businessman (see *Chambers County Estray Book, 1833-1839,* pp. 97-98; *Chambers County Bond Book of Public Officials, 1833-1841, passim*).

7. *Tallapoosa County Deed Record Book, February 4, 1835-June 20, 1842*, A, 219, 274, 328, records land sales from Young to Stone and others; *ibid.*, A, 105, 160, 180, 204 and *passim*, lists Hanrick's many transactions; *ibid.*, *1843-1844*, C, 53, 301, 315 records various trades made by Holly; and *Chambers County Administrator's Guardian and Will Record*, IV, 181-191 [December 3, 1849], recopied in *Chambers County Will Record*, I-II, 304-305, lists data on Baugh, Richardson, and the Holifields. Judging from these records and others too numerous to list these men were among the leading citizens of the new country.

8. On March 9, 1835, the County Commissioner "ordered that rates and prices to be paid at all taverns . . . be established as follows:

At Houses of Entertainment

Breakfast or Supper	$0.37½	Man & Horse per day	
Lodging	.12½	(24 hours)	1.75
Dinner	.50	Horse Feed	.37½
Board & Lodging		Horse all night or 12 hours	.62½
perday (24 hours)	1.00	Horse all day & night	
		or 24 hours	1.00

At Retailers of Liquors

Whiskey per half pint	.12½	West Indian Rum	.25
Peach or Apple Brandy	.12½	New England Rum	.12½"
Cogniac Brandy	.25		

(*Chambers County Commissioners Court Record, April, 1833-November, 1837*, p. 74).

9. The following bill of sale to Hooper is taken from an unidentified ledger on deposit in the Tallapoosa County Court House, Dadeville, p. 197:

	1837			
June	26	to	1 Curb Bridle	.75
			1 pr. Martingales	1.00
July	6		1 pocket comb	.06
	19		1 Runabout	2.00
			1 fine saddle	16.00
	31		1 pr. fine Shoes	2.25
Aug.	5		1 large knife	1.50
	24		1 silk Handkf	1.25
	26		1 pr. socks	.50
	31		1 watermelon	.13

10. This extremely interesting correspondence between Jackson, Peggy, Catherine and Joseph A. Johnson and James Moore and the diary-expense book kept by Johnson are owned by and used with the kind

permission of C. S. Johnson of Jacksonville, Florida, grandson of Joseph A. Johnson. The letters from Jackson to his father are dated Maplesville, Alabama, June 8 and Jefferson County, Mississippi, June 28; James Moore's to his son, Dudleyville, Alabama, September 3; Catherine Moore's to James Moore, Ouachita Parish, Louisiana, August 1; and the two letters, Johnson to Moore, Russellville and Shreveport, Louisiana, September 30, November 18, 1837. The diary-expense book covers September 10-October 3, 1837. These documents, photostats of which are in the University of Alabama Library, are scheduled for publication in *The Alabama Review.*

11. Letter, Hooper to Joseph A. Johnson, Charleston, South Carolina, October 3, 1838 (in possession of and used with the kind permission of C. S. Johnson, Jacksonville, Florida). This writer is indebted to Mr. Johnson for his help in identifying personalities mentioned in the correspondence, as well as for other favors (see his letters, February 7, 14, 19, 27, 1951, and photostatic copy of Hooper's letter in University of Alabama Library).

12. In *Tallapoosa County Bench Trial Docket, Fall Term, 1838,* n. p., this mysterious entry appears without explanation or details: "Johnson J. Hooper *vs.* John Setters, Sr." It may have been his first law case. See also *Tallapoosa County Bond Book,* [1829-1848] II, 11. This bond was registered June 10, 1840.

13. Hooper's visit to Tuscaloosa at this time is an assumption based on the following facts. From April 4-25, 1838, the Tuscaloosa *Flag of the Union* carried the name of "John J. Hooper" in its "List of Letters Remaining in the Post Office, Tuscaloosa," and from July 4-August 1, 1838, the name of "Johnson Hooper." Before April 4 and after August 1 neither name appears. In all probability Hooper visited Tuscaloosa prior to April 4, but was not in town to receive his mail after that date. That he afterwards visited Tuscaloosa is of course obvious (for examples, see *Spirit,* XV, 372-373, October 4, 1845; XX, 117, April 27, 1850; and *Simon Suggs,* pp. 52ff.).

14. *United States Census* (Sixth), 1840 [Original MSS. Returns], Alabama, VII, 173; see also *Simon Suggs,* pp. 151-154.

15. *Ibid.,* pp. 149-150.

16. *United States Census* (Sixth), 1840 [Original MSS. Returns], Alabama, VII, 161-188. The petition for "highest compensation," dated October 20, 1840, was signed by "Job Taylor, Col. Comg. T. C., W. L. Justis, Clerk Circuit Ct., Irvine Lawson, Judge, Co. Col. T. C., and J. McClendon, T. Co. Surveyor." See also *Sixth Census or Enumeration of the Inhabitants of the United States, as Corrected at the Department of State, in 1840,* pp. 244-245, and Williams, *op. cit.,* I, 292-293 (October, 1948).

17. *Spirit,* XIII, 326 (September 9, 1843).

18. *Tallapoosa County Record Book, 1839-1842,* B, 350.

19. *Tallapoosa County Trial Docket, Spring Term, 1841,* pp. 35, 70, 76, 82; *ibid, Fall Term, 1841,* p. 114; *ibid., Spring Term, 1842,* pp. 176-178, 190, 195, 201 and *passim.*

20. *Chambers County Appearance Docket, January Term, 1842, passim; Chambers County Trial Docket, April Term, 1843-October Term, 1844,* p. 57; *Tallapoosa County Trial Docket, Spring Term, 1842,* pp. 200, 203, 205; and *The* [La Fayette] *Alabama Standard Account Book, 1842,* which on April 2, 1842, has this entry: "G. & J. Hooper Dr. For 4 insertions Chancery notice 'Jacob Bailey' *vs* William Gragg and others 5 sqs. 12[50]" (MSS. volume owned by W. B. Wood, Jr., Lafayette, Alabama).

21. Jonathan Johnston and Green D. Brantley conducted a mercantile business in La Fayette known as "Brantley and Johnson" (see *Chambers County Deed Record, 1837-1839,* II, 86). In 1839 Brantley had served as justice of the peace of La Fayette and later (1845) was elected to the state legislature. He served two terms, 1845-1848 (see Brewer, *op, cit.,* p. 164). The Brantleys had eighteen children, sixteen of whom lived to maturity.

22. Personal data obtained from an interview with Anne H. Augustus, Macon, Mississippi, a niece of Mary and Ann, who, of course, knew the sisters in their latter years only. See also, letter, C. A. Hooper to Marion Kelley, May 31, 1934 (Kelley, *op. cit.,* p. 35).

23. *Chambers County Record of Marriage, November 8, 1839-September 19, 1843,* II, 278.

24. *Ibid.,* II, 286. See also Mary Brantley Hooper's *Autograph Book* (Johnson Jones Hooper Collection, Evans Memorial Library, Aberdeen, Mississippi). Mary Mildred Brantley was born in Jasper County, Georgia, November 20, 1826, according to the Hooper Family *Bible.*

25. Letter, Green D. Brantley to Ann B. Heard, La Fayette, Alabama, December 25, 1842. (Unless otherwise stated, this and all manuscripts cited in this chapter are owned by Anne H. Augustus, Macon, Mississippi, and were used with her kind permission.)

26. Letter, Ann B. Heard to "My Dear Sister," La Fayette, January 21, 1850.

27. Letters, Ann B. Heard to her sister, Amelia M. Brantley, Mobile, December 3, 18 [?]; to her mother, Elizabeth Brantley, Cahawba, Alabama, July 3, 184[?], Mobile, January 18, December 26, 1845; to her father, G. D. Brantley, Mobile, December 19, 1848; and to her sister, Sarah, New Orleans, May 6, 1853, February 15, 1861, May 4, 1862, are but a selected few of the many preserved.

28. Diary of Mrs. Annie B. Heard, February 24, 1858-October 1863.

29. See *infra,* p. 210, n. 57.

30. *Chambers County Administrator's Guardian and Will Record,* IV, 188-191; recopied in *Chambers County Will Record,* I-II, 304-305 (dated December 3, 1849). However, see letter, Ann B. [Mrs. T. R.] Heard to "My Dear Sister," La Fayette, Alabama, January 21, 1850, in which she states that her husband, Thomas R. Heard, was "executor" of Green D. Brantley's estate. Upon his death Brantley left each of his daughters "a sound, likely, and intelligent negro girl" and $80, but "my daughter Mary M. Hooper shall not be entitled to receive said sum of eighty dollars, she having already commuted therefor."

31. Letter, Hooper to Alsea K. Brantley, La Fayette, Alabama, October 7, 1849; letters, Green D. Brantley to Alsea K. Brantley, La Fayette, Alabama, August 11, 18[?], and to Elizabeth Brantley, his wife, Walnut Hill, Arkansas, April 27, 1849. In the last, Brantley mentions having recently received a letter from "Mr. Hooper" and sends love "to Mary and Mr. Hooper and their children."

32. Letter, Hooper to Sarah J. Brantley, Montgomery, Alabama, April 9, 1854. Miss Augustus also owns a copy of *Don Quixote,* bearing Hooper's coat-of-arms bookplate ("nil conscire sibi") and inscribed "To Sarah Brantley from Johnson Jones Hooper." On page 50 of the volume is written "Sarah Brantley—from her brother Johnson J. Hooper." According to Miss Augustus Sarah Brantley was a very talented teacher and writer and one of the most beloved members of the large Brantley family. A manuscript volume of her poems as well as several letters written by her to her various relatives are in Miss Augustus' possession.

33. Letter, Hooper to Mrs. T. R. Heard, Montgomery, Alabama, August 22, 1850. See also letter, Mrs. Annie B. Heard to her sister, Sarah, New Orleans, May 6, 1853, in which she invites her to spend the summer.

34. *Songs and Poems of the South* (New York, 1857), pp. 23-24. For verification of this dedication see *Spirit,* XVI, 552 (January 9, 1847): "*The Rose of Alabama* - We are indebted to Mr. Bouliemet of Mobile, and Mr. Mayo of New Orleans, for a copy of this popular melody, with *new words* by the Hon. A. B. Meek, of Ala., which are respectfully dedicated to Mrs. J. J. Hooper, of Montgomery—the accomplished lady of our occasional correspondent, the author of 'Capt. Simon Suggs,' etc., who is now an associate editor of the 'Alabama Journal.' The 'new words' were originally published in the 'Planter' of Mobile, the editor of which, like ourselves, considers the composition as charming as the music is full of pathos. Married, as it now is, to immortal verse, this simple air we trust will find a resting place among the native melodies of the land." See also the Mobile *Advertiser,* December 24, 1846.

35. Letter, Hooper to Mrs. T. R. Heard, Montgomery, August 22, 1850.

36. Dates taken from Hooper Family *Bible*. See also letter, C. A. Hooper to Marion Kelley, May 31, 1934 (Kelley, *op. cit.*, p. 36).

37. William DeBerniere Hooper joined the Confederate Army in the spring or summer of 1861 and was made a second lieutenant. He was at first stationed at Fort Morgan, near Mobile (see *supra*, p. 162).

38. *The War of the Rebellion: A Compilation of the Official Records of the Union and Confederate Armies* (Washington, 1880-1901), 1st Series, XII, Pt. 2, 702; *ibid.*, XIX, Pt. 1, 807, 1000; Whitaker, *op. cit.*, V, 70-71 (July, 1905); Thomas McAdory Owen, *History of Alabama and Dictionary of Alabama Biography* (Chicago, 1921), I, 838-839. A third son, John DeBerniere Hooper, born in 1853, was first inspector of mines of Alabama.

39. To William and Carrie Smith Hooper were born three children: Johnson Jones (born 1869), Nancy Ragsdale (1871-?), and William DeBerniere (1875-?). All of these, as well as Mrs. Johnson J. Hooper, are buried in Aberdeen, Mississippi. There are no living descendants. See *Roster of Cemeteries and of Persons in Marked Graves in Monroe County, Mississippi* (in Evans Memorial Library, Aberdeen, Mississippi), pp. 36, 219, 227, 253.

40. Diary of Mrs. Annie Brantley Heard, n.d., states that Adolphus S. Hooper studied accounting in New York City, living at 74 Warren Street.

41. July 29, 1875; Mobile *Daily Register*, July 30, 1875. The *Examiner* added that Hooper "was the eldest son of the late Johnson Hooper, of Montgomery, Alabama, whose reputation as a writer and editor is familiar to all our readers."

42. Whitaker, *op. cit.*, V, 70-71. The Hooper Family *Bible* gives the date April 24, 1890.

43. Two letters written by Mrs. [Mary Mildred] Hooper from Aberdeen, November 24, December 1, 18[?], to her sisters, Mrs. Heard and Mrs. Kate B. Augustus, are owned by Anne H. Augustus, Macon, Mississippi.

44. Letter, Mrs. Kate B. Augustus to her son, George, Macon Mississippi, March 18, 1884, states ". . . you must mind Aunt Annie and Aunt Mary and do everything they tell you to do."

45. Letter, Anne H. Augustus to Marion Kelley, July 19, 1934 (Kelley, *op. cit.*, p. 247).

46. See letter, Mrs. Willie L. (James A.) Anderson to this writer, Tuscaloosa, Alabama, January 1, 1949; letter, Richard C. Foster to Miss Caroline A. Hooper, University, Alabama, February 26, 1938; and letters, Anne H. Augustus to Lawrence M. Foster and this writer, Macon,

Mississippi, June 11, 1945, in University of Alabama Library. Anne H. Augustus, Macon, Mississippi, owns daguerrotypes or photographs of William DeBerniere and Adolphus Sanford, Johnson J. Hooper's sons, Major T. R. Heard, C.S.A., Sarah J., Alsea K., John F., and Greene Brantley, Jr., and Mrs. Ann B. [T. R] Heard. Alsea K. Brantley was drowned in the Yazoo River, May 10, 1867, Sarah J. Brantley died in New Orleans, July 27, 1870, and Ann B. Heard died in Montgomery, Alabama, November 23, 1898.

CHAPTER THREE

1. The earliest issue of the *East Alabamian* located by this writer is I, No. 30 (July 8, 1843). By counting back from this date the first issue would normally have fallen on December 17, 1842, as stated above. Volume II, No. 1 (Whole Number 53), is dated December 16, 1843, a fact which substantiates this belief. However, W. B. Wood, Jr., of Lafayette, Alabama, owns an unidentified newspaper clipping, dated April 1, 1842, which advertises "Lewis Stells, Boot & Shoemaker, at the Sign of the Boot, opposite *East-Alabamian* office," indicating that the paper was in operation at least *nine months before* December, 1842. Mr. Wood also has receipts from the "Office of the [La Fayette] Alabama Standard," dated March 12, June 14, and December ?, 1842, and *The Alabama Standard Account Book, 1842,* a manuscript ledger which opens with an entry under volume I, no. 1, March 7, and closes with volume I, no. 23, August 13, 1842. It is possible that the two papers were begun at approximately the same time in early 1842. Rhoda Coleman Ellison (*A Check List of Alabama Imprints, 1807-1870,* University, Alabama, 1946, p. 11) lists both titles but states "no file located" for the *Standard.*

2. Whether Hooper became editor of the *East Alabamian* at its very beginning has not been established. He was editor on July 8, 1843, for his name appears in that issue, and the advertisement stating that his law office was "at the office of the *East Alabamian*" was first dated March 18, 1843, a fact which evidences his connection with the paper at that time. It is quite likely that he was editor from the beginning in December, 1842, if indeed that was the beginning.

3. George D. Hooper formed a partnership with H. L. McGregor late in 1842 as "Attorneys at Law and Solicitors in Equity." On July 21, 1843, he was elected secretary of "The La Fayette Bar and Officers of the Court." See *ibid.,* July 29, 1843; *Chambers County Trial Docket, April, 1843-October, 1844,* pp. 122, 139, [October, 1844].

4. *East Alabamian,* July 8ff., 1843.

5. Heretofore, sketches of Hooper have stated that his first newspaper work was as editor of the Dadeville (Alabama) *Banner* in the early 1840's (see for examples, Brewer, *op. cit.,* p. 465; *Dictionary of Ameri-*

can Biography, IX, 202; Peter A. Brannon, *op. cit.,* p. 52; B. F. Riley, *Makers and Romance of Alabama History,* n. p., 1915?, pp. 67-72, and others). Unless there were *two* separate and distinct Dadeville *Banners,* one in 1840-1842 (of which there is no record) and the other, begun in 1852 (of which there are copies extant), this statement cannot possibly be true. According to all available data, such as the following, there never was but one, the 1852 *Banner*: "The first newspaper published in Tallapoosa County was 'The Dadeville Banner,' and a copy in the 'Record' office shows that Volume 2 was issued September 7, 1853, which would have shown Volume I to have been published in September, 1852" (Dadeville *Record,* June 22, 1933). "Dadeville Banner—first number of a neatly printed sheet bearing the above title . . . has been received . . ." (Wetumpka, Alabama, *State Guard,* September 10, 1852; see also *Macon,* Alabama, *Republican,* September 9, 1852.).

6. Letter, Hooper to Joseph A. Johnson, Chambers Court House, n. d. (in possession of and used with kind permission of C. S. Johnson, Jacksonville, Florida), photostatic copy in University of Alabama Library.

7. *Spirit,* XIII, 326, 505 (September 9, December 23, 1843); *East Alabamian,* August 19, 1843. Only ten issues of the *East Alabamian* (July 8, 29, August 11, 19, September 9, 23, October 21, November 4, December 2, 16, 1843) are known to exist.

8. This story did not appear in any of the extant issues of the *East Alabamian.* Since it was reprinted in the *Spirit* of September 9 (XIII, 326), it obviously appeared in Hooper's paper before that date; i.e., August 5 or 26 or July 15 or 22, 1843.

9. *Ibid.,* XXIX, 1 (February 12, 1859).

10. The *Spirit* was begun December 10, 1831, and ended June 22, 1861. For a summary of title changes, editorships, etc., see Frank Luther Mott, *A History of American Magazines, 1741-1850* (New York, 1930), pp. 479-482.

11. *Spirit,* XVII, 262 (March, 1841); XV, 223 (January 6, 1838).

12. Francis Brinley, *Life of William T. Porter* (New York, 1861), *passim.*

13. *Dictionary of American Biography,* XV, 107-108.

14. For an excellent summary of Porter's ability and influence see Meine, *op. cit.,* pp. xxvii-xxix, 449-454.

15. The *Spirit* is filled with conversational chit-chat between Porter and his friends, his contributors. For examples, on September 13, 1845, (XV, 333) he addressed Hooper: "*J.J.H.* Please send us the back numbers of the 'Whig' from the date you have been connected with it"; on October 4, 1845, (XV, 369): "J.J.H. Have seen the 'notice.' The 'dog-ra-type' shall be forwarded sure,' with many thanks"; and on

March 4, 1848 (XVII, 573): "J.J.H. Will send you the Dorkings next week. The books ordered from London have not been received."

16. *Ibid.*, XIV, 547 (January 11, 1845).

17. *Ibid.*, XIII, 326 (September 9, 1843). "Cousin Sally Dillard," by Hamilton C. Jones, was "one of the most-widely read of all the humorous stories" (Meine, *op. cit.*, pp. 39-43).

18. September 23, 1843.

19. *Spirit*, XIII, 505 (December 23, 1843).

20. *Ibid.*, XIV, 104 (April 27, 1844). See also *The American Penny Magazine*, I, 387-388 (July 26, 1845).

21. *Spirit*, XIV, 241 (July 20, 1844), quoted from the *East Alabamian.*

22. *Chambers County Trial Docket, April Term, 1843-October Term, 1844*, pp. 96, 110, records Hooper as a practicing attorney both with his brother George and alone in April, 1844.

23. W. W. Ellison, "Noted Author Once Lived in La Fayette, Ala.," Columbus (Georgia) *Ledger Magazine*, June 19, 1927, p. 1.

24. *Spirit*, XIV, 558 (January 18, 1845), quoted from the *East Alabamian*, January 1, 1845.

25. This personal description of Young is recorded in a letter from George E. Brewer, who knew him, to Peter A. Brannon, Montgomery, Alabama, dated Columbus, Georgia, October 15, 1919, and now in possession of and used here with the permission of the addressee. See Brewer, *op. cit.*, p. 548; Brannon, *op. cit.*, p. 52, and "Little Journeys Through Alabama," *Alabama Highways*, IV, 3-6 (April, 1930). The last-named contains a picture of Young, captioned "the original of Hooper's Captain Simon Suggs," as does Owen, *op. cit.*, I, 577.

26. See *supra*, p. 31.

27. Letter, A. F. Young to Marion Kelley, July 12, 1934 (Kelley, *op. cit.*, pp. 260-261). Bird H. Young died in October, 1866.

28. *Tallapoosa County Record Book, 1839-1842*, B, 601; *Tallapoosa County Bond Book of County Officers, 1849-1859*, pp. 8, 62, 125; *Tallapoosa County Trial Docket, 1844-1849, Spring Term, 1844*, p. 6; and *Tallapoosa County Bench Trial Docket, Fall Term, 1838*, n. p.

29. In 1847 Young ran for doorkeeper of the state Senate against eight other contestants and received only four votes (*Journal of the Senate of the State of Alabama . . .* [1847-1848], Montgomery, 1848, pp. 6-7).

30. Brewer, *op. cit.*, p. 548. This writer owns an official form, dated Fall, 1840, authorizing payment to Bird H. Young for his services as "Pettit Juryman" in the Tallapoosa County Circuit Court.

31. *Tallapoosa County Record of Circuit Court, Fall Term 1834-Spring Term, 1836*, I, 23, 39, 59.

32. Kelley, *op. cit.*, p. 263, quotes the following sentence from the fly-leaf of an unidentified business ledger, dated 1858, in the basement of the Chambers County Courthouse: "I hereby swear that I will not credit Bird Young any more so long as life in [?], by God." This writer was unable to locate the ledger in 1948-1951.

33. Upon this writer's visits to East Alabama in 1948-1951 he mentioned Bird H. Young to at least a dozen people, each of whom was familiar with "legends" about him and promptly identified him with "Simon Suggs." It is a tribute to Young as well as to Hooper that both "characters" are still bywords in the community after more than a hundred years.

34. Letter, George E. Brewer to Peter A. Brannon, October 15, 1919. In quoting personal interviews with J. H. and J. F. Johnston and J. P. Oliver, who also remembered Young, Kelley (*op. cit.*, pp. 262-265) says that on one occasion Young led some of his drinking cohorts in a dance around blazing fires built on the Courthouse Square in Dadeville. The game was called "Follow the Leader." Young threw an old, borrowed hat into the fire, whereupon his followers threw their good hats. Young then pulled his good hat out of hiding and walked away, laughing. A favorite trick of Young's was inviting friends to have drinks with him, then walking off, leaving the bills unpaid. When he needed a new pair of shoes, it is said, he would "borrow" a pair from a hotel guest who had left them in the corridor for blacking. Several such yarns are yet repeated in the "Young country." See also letter, Pearl C. Partridge to this writer, Boligee, Alabama, July 22, 1948 (in University of Alabama Library).

35. Letter, Brewer to Brannon, October 15, 1919.

36. *Spirit*, XV, 471 (November 29, 1845).

37. Hollingsworth, *op. cit.*, p. 3.

38. Letter, Brewer to Brannon, October 15, 1919.

39. *Spirit*, XIV, 606 (February 15, 1845).

40. *Ibid.*, XV, 21 (March 15, 1845).

41. *Ibid.*, XIV, 547 (January 11, 1845). In reprinting the first of the stories Porter gave it the title "Captain Suggs of Tallapoosa" and omitted the introductory paragraphs by beginning with "Until Simon entered his seventeenth year . . ." His excuse for so doing was lack of space and the fact that it had not "been written expressly for this paper."

42. *Ibid.*, XIV, 571, 583 (January 25, February 1, 1845). Hooper's letter as well as his editorial in the *East Alabamian* are here quoted.

43. *Ibid.*, XV, 9, 21-27, 38, 57, 296 (March 8, 15, 22, April 5, August 16, 1845). The New Orleans *Delta*, the Boston *Yankee Blade*, the Cincinnati *Great West*, the Baltimore *Republican and Daily Argus* were a few of the larger papers which frequently reprinted Hooper's stories.

44. William T. Porter, *op cit.*, pp. 62-79; *Spirit*, XV, 33, 57, 69, 90, 126 (March 22, April 5, 12, 19, May 10, 1845). The *Big Bear* was widely acclaimed and is still considered one of the outstanding volumes of early American humor. Upon its appearance the Boston *Daily Times* wrote: "We have read and re-read many of [the *Big Bear* stories] till tears of delight and screams of laughter brought on syncope; and we have offered to back 'Simon Suggs,' 'That Big Dog Fight at Myers's,' and 'Chunkey's Fight with the Panthers,' against the same amount of printed matter to be culled from any other volume, for fun, spirit and force, to the 'extent of our pile,' time and again, without finding any 'takers.'" See also *Knickerbocker Magazine*, XXVI, 94 (July, 1845).

45. *Carey & Hart Record Book*, II, 74, dated April-May, 1845 (MSS. volume in the Historical Society of Pennsylvania). The complete entry follows:

3000	Simon Suggs	
May	Presswork	
	34 Reams	
" 22	Stereotyping	126.80
Apl. 24	Designing 10 cuts	70.00
	Engraving 6 cuts	72.00
Cost to this date added to Stich June 16, 1845.		$268.80

Obviously Carey & Hart's advertisement of the completed *Simon Suggs* in the *Spirit* (XV, 90, April 19, 1845) was weeks premature.

46. *Ibid.*, XV, 21 (March 15, 1845). In reply to an obvious inquiry, Porter wrote Hooper, "Of course you are at liberty to make any disposition you choose of your sketches published in this paper."

47. *Ibid.*, XV, 45 (March 15, 1845). "[Carey & Hart] have in press '*The Life and Adventures of Simon Suggs*, the Shifty Man', complete in one volume, with a portrait of *Simon*, taken on the spot, and numerous illustrations by Darley. We have *a-sort-of-a-promise* on the part of both Hooper, the author, and his courteous publishers, of a sketch or two in advance, for the especial gratification of the readers and correspondents of the '*Spirit*.'"

48. Letters, Porter to Carey & Hart, March 3, 13, April 10, 1845 (in New York Historical Society Library), quoted in Nellie Smithers, *Library of Humorous American Works* (unpublished Master's thesis, Columbia University, 1936), pp. 10, 13, 15.

49. *Spirit*, XV, 21-27 (March 15, 1845). Hooper in a "private letter" apologized for "Daddy Biggs" as a "miserable performance," and added that he had not of late felt "'i' the vein for writing.'"

50. *Ibid.*, XV, 69, 201, 333, 369, 465 (April 12, June 28, September

13, October 4, November 29, 1845). More than once Hooper asked Porter for a 'dog-ra-type minnichure' [daguerreotype miniature?] of himself, and other favors.

51. *Ibid.*, XV, 131, 237-238 (May 17, July 19, 1845). "Simon Becomes Captain" appeared in the *South Carolinian* (Columbia), June 26, 1845.

52. *Spirit*, XV, 98, 158, 202 (April 26, May 31, June 28, 1845). A confusion between Hooper's story in the *Big Bear* and his own book, *Simon Suggs*, seems to have existed. Hooper himself stated in the *East Alabamian* that the Talladega (Alabama) *Reporter* had advertised the *Big Bear* incorrectly and that "the 'Capting'" was forthcoming in "a volume of his own" (*ibid.*, XV, 158, May 31, 1845).

53. *Ibid.*, XV, 246, 296, 333 (July 19, August 16, September 13, 1845).

54. *Ibid.*, XV, 356 (September 20, 1845). The volume contained twelve chapters of *Simon Suggs*, "Taking the Census" (two parts) and "Daddy Biggs's Scrape."

55. *Ibid.*, XV, 434 (November 8, 1845), quoted from the *Journal*. The writer also added, *Simon Suggs* "leaves Longstreet *[Georgia Scenes]* 'no whar.' If there is any truth in the old song of 'laugh and grow fat' . . . the reader may put himself down as 'bound' for a gain for two clear inches on each rib."

56. I, 284 (October 11, 1845).

57. *Spirit*, XV, 471 (November 29, 1845), quoted from the New Orleans *Commercial Times*. Thorpe referred to *Simon Suggs*, Chapter XI, pp. 69-72, the introductory section.

58. *Spirit*, XV, 369 (October 4, 1845).

59. *Carey & Hart Record Book*, III, 120 (MSS. volume in the Historical Society of Pennsylvania). Under date of August 25, 1845, the following entry appears:

5000 Simon Suggs			
50 Reams Paper 24x38	@475		237.50
20 Do. Plate Paper	252		50.00
Presswork 160 Token	40		64.00
Do on 5000 covers & alterations			8.00
Com paper 2 Reams	7		14.00
Prg 5000 Plates 10 each 34 Tokens @152			51.00
Composition at foot of wood Cuts			4.50
Stereotyping	$125.00)		
Designing 10 cuts	70.00)		
Engraving 10 Do	130.00)	say	276.82
Copyright	250.00)		
Binding 1/8			56.25

Copies for Editors &c &c &c	37.95
Cr (Plates, copyright, cuts &c &c &c vald at 300 after this edition)	$800.00

60. *Spirit,* XV, 436, 458, 465 (November 8, 22, 29, 1845). See also *ibid.,* XVI, 102 (April 25, 1846).

61. *Ibid.,* XV, 470 (November 29, 1845), quoted from the Wetumpka *Whig,* of which Hooper had become editor.

62. Wetumpka, a flourishing town, was itself in 1845-1846 being seriously considered as the capital of the state. See Malcolm Cook McMillan, "The Selection of Montgomery as Alabama's Capital," *The Alabama Review,* II, 79-90 (April, 1948).

63. *Spirit,* XV, 344 (September 13, 1845).

64. In *Boyle and La Wall & Co. Tailors' Record* [La Fayette, 1845], a manuscript ledger in possession of W. B. Wood, Jr., of Lafayette, Alabama, one entry indicates that Hooper had a pair of pants made to order and that his father-in-law, Green D. Brantley, bought "frock coat & pants" at this time.

CHAPTER FOUR

1. Regretfully, only two issues of the Wetumpka *Whig* published during Hooper's short term of editorship are known to exist and it is impossible to follow his activities on this weekly, except as they were mirrored elsewhere, especially in the pages of his loyal friend Porter's *Spirit.* These issues are dated November 13, 1846, and January 15, 1847. The first is volume III, no. 20, indicating that the *Whig* was begun in the summer (June?) of 1844.

2. XV, 333, 386, 470 (September 13, October 11, November 29, 1845).

3. *Ibid.,* XV, 356, 369, 381, 434, 436, 458, 465, 471 (September 20, October 4, 11, November 8, 22, 29, 1845); XVI, 102 (April 25, 1846).

4. *Carey & Hart Record Book,* III, 143 (MSS. volume in the Historical Society of Pennsylvania). Under date of February 21, 1846, the following entry appears:

1000 Simon Suggs		
9 Reams Paper	@4.50	40.50
Presswork 32 Tokens	40	12.80
1000 Setts Cuts		16.00
Proportion of Ster Plates		50.00
Binding &c 1/8		11.25
CM		$130.55

Plates, Cuts & Copyright valued at $ued after this edition.

5. March 7, 1846. The *Reveille* also frequently quoted the *Spirit*. A month after the paper was begun Field had asked Porter to put him on the mailing list (*ibid.*, June 16, 1844).

6. XVI, 145 (May 23, 1846). Sixteen months later there appeared in the *Spirit* (XVII, 335, September 4, 1847) a piece called "Curnel Jeemes Hummy's First & Last Speech in the Alabama Legyslatry," signed "Didelphis." This has not been identified as Hooper's, however.

7. *Ibid.*, XVI, 186 (June 13, 1846).

8. *Chambers County Bar Trial Docket, October Term, 1843, passim; ibid., April-October Term, 1845, passim. Chambers County Orphans Court Record, 1845-1849,* has "J. J. Hooper" written across the cover in a bold hand, but Hooper's name does not appear in the volume.

9. *Acts Passed at the Annual Session of the General Assembly of the State of Alabama* . . . [1845-1846], (Tuscaloosa, 1846), p. 253.

10. McMillan, *op. cit.*, I, 79-90 (April, 1948).

11. *Acts of the General Assembly, 1845-1846,* pp. 28, 243; *Journal of the House of Representatives of the General Assembly of the State of Alabama* . . . [1845-1846], (Tuscaloosa, 1846), p. 399. The other four were M. W. Abernathy, George Steele, Daniel Pratt, and A. B. Clitherall.

12. W. W. Screws, "Alabama Journalism," in *Memorial Record of Alabama* (Madison, Wisconsin, 1893), II, 182. This paper, established January 6, 1821, as the Montgomery *Republican*, became the *Alabama Journal* in 1825, under the editorship of G. W. B. Towns. Bates and Sayre acquired it in the early 1840's. The latter was a "strong writer" and Bates "a strong and vigorous writer and thoroughly informed on public questions. He never varied in his advocacy of whig doctrine, and persistently refused to support the know-nothing or native American party, to which so many of his party associates gave in their adhesion, with the hope that it would break down the democratic party."

13. XVI, 145, 186 (May 23, June 13, 1846).

14. *Alabama Journal*, January 19, 1849.

15. Screws, *op. cit.*, II, 182, states that Hooper "proved quite a valuable acquisition [to the *Journal*] because of his capacity as a writer, and his humorous way of treating matters and things." Hooper and Bates also published books (see Ellison, *op. cit.*, item 586, p. 70).

16. *Spirit*, XVI, 235, 421 (July 25, October 31, 1846). Porter charged Hooper 5 per cent commission "for filling the [$300] orders."

17. Mobile *Advertiser*, December 5-8, 1846, January 9, 1847.

18. *Spirit*, XVI, 529, 552 (January 2, 9, 1847). See *supra*, pp. 40, 197, n. 34.

19. *Ibid.*, XVII, 477 (December 4, 1847); XVIII, 13, 167, 301 (March 4, May 27, August 19, 1848); XIX, 55 (March 24, 1849).

20. *Ibid.*, XVII, 78 (April 10, 1847); XVIII, 217 (July 1, 1848).

Letter, Samuel Lover to Johnson J. Hooper, Montgomery, Alabama, February 25, 1847 (in Johnson Jones Hooper Collection, Evans Memorial Library, Aberdeen, Mississippi).

21. Hooper was defeated by J. F. Marrast, 17 to 8 (*Journal of the Senate of the State of Alabama, At the First Biennial Session Begun and Held in the City of Montgomery, on the First Monday in December, 1847*, Montgomery, 1848, p. 4). Alexander B. Clitherall was elected clerk of the House (*Journal of the House of Representatives of the State of Alabama, at the First Biennial Session Begun and Held in the City of Montgomery, on the First Monday in December, 1847*, Montgomery, 1848, p. 4).

22. *State Guard*, August 24, 1847. See also copied material from Huntsville *Democrat* and *Chambers Herald*.

23. *Alabama Journal*, January 27, 1849. *Alabama Daily State Gazette*, June 24, 1848, contains a letter from R. T. Scott in reply to an attack upon him by Hooper. Scott claimed Hooper's "whole article is a tissue of falsehood, misrepresentation, and uncharitable insinuations."

24. *Alabama Journal*, January 19, 1849. Upon Hooper's withdrawal a new partnership, "Bates & Sayre, Editors, Publishers, and Proprietors," was formed. For several weeks the *Journal* thereafter carried the announcement that "The copartnership of Bates, Hooper & Co." had been dissolved "by mutual consent."

25. January 13, 1849.

26. *Alabama Journal*, January 24, 1849.

27. *Carey & Hart Record Book*, III, 60 (MSS. volume in the Historical Society of Pennsylvania). Under date of April 5, 1848, the following entry appears:

1000 Simon Suggs	
Presswork 32 tokens @40c	12.80
Paper 9⅓ reams @4.50	42.00
Plates 2 reams paper 7=$14-pressW $6.00=	20.00
Proportion Stereotype Plates	50.00
Binding /⅛=	11.25
	$136.05

Plates &c valued at $udd after this edn

28. Twenty-four numbers of "Chambers Gossip" appeared in the *Alabama Journal* between January 23-September 28, 1849. They began on a weekly basis, but became irregular after midsummer. A few of the better pieces Hooper used again (see *supra*, p. 72). The majority of the pieces were written from La Fayette, but Numbers 10 and 11 (April 2, 7) were from Crawford, Russell County, dated March 28 and April 2; Number 12 (April 14) was from Columbus, Georgia, dated

April 11; and Number 13 (April 18) was from Girard, Alabama, dated April 15, 1849.

29. XIX, 56, 87-88, 100, 231 (March 24, April 14, 21, July 7, 1849). These were copied from the *Alabama Journal,* March 5, 27, February 21, May 4, 1849.

30. *Spirit,* XIX, 25 (March 10, 1849).

31. *Ibid.,* XIX, 55 (March 24, 1849). The *Alabama Journal,* taking advantage of Hooper's affiliation as correspondent, played up "The Muscadine Story" in two issues (April 8, 10, 1849).

32. For example see *The World We Live In* (New York), III, 248 (May 15, 1849). P. 259 of the same issue also contains a brief story, "Worse and Worse," attributed to the *Alabama Journal.*

33. *Spirit,* XIX, 270 (July 28, 1849). The essay is dated La Fayette, June 7, 1849. William Garrett, *Reminiscences of Public Men in Alabama for Thirty Years* (Atlanta, 1872), pp. 526, 745, insinuates Hooper's candidacy by stating "after a stubborn contest in the Legislature, in the session of 1849 . . . ," and names the victors: Joseph Barrow, F. M. Chisolm, Benjamin L. Goodman and John M. Kennedy. Hooper probably ran in the place of Robert Curry who had voluntarily withdrawn from the race (*Alabama Journal,* July 20, 1849), though, in reporting the results of the election in his "Chambers Gossip No. 21," August 11, 1849, he makes no mention of his own defeat (see *ibid.,* August 8, 10, 15, 24, 1849).

34. *Ibid.,* August 24, 1849; Mobile *Advertiser,* September 8, 1849. So far as is known by this writer no complete file of the *Tribune* exists. The only four issues seen are those of November 9, 1849 (I, No. 11), July 5, 1850 (I, No. 45), December 9, 1853 (V, 16), and June 10, 1859. The paper was "Devoted to Politics, Agriculture, and Commercial and General Intelligence."

35. *Alabama Journal,* September 10, 1849. Bates recommended the *Tribune* as a fine advertising medium in the "up country."

36. The last column, No. 24, in the *Journal* (September 28, 1849) was devoted to "Murder; Attempt to Commit Rape; Another Murder Case; Larcency; Assassination." It was dated La Fayette, September 23.

37. *Alabama Journal* (Tri-weekly), October 17, 1849, quotes one of Hooper's "graphic sketches."

38. Quoted in the *Spirit,* XIX, 388-389, 423-424, 450, 460 (October 6, 27, November 10, 17, 1849); XX, 28 (March 9, 1850). "The Widow Rugby's Husband" was copied by the *Spirit* from the Cincinnati *Great West.*

39. *Spirit,* XIX, 399 (October 13, 1849).

40. Quoted in *ibid.,* XIX, 436-437, 471, 483 (November 3, 24, December 1, 1849). In each case the *Delta* is given as the source.

41. Brewer, *op. cit.*, pp. 514-515; Garrett, *op. cit.*, p. 529. Garrett states that Latham left for California after his defeat for the judgeship, declaring that "he would not live in a State where Johnson Hooper could beat him for solicitor."

42. Brewer, *op. cit.*, p. 538; Garrett, *op. cit.*, pp. 425, 529. The other two were A. M. Presley of Chambers and an unidentified Mr. Spyker, in all probability B. H. Spyker of Talladega, co-owner of the (Talladega) *Alabama Reporter.*

43. Kelley, *op. cit.*, p. 64.

44. *Alabama Journal,* November 22, 1849; Garrett, *op. cit.*, p. 526.

45. C. C. Clay, *A Digest of the Laws of the State of Alabama . . .* (Tuscaloosa, 1843), p. 516. Beginning in 1854 Circuit Court judges were paid $2000 (*Acts of the Fourth Biennial Session of the General Assembly of Alabama . . .* [1853-1854], Montgomery, 1854, p. 64.). Hooper, it will be recalled, wrote Mrs. T. A. Heard, August 22, 1850, that he hoped "the next riding" would pay him $600 (see *supra,* p. 40).

46. W. B. Wood, Jr., of Lafayette, Alabama, owns an original "Capias Warrant," signed by "Hooper State's Attorney, February 27-28, 1851, Chambers County Circuit Spring Term, 1851," covering the case of "The State *vs* Jere Harris & Smith Drinkard." *Chambers County Circuit Court Minutes, Spring Term, 1850-Fall Term, 1853,* VI, 18ff., and VII, 140ff., lists many cases in which Hooper defended the state.

47. Johnson J. Hooper, *The Widow Rugby's Husband, A Night at the Ugly Man's, and Other Tales of Alabama* (Philadelphia, 1851), p. 65.

48. *Ibid.*, p. 66. See also *Tallapoosa County Circuit Court Minutes,* E, 102 [1850], for an illustrative case, the "State *vs* William White being called to come into the court to answer to a charge preferred against him for an Assault and Battery."

49. The Union (or United States) Hotel (later called the Dennis Hotel), built in 1836 and yet standing (1951), is mentioned because of its historical interest and because it is locally closely identified with Hooper (see Varian Feare, "In Search of a Book, a Man, an Inn," Birmingham *News-Age-Herald Magazine,* October 6, 1935, p. 10, and letter, Jere C. Dennis to Varian Feare, Dadeville, Alabama, October 7, 1935, a copy of which is in the Jere C. Dennis Papers, University of Alabama Library). Major Dennis is the present owner of the hotel which has been in his family for more than 100 years.

50. The Dadeville Courthouse, typical of those in which Hooper worked was constructed in 1839. It is described in *Tallapoosa County Bond Book* 2, 28-29 [1839] and in *Index to the Map of the Town of Dadeville* [1838-1840], pp. 28-29, as follows:

" . . . Court House to be built of the same size and built in the same manner as the Court House in the town of La Fayette, Chambers

County, Alabama, the Jail to be eighteen feet by thirty-four feet from outside to outside to be divided into four rooms two below and two above, the first story to be ten feet pitch of Bricks, two Bricks in thickness or eighteen Inches thick, the upper story to be built of Logs twelve Inches wide and seven Inches thick in the inside and the outside to be of Brick nine Inches thick. The Dungeon room to be eleven feet by fifteen feet made secure with Iron after the manner of the Jail in the Town of La Fayette, Chambers County, Ala, the balance of the upstairs with the exception of an entry of four feet running across the room to be formed into a debtors room which is to be finished after the manner of the debtors room in La Fayette, Chambers County, Alabama, there is to be two fire places in the Jail one below and one upstairs in the debtors room."

51. See *supra*, p. 12.

52. *Widow Rugby's Husband*, pp. 64-65.

53. Mobile *Advertiser*, December 5, 1850. This writer added that Hooper was editing the *Tribune* "as none but he could edit a paper." Williams, the printer, is not mentioned and it must be assumed that he was somehow forced out by the deal. See also *Alabama Journal*, December 3, 1850.

54. The firm of Holifield, Hooper & Co. also did job-printing. For instance, see Rhoda Coleman Ellison, *op. cit.*, p. 81 [item 755].

55. The only known copy of this exceptionally rare volume, *A Ride with Old Kit Kuncker, and Other Sketches, and Scenes of Alabama* (Tuscaloosa, 1849), is owned by this writer. Two years later the volume was copyrighted by A. Hart of Philadelphia (successor to Carey & Hart) and reissued as *The Widow Rugby's Husband, A Night at the Ugly Man's and Other Tales of Alabama.* This second edition contained the same stories, but in different order, with illustrations and four additional sketches, "The Bailiff that 'Stuck to His Oath,'" "Jim Bell's Revenge," "Mrs. Johnson's Post Office Case," and "A Fair Offender" (see *infra*, p. 72). In *A Ride with Old Kit Kuncker* the title story was first in the volume, "The Muscadine Story" second, and "The Widow Rugby's Husband" third, and "A Night at the Ugly Man's" fourth; in the 1851 edition these four stories were placed in tenth, fifth, first, and fourth positions, respectively.

56. *Alabama Journal*, January 29, 1850.

57. Rhoda Coleman Ellison, "Early Alabama Interest in Southern Writers," *The Alabama Review*, I, 101-110 (April, 1948). Anne H. Augustus, Macon, Mississippi, owns an unidentified newspaper clipping (among the papers of Mrs. Annie B. Heard) in which the following interesting sidelight on Hooper's friendship for Meek is revealed: "*Letter from Hooper to Meek.* Through the kindness of a friend (says

the Selma *Times*) we have been favored with the following, in the shape of a letter with superscription from the renowned and genial humorist, the lamented J. J. Hooper, to his friend, the late Hon. A. B. Meek.

Mon Ami, de Mique.
Hav you got von grand pique,
At your friend?
Ah!
Be Gar!
Your mannaire must mend

Not von single lettaire
Hav you write to me, sair,
Sacre damn!
Ca!
Bah! Bah!
Not any more flam!

Sins way off last spreeng,
I hav not have notting
From you!
Mail
Not fail—
But You do—Pambleu!

So write to me queek,
Mon cher, monsieur Mique!
Cuss your pet!
Eh?
what say
To 'Yours' in La Fayette?
[Signed] *Hoopaire*

Advertised Forwd Mons'r Alexander B. Mique, Advocate des Etats Unis, Tuscaloosa, Alabama—Aif Mr. Mique has no longer raside in T. will monsieur le amiable maitre de la Poste follow this after him sans delai and oblige, *Victor Bonbonniere*."

58. See *supra*, pp. 41, 196, n. 21.

59. *Spirit*, XX, 28, 41, 56, 69, 117, 231 (March 9, 16, 23. 30, April 27, July 6, 1850). The last-named was copied by Porter from the *Yankee Blade* (Boston).

60. *Spirit*, XIX, 593 (February 2, 1850).

61. *Ibid.*, XX, 579-580 (January 25, 1851).

62. *Alabama Journal*, February 26, 1850; *Spirit*, XX, 52 (March 23, 1850). The sketch, which Hooper had read and sanctioned before printing, is as follows:

"A kiln-dried specimen of humanity, about 5 feet 10 inches in height, a cross between an Egyptian mummy and a shriveled pumpkin, conveys to the mind a faint idea of Johnse . . .

"An old silk which has honestly won, and boldly wears the title of 'a shocking bad hat,' covers a small bullet-shaped head; a sack coat of grey tweeds covers, while it displays to perfection, a hump which would excite the envy of an Eastern dromedary, or Parisian belle; a striped vest buttoned closely to the throat, hides a shirt which the washerwoman has but a slight acquaintance; breeches, whose original color is '*questio vexata*,' encase a pair of legs formed in humble imitation of the Jack of Diamonds—below the termination of the breeches are a pair of pigeon-toed feet, covered with yarn socks, one of which is always worn wrong side outwards, and a pair of kip brogans, as inconscious of blacking as their owner's face is of soap.

"Hooper's face can 'better be imagined than described.' In attempting to take his Daguerreotpye, Park has broken two cameras! . . . His hair is sun-burnt brown, seldom combed, never oiled; his fore-head is bold and intellectual, it is the sole mark by which you can recognize his face as human; his eyes are foxy . . . his lips full and sensual show little firmness, but much ambia; his nose a counterpart of that portion of Montgomery known as Jerusalem; his cheekbones are strongly defined, and his cheeks sunken . . .

"Hooper is ugly—theoretically, practically, decidedly ugly. This misfortune made him solicitor of the seventh. In his recent canvass before the Legislature, his friends argued that so much ugliness fortified by bills of indictment and writs of capias, would drive old offenders from the circuit, and deter the rising generation from crimes and misdemeanors. The argument held good, and Hooper was elected . . . Hooper is ugly simply because he can't help it. From self defence, he has cultivated a bold and original style, with a fine appreciation of the ridiculous . . . But we must say that he pursues his foes with as much zeal as he serves his friends, be the injury great or small, the punishment is in full. He never forgets an Offence, and never forgives one."

[Signed] "Big Ugly"

63. *Macon Republican* (Tuskegee), January 31, 1850, states that during this time Hooper was writing a series of sketches for the *Tribune* called "Capital Sketches."

64. *United States Census* (Seventh), 1850 [Original MSS. Returns], Alabama, II, 233, records Hooper as 34 years old, his wife Mary 25, and his sons William D. and Adolphus S., six and three, respectively.

65. Hooper was also practicing law at this time (see case of G. G. Hudson *vs* T. E. Landrum, *Chambers County Appearance Docket, Spring Term,1849-Spring Term, 1855,* n. p, *passim*).

66. *Carey & Hart Record Book,* IV, 4 (MSS. volume in Historical Society of Pennsylvania). Under date of March 6, 1850, the following entry appears:

	1000 Simon Suggs	
	Presswork 23 tokens @30c	9.60
•	Reprinting wood cut title 11.85 say	5.00
Plates	Paper 9 reams @4.00 (40lbs)	36.00
$125	Covers	30.00
	Binding	15.00
	500 sets cut to be printed	10.00
	10½ cts	$105.60

67. *Ibid.*, IV, 9. Under date of September 30, 1850, the following entry appears:

1000 Simon Suggs.	
Presswork 32 tokens @30c	9.60
Paper 9 reams 4.00	36.00
Covers	25.00
Plates Pr. $12. P. 2 r. @$5.00=$10.=	22.00
Binding	15.00
Prop, Ster Plates "Modern Chivalry"	30.00
	$137.60
14 cts per copy	

68. *Spirit*, XXI, 150 (May 17, 1851). These editions were entitled *Some Adventures of Captain Simon Suggs, Late of the Tallapoosa Volunteers, Together with "Taking the Census," and Other Alabama Sketches;* with a portrait of the Author, and Other Illustrations, by Darley. They were illustrated "with excellent wood-engravings, and published at the small charge of 50c." *The Literary World*, IX, 233 (September 20, 1851) announced the Getz & Buck edition as follows: "Getz & Buck, Philadelphia, offer to the trade . . . their humorous works, with humorous designs by Darley, at humorously cheap prices, and in humorously pleasant succession . . . In various humorous advertisements are the trade and public invited to order and to read the famous Simon Suggs, Breckinridge's Teague O'Regan, Chronicles of Pineville, Stray Subjects, Bear of Arkansas, &c." No copy of the Stringer and Townsend edition has been seen by this writer, however.

69. *The Widow Rugby's Husband, A Night at the Ugly Man's, and Other Tales of Alabama.* By Johnson J. Hooper, author of "Adventures of Capt. Simon Suggs." With Engravings from Original Designs by Elliott. Philadelphia, A. Hart, 1851. See *The Literary World*, VIII, 137, 179, 523 (February 15, March 1, June 28, 1851) and *supra*, p. 72.

70. See, for example, the Florence (Alabama) *Gazette*, March 30, 1850.

71. See, for examples, "The 'Frinnolygist' at Fault," *Wheler's Southern Monthly Magazine* (Athens, Georgia), II, 25-28 (January, 1850); "Shifting the Responsibility," *Little Scissors* (New York), II, n. p. (February, 1857); "A Visit to the Ugly Man's," "Sloshin' About," "Shifting the Responsibility," "In Favor of the Hog," and "Another Hatful Joel," *Yankee Notions, or Whittlings from Jonathan's Jack-Knife* (New York), II, 310-311 (October, 1853); III, 205 (July, 1854); V, 125, 263 (April, September, 1857); VII, 358 (December 1858). For other stories, unsigned but possibly Hooper's, see "An Alabama Incident," "Staying All Night," "An Alabama Daniel Come to Judgment," and "Bugging an

Overseer," *ibid.*, I, 284 (September, 1852); V, 272 (September, 1856); VII, 330 (November, 1858); and IX, 92 (March, 1860).

72. Thomas A. Burke, editor, *Polly Peablossom's Wedding; and Other Tales* (Philadelphia, n. d.), pp. 143-145. The first (1851) edition, published by "A. Hart, Late Carey & Hart," although bearing the identical dedication, does not contain "Shifting the Responsibility." The undated edition referred to here was published by T. B. Peterson, Philadelphia, and does contain both the dedication and Hooper's piece, as stated. See also *Spirit,* XXI, 74 (April 5, 1851).

73. (New York, 1853), pp. 114-141. As a frontispiece *Flush Times* has a picture of "Simon Suggs, Jr.," which bears a great likeness to his "father," Hooper's original character. See Samuel Boyd Stewart, *Joseph Glover Baldwin* (unpublished Ph. D. thesis, Vanderbilt University, 1941), pp. 193-195, for a brief comparison of these two characters.

74. December 3, 1850.

75. April 11, 1850. See also December 29, 1853.

76. Interesting sidelights on Hooper's social activities during this affluent period are to be seen in his Masonic affiliations. In *Minute Book Solomon's Lodge No. 74, La Fayette, Alabama, December 27-1848-June 1, 1855,* under date of October 31, 1851, is found this note: "[Johnson J. Hooper] who had been initiated as an E. A. Mason in Montgomery Lodge No 11, and having produced satisfactory evidence from that Lodge of their willingness for him to have the F. C. & M. M. degrees conferred upon him in this Lodge petitioned for further light on Masonry by being passed to the F C D and on motion it was unanimously made a case of emergency in consequence of Bro. Br [J.M.] Branridge the Grand Leader of the Grand Lodge . . ." [he] "was balloted and duly elected to receive the M M degree & was introduced & regularly raised to the sublime degree of M Mason in due form . . ." Hooper attended Solomon's Lodge regularly throughout 1853, and on two or more occasions served as Secretary *pro tem.*

The *Secretary Book No. 1 Concord Chapter No.* 37 [Royal Arch Masons] *La Fayette, Alabama July 19, 1848-April 22, 1865* indicates that this lodge was organized in 1848 with Hooper's friend, P. H. Brittan, as a charter member. Hooper was a member of the chapter and on April 17, 1852, was "advanced to honorary degree of M. M." He attended meetings from July 5, 1852, to the end of 1853 with regularity. Both above manuscript volumes are in possession of W. B. Wood, Jr., Lafayette, Alabama, and are here used with his kind permission. See *supra,* pp. 107, *infra,* 226, n. 59.

77. *Spirit,* XXI, 601 (February 7, 1852); XXIII, 253, 277, 373, 469 (July 16, 30, September 24, November 19, 1853). On one occasion (September 24) Porter added: "Of course we charge you no commis-

sion, but one of these days we will take a chew of tobacco or a mint-julep with you, while we enquire for 'Simon Suggs' and 'Daddy Biggs.'" See also *ibid.*, XXIV, 85 (April 8, 1854).

78. *Ibid.*, XXIII, 254, 446 (July 16, November 5, 1853).

79. *Ibid.*, XXIII, 553 (January 7, 1854).

80. *Ibid.*, XXIII, 289, 392, 446, 553, 589 (August 6, October 1, November 5, 1853, January 7, 28, 1854). The stories were entitled "An Otter Story," "Quail in Alabama," "Electioneering in Alabama," "Dog Story Extraordinary," and "Sporting Epistle in Alabama." See also *ibid.*, XXIII, 337 (September 3, 1853).

81. XXIII, 303-304 (August 13, 1853). The sketch, as "A Night at the Ugly Man's," had first appeared November 24, 1849, (XIX, 471), copied from the New Orleans *Delta.*

82. *Macon Republican,* June 30, 1853, chides Hooper for his fence-straddling politics, accusing him of having "one eye towards Montgomery, and one towards Chambers."

83. That Hooper gave up the editorship of the *Tribune* during these weeks is very doubtful. The assumption that he temporarily transferred at least a part of the work to another is based on an editorial in that paper, quoted by the *Spirit*, XXIII, 591, (January 28, 1854), for which see *supra*, p. 74.

84. *Chambers County Record of Commissioners Court, August 20, 1849-December, 1868,* IV, n. p., under date of August 15, 1853, has notation that Holifield and Hooper were paid $12 for advertizing by the County. W. B. Wood, Jr., of Lafayette, Alabama, has a receipt dated November 9, 1852, signed by "Chambers Tribune, Holifield and Hooper." The bill is to J. L. Williams and is marked "*paid.*" Phillips and Prather probably bought the *Tribune* in mid-1853, for Mr. Wood owns a receipt signed by those men, dated August 12, 1853.

85. *Alabama Journal,* November 12, 1853. In this news item "the bloody 7th" is given instead of "the bloody 9th." Obviously a misprint, the figure has been changed by this writer to prevent confusion. Bate's comments are followed by a long description of Hooper's visit to Montgomery, quoted from the *Chambers Tribune.*

86. Garrett, *op. cit.*, pp. 525-526, 766; Brewer, *op. cit.*, pp. 540-541. Woodward was reelected in 1857 for a second term. Hooper's father, it will be recalled, died at this time, at George's home in Crawford, September 25, 1853.

87. Montgomery *Advertiser and State Gazette,* December 31, 1853. This letter, entitled "Hooper on the Solicitorship," written to W. G. Clark, editor, Mobile *Advertiser,* in which paper it first appeared, December 22, 1853.

88. *Spirit,* XXIII, 591 (January 28, 1854), from *Chambers Tribune.*

89. *Spirit*, XXIV, 52, 85 (March 18, April 8, 1854), quoted from the *Chambers Tribune.*

90. March 9, 1854.

91. March 3, 1854.

92. Letter, J. J. Hooper to Sarah J. Brantley, Montgomery Alabama, April 9, 1854. Screws, *op. cit.*, II, 191-192, says that the delays were due to the fact that the ship bringing Hooper's paper and supplies from New York was seized at Havana *en route* to Mobile.

93. *Spirit*, XXIV, 73 (April 1, 1854).

CHAPTER FIVE

1. For a background of Alabama party politics prior to 1861, the reader is directed to Abernethy, *op. cit.*, pp. 102-121; Moore, *op. cit.*, pp. 159-207, 238-268; Theodore H. Jack, *Sectionalism and Party Politics in Alabama, 1819-1842* (Menasha, 1919); Lewis Dorman, *Party Politics in Alabama from 1850 to 1860* (Montgomery, 1935); J. E. D. Yonge, "The Conservative Party in Alabama, 1848-60," *Transactions of the Alabama Historical Society,* IV, 501-526 (Montgomery, 1904); C. P. Denman, *The Secession Movement in Alabama* (Montgomery, 1933); Arthur C. Cole, *The Whig Party in the South* (Washington, 1913); and studies of the several prominent political personalities of the period.

2. *Alabama Journal,* September 3, 1851. See also the *Advertiser and Gazette* (Montgomery), December 21, 1851. Hooper was at this time against secession, however: "Hooper, (in the Chambers *Tribune*) is cutting and slashing the disunionists up in those diggins, at a rate that must soon make dogsmeat of the whole concern," stated the *Macon Republican,* July 10, 1851. "Jonce must have split his pen with a grubbing-hoe, and sharpened it with a meat-axe."

3. Various sources give Thursday, April 13, 1854, as the date of the first issue of the *Weekly Mail* (for example, M. P. Blue [and others], *City Directory and History of Montgomery, Alabama, with a Summary of Events in that History, Calendarically Arranged, besides Other Valuable and Useful Information,* Montgomery, 1878, p. 56), but Hooper himself wrote Sarah J. Brantley on April 9, 1854, that the paper "will be issued next Wednesday," which was the twelfth (see *supra*, pp. 78, 216, n. 92). Screws, *op. cit.*, p. 191, says the first issue appeared "about the 13th of April." Since no copy has been located, it is impossible to prove the point.

4. Letter, Hooper to Sarah J. Brantley, Montgomery, April 9, 1854: "Joe and his wife are only tolerably well pleased with Montgomery. They are within one door of Reub's [probably Reuben C. Holifield, Jr., an editor on the Montgomery *Times*] and I board with them . . ." See Screws, *op. cit.*, p. 190. The baptisms are recorded in Parish Register,

St. John's church (MSS. vol. in Alabama State Department of Archives and History, Montgomery), I, 21 (November 30, 1854).

5. *The Seventh Census of the United States: 1850* (Washington, 1853), p. 241, gives the county a total population of 29,711—10,169 whites, 115 free colored, and 19,427 slaves.

6. Baldwin submitted an article to the *Mail*, instructing Hooper to print it, if he wished. Baldwin also thanked the editor for his favorable review of *Flush Times* and offered to send him a copy of his forthcoming *Party Leaders* (letter, Baldwin to Hooper, Livingston, Alabama, June 10, 1854, in Lester-Gray Collection, owned by Robert McDonald Lester, 414 East 52nd Street, New York City, quoted by Stewart, *op. cit.*, pp. 186, 278).

7. The earliest issue of the *Tri-Weekly Mail* located by this writer is dated May 1, 1856 (II, 140). It is therefore reckoned that the first issue appeared Saturday, June 10, 1854.

8. XXIV, 161, 172, 197, 200, 209, 273, 348, 380 (May 20, 27, June 10, 17, July 15, 22, September 2, 23, 1854). In the issue of July 15 (XXIV, 253) Porter announced that he had received "a Daguerrotype of the author of 'Simon Suggs'" but was doubtful of its authenticity—"a pretty good likeness of 'N. of Arkansas,'" he wrote. "'No tricks upon travellers,' mind."

9. April 20, 1854.

10. IX, 701 (October, 1854). See also footnotes 17 and 47 below.

11. Lack of a file of the Montgomery *Weekly Mail* renders a positive statement impossible. In the November 17, 1854, issue of the Montgomery *Daily Mail* (I, No. 2) the statement is made that the weekly had been suspended "through fear of the yellow fever." Porter's *Spirit* quotes the *Weekly Mail* on July 2 and September 23 (XXIV, 273, 348, 380) but nothing thereafter until December 9 (XXIV, 505). The earliest issue of the weekly located by this writer is dated Friday, March 9, 1860 (VI, No. 45), the publication day having been moved up during the years from Thursday to Friday. If publication had been steadily consistent for six years, the March 9, 1860, issue would have been Volume VI, Number 49. Instead, it is number 45, clearly indicating that four weeks of publication had been skipped. Hence, the deduction that the *Weekly Mail* missed four issues during the fall of 1854, probably during October.

12. Quoted in the *Daily Mail*, December 7, 1854.

13. The Montgomery *Daily Mail*, the first extant issue of which is dated November 17, 1854 (I, 2), sold for $8 per year, and the *Weekly Mail* for $2.50.

14. November 23, 1854.

15. Quoted in the *Daily Mail*, December 7, 1854.

16. *Ibid.*, November 18, 21, 22, 24, 1854, contains sketches entitled "Matched to a Hair," "Tail Told," "The Town Cow," and "Valor and Prudence—but Mostly Prudence," for examples. "Matched to a Hair" also appeared in the *Spirit*, XXIV, 521 (December 16, 1854).

17. It is interesting to note (*Daily Mail*, December 2, 1854) that Hooper wrote: "The last *Harper's* publishes a little sketch written by us, years ago, entitled 'The Georgia Major,' and credits it to Judge [Augustus Baldwin] Longstreet. Of all the undeserved compliments we ever received, this is the highest." Hooper was mistaken in saying the piece was credited to Longstreet. "We have forgotten precisely who the 'Georgia Major' was," stated *Harper's New Monthly Magazine*, X, 133 (December, 1854), "but we believe he was an intimate acquaintance of the quaint, humorous, and accomplished Judge Longstreet, of that region of the country."

18. *Daily Mail*, November 20, 24, December 1, 6, 8, 1854.

19. *Ibid.*, December 12, 1854, January 8, February 24, March 3, 26-29ff., 1855. Tuomey was author of the *First Biennial Report on the Geology of Alabama* (Tuscaloosa, 1850).

20. *Daily Mail*, January 27, 1855.

21. *Ibid.*, May 25, 1855.

22. *Ibid.*, May 9, 1855.

23. *Ibid.*, January 3, 26, 1855.

24. *Ibid.*, January 13, 22, 1855. On this visit Hooper met the former President of Texas, Mirabeau B. Lamar, interviewed Dion Boucicault and Agnes Robertson who were playing *London Assurance*, and talked with Clark Mills, the "widely famous" sculptor of the "equestrian statue of Jackson."

25. See Dorman, *op. cit.*, pp. 106-107. Briefly, the party supported "native Americans," the right of "freedom of worship," the "non-intervention by the Federal government with slavery," "perpetuity of the Union upon the the principles of the Constitution," and "purity of the ballot box." It opposed "immigration of paupers and criminals" and "political franchise to foreigners."

26. *Daily Mail*, May 28, 1855. Hooper met and was entertained in Atlanta by Mayor A. Nelson.

27. *Ibid.*, May 29-June 27, 1855.

28. Frequent gifts, especially tomatoes, strawberries, watermelons, etc., were sent to Hooper by his readers (*ibid.*, June 4, 1855).

29. Montgomery *Advertiser*, June 14, 1855.

30. *Daily Mail*, June 25, 26, 1855. Besides Shortridge and Watts, the *Mail* also announced its support of Daniel Pratt for senator, J. H. Clanton and J. E. Belser for the House of Representatives, and James Y. Brame for sheriff of Montgomery County.

31. *Ibid.*, June 12, 13, 1855. See Dorman, *op. cit.*, pp. 101-124, for a detailed analysis of "The Know-Nothing Campaign of 1855."

32. *Daily Mail,* April 27, 1855. See also "The Temper of the South," *ibid.*, April 15, 1855.

33. *Ibid.*, May 3, 1855.

34. *Ibid.*, July 15, 1855. During all this while Hooper kept up a continuous editorial fight with Brittan of the *Advertiser,* who was supporting the candidacy of Winston. Hooper frequently referred to "Britt" and his Democrats as "Bogus Democrats."

35. *Daily Mail,* July 3, 1855.

36. In the 1855 elections 61 and 20 Democrats and 39 and 13 "Know Nothings" were sent to the legislature and senate, respectively, from the state at large (see Dorman, *op. cit.*, p. 122).

37. *Daily Mail,* August 7, 9, 10, 1855.

38. *Ibid.*, July 11, August 3, 9, 14, 20, 1855. During Hooper's absences the quality of the *Mail's* editorials noticeably deteriorated. They were written by "kind friends," he said.

39. *Ibid.*. September 3, 10, 24, 26, 27, October 6, 8, 10, November 2, 1855. In November Hooper was elected secretary of the "Aid to Virginia Cities" (yellow fever) committee and to the "Committee on Terrier Dogs" for the State Fair which was held annually in Montgomery. It is significant that Thomas H. Watts, Hooper's political friend, was chairman of the first-named group and J. C. Bates, his political rival, a member of the second.

40. (Montgomery, 1855). The only copy seen of this rare pamphlet is in the J. L. M. Curry Collection (volume 22), Alabama State Department of Archives and History, Montgomery. It was printed by Barrett and Wimbish.

41. *Daily Mail,* November 20, 1855.

42. *Spirit,* XXVI, 221 (June 2, 1856) quoted from *Freeman's Journal* which had copied it from the *Mail.* Curiously enough, this same quotation appears in the St. Louis (Missouri) *Reveille* (edited by Joseph M. Field and Charles Keemle), August 27, 1844, copied from the Wetumpka *Whig,* the paper which Hooper had edited eleven years earlier. Stated the Reveille: "*Taking it in Good Humor.* The editor of the Wetumpka (Ala.) *Whig* places the following caption to his election news in that State: 'we have met the Enemy! and—*we are theirs!*' How much pleasanter must be the feeling of such an editor, than those of one who flies into a fit of displeasure, and vents his disappointment in wrangling and personal invective? Let politicians take a lesson from this."

43. *Southern Times* (Montgomery), March 31, 1855, contains a 1½-column story, "How Widder Westbrook 'Took' the Sheriff," written "for the *Southern Times* by Johnson Jones Hooper, Esq."

44. Hooper's climactic denunciation of "Simon Suggs," which allegedly occurred in December, 1856, will be discussed in more detail later (see *infra,* pp. 102-103).

45. *Spirit,* XXV, 164, 343, 387, 486, 495, 513 (May 19, September 1, 22, November 24, December 1, 8, 1855). Not all these were written by Hooper. "Fish Breeding in Alabama" is not his and "Old Charley," quoted from the *Mail,* is signed "Omega," John G. Barr, of Tuscaloosa, one-time professor of mathematics at the University of Alabama and a frequent contributor to the *Spirit* and other papers (see *infra,* p. 229, n. 28).

46. *Ibid.,* XXIV, 505 (December 9, 1854); XXV, 205 (June 16, 1855). In the last Porter asked, ". . . why the 'Mail' does not reach us?"

47. *Ibid.,* XXV, 557 (January 5, 1856). See *supra,* p. 83.

48. The location of the first *Mail* office is unknown to this writer, but in February, 1855, it was moved to "Freeman's Building, on the Public Square, above the Auction rooms of Lee & Norton." The address given was "Court Square, North of Artesian Basin." "Whenever we say 'square', in this connection," wrote Hooper, "we always mean the open space in the center of our town, wherein the old Court-house used to stand, and which is not in the power of geometry to describe" (*Daily Mail,* February 12, March 25, 1855).

49. *Ibid.,* April 16, 27, 1855.

CHAPTER SIX

1. *Minutes of the City Council of Montgomery, Alabama, June 2, 1856-September 10, 1860,* pp. 37, 39, 41, 42, December 29, 1856 (MSS. volume in the University of Alabama Library). The *Mail* kept this account until 1860 (*ibid.,* pp. 113, 124, 325, 375).

2. Screws, *op. cit.,* II, 192. Riggs was also a friend of George D. Brantley (see letter, Joel Riggs to Brantley, Montgomery, June 3, 1848, in possession of and used here with the kind permission of Anne H. Augustus, Macon, Mississippi). Riggs died in Montgomery, November 16, 1865.

3. *Montgomery County Conveyance,* O. S. VII, 64-65. The $2300 was not paid in full until January 4, 1859. For Hooper's sale of his interest in this property see *ibid.,* XII, 197 (March 12, 1860).

4. Screws, *op. cit.,* II, 192; *Daily Mail,* November 5, 1856. At this time the *Mail's* office was still on "Court Square, North of Artesian Basin," but the office of the *Tri-Weekly* was given as "Over Bell's Store, Market Street" (*ibid.,* September 23, 1856).

5. Lack of a file of the *Mail* during most of 1856 prevents a detailed reporting of Hooper's activities. This writer has located no issues of the *Daily Mail* or *Weekly Mail* between November 6, 1855-November 5, 1856, and only a few scattered issues of the *Tri-Weekly.*

6. For an excellent discussion of Alabama politics in 1856, see Dorman (*op. cit,* pp. 125ff.), which has been used here as a primary source for this brief summary.

7. Montgomery *Advertiser,* February 1, 1856. The other leaders were C. C. Langdon, J. E. Belser, L. E. Parsons, B. S. Bibb, J. H. Clanton, and B. M. Woolsey.

8. J. W. DuBose, *Life and Times of William Lowndes Yancey . . .* (Birmingham, 1892), p. 313.

9. Montgomery *Independent American,* June 4, 1856; *Clarke County Democrat,* September 18, 1856.

10. *Tri-Weekly Mail,* May 1, 1856.

11. *Ibid.,* June 10, 1856. On June 20 the committee scheduled a mass meeting of the party at Shelby Springs. James E. Belser, B. S. Bibb, H. P. Watson, Thomas H. Watts, Edmond Harrison, A. W. DeBardelaben, B. L. Posey, Daniel Pratt, A. Kimball, J. T. Holtzclaw and Walter Echols were the other members. In August Hooper attended an American rally at Butler Springs (see *ibid.,* September 2, 1856).

12. *Ibid.,* June 7, 1856. The Alabama Democrats had recommended the re-election of Pierce, whom they considered a friend of the South.

13. *Ibid.,* July 3, 1856.

14. December 5, 1856.

15. *Daily Mail,* November 25, 1856.

16. *Ibid.,* November 7, 1856.

17. Throughout these years the *Mail,* as well as other Alabama papers, was filled with flattering comments about everything "Southern" —theatricals, industries, mining, books, cities, railroads, etc. They appeared with increasing frequency until 1861. Even a casual reading of Minnie Clare Boyd, *Alabama in the Fifties* (New York, 1931) will supply ample evidence of this almost fanatical fervor of sectionalism.

18. *Spirit,* XXVI, 186, 221 (May 31, June 21, 1856); XXVII, 183 (May 30, 1857). The June 21 issue contained " 'Seeing the Elephant' and other Scraps," copied from *Freeman's Journal,* and the May 30, "Old Mammy Halladay's Experience" copied from the *Mail.*

19. *Spirit,* XXVI, 354 (September 6, 1856). Edward E. Jones became Porter's successor on the *Spirit,* when the latter began *Porter's Spirit of the Times,* the first issue of which dated September 6, 1856. This journal ran until February 19, 1861, at which time it merged into *Wilkes' Spirit of the Times.* By 1858, however, *Porter's Spirit* had degenerated into a horse-racing and chess weekly. *Knickerbocker Magazine,* XLVIII, 437 (October, 1856) states that *Porter's Spirit* began with a subscription list of "over 24,000."

20. Hooper published Porter's letter verbatim in the *Mail,* August 26, 1856.

21. *Porter's Spirit*, I, 14 (September 6, 1856). Hooper continued: "If not for the first number, very soon thereafter, although I hope to get something up for that just to see myself in it. When you say the word, I'll let our boys know it, and the 'Spirit of the Times,' 'made perfeck,' by the prefix of 'Porter's,' will become a 'harp of a thousand strings,' on which we will all want to play." Significantly, the letter was signed "Simon Suggs."

22. *Ibid.*, I, 69 (October 4, 1856). This short sketch, entitled "Simon Suggs Rejecting the Flattering Unction," was obviously not written by Hooper. It is quoted below because of the added light it throws on the prototpye of "Simon Suggs," Bird H. Young:

"Every body has read or heard of Simon Suggs, whom 'Jonce' Hooper immortalized; and almost every body is aware that the veritable original *Simon* (whose real home need not be mentioned, because that is nobody's business, no-how), still lives, in Alabama. A year or two since, he came to Tuskegee, with an almighty long face, and a yard of crape *[sic]* round his hat, and met his friend, Ned—[Hanrick?], when the following remarks were made.

"Byrd," said Simon's friend, "what ails you? You look solemn and serious, as if you had met with some misfortune."

"You know, Ned," said Simon, "that I have lost my companion." (He had recently lost his wife, a most pious and estimable lady, by death); "and besides that, I have been thinking a good deal, lately about my latter end, and the next world."

"You," said Ned. "I always thought you were a Universalist."

"So I was," said Simon, perfectly serious and evidently impressed with the solemnity of the subject; *"but I tell you, Ned' there aint nary a pair in that hand. It aint any use to bluff agin Old Master. He sees every card in your hand."*

23. Porter died July 15, 1858, at the age of 48. See *Dictionary of American Biography*, XV, 107-108; *Spirit*, XXVIII, 288 (July 21, 1858); and *Porter's Spirit*, IV, 328 (July 24, 1858).

24. *Daily Mail*, July 24, 27, 1858. It is interesting to note, however, that other Alabama humorists were at this time contributing to *Porter's Spirit*. One, "Omicron" (of Pickens County) wrote "Bubbles for *Porter's Spirit*" (I, 99, October 11, 1856); and "Omega" (John G. Barr, of Tuscaloosa, a friend of Hooper's) contributed "New York Drummer's Ride to Greensboro" (I, 6-7, September 6, 1856), "Jemmy Owen's Fifty Dollar Note; or Moind Whay ye Say" (I, 35-36, September 20, 1856), and several other stories. See *infra*, pp. 145, 229, n. 28.

25. William Watson Davis, "Ante-Bellum Southern Commercial Conventions," *Transactions of the Alabama Historical Society*, V, 153-202 (Montgomery, 1906).

26. *Daily Mail,* November 17, 18, 28, December 18, 1856; *Weekly Alabama Journal,* November 29, 1856. David Hubbard was chairman of the Alabama delegation. The other Montgomery delegates, in addition to Mayor C. R. Hansford, were H. P. Watson, C. T. Pollard, F. M. Gilmer, J. H. Murphy, William Knox, Seth Robinson, Richard Jones, B. S. Bibb, John C. Bates, Fort Hargrove, Dr. N. B. Cloud.

27. *Daily Mail,* November 12, 17, 1856.

28. December 13, 1856.

29. Quoted in *Daily Mail,* November 22, 1856.

30. *Ibid.,* December 6, 9, 1856.

31. December 8, 1856. The *News* added that the delegates "have been pouring into the city by every steamer and every train of cars, until our hotels are overflowing . . ."

32. *Daily Mail,* December 9-12, 1856; *DeBow's Review,* XXII, 81 (January, 1857).

33. *Daily Mail,* December 11, 1856; *Weekly Alabama Journal,* December 13, 1856; *DeBow's Review,* XXII, 82 (January, 1857). The other nine states, with their representatives were: Thomas L. Gholson (Virginia), William T. Dortch (North Carolina), William A. Cooper (Georgia), William G. McAdoo (Tennessee), Albert L. Webb (Maryland), Arthur L. Nevitt (Louisiana), D. F. Jemison (South Carolina), A. Mc Leod (Texas) and J. S. Maxwell (Florida).

34. This report of the convention scene is based on Garrett, *op. cit.,* pp. 528-529 (written in 1872) and on Riley, *op. cit.,* pp. 70-71, who obviously copied his predecessor. Both name John A. Jones as the man who called on Hooper, Riley referring incorrectly to Jones as the author of *Major Jones' Courtship.* J. D. B. DeBow, delegate from Louisiana, who covered the convention for his *Review* makes no mention of the "Simon Suggs" incident; in fact, he throws doubt on the whole story by suggesting that the "delegations from each State" were appointed to name the Joint Committee. In such case, Hooper, as a member of the Alabama delegation, would have been out of the hall during the interim. If the rest of the story is true, Hooper was not in the assembly at the time "Mr. Suggs" was asked to "give an account of himself." Brewer, *op. cit.,* p. 466 (also written in 1872) says merely that Hooper "regretted" having written *Simon Suggs.* On June 28, 1862, shortly after Hooper's death, the *Weekly Mail* quoted the Milledgeville (Georgia) *Recorder*: "Mr. Hooper was well known to the country as the author of 'Simon Suggs,' a work of unsurpassed humor and of great popularity. He has been known to express his regret, however, for having [written it], because, as he conceived it, it identified his name with a class of literature which was an obstacle to his advancement in the more ambitious walks of life, of which he had a just sensibility."

35. *Daily Mail,* December 11-18, 1856.

36. *Ibid.,* December 24, 1856. At this time the Grenada (Mississippi) *Locomotive* stated, "The *Weekly Mail* is the very handsomest paper in Alabama" (quoted in *Daily Mail,* February 10, 1857). At this time the *Mail* had "authorized agents" in New York, Boston, Philadelphia, and many Southern cities.

37. *Ibid.,* May 7ff., 1857, contains notices of the "American and Whig Parties" county convention during circuit week. Thomas J. Judge, William H. Rives, C. H. Molton, and J. R. Dillard, American-Whig candidates, received the *Mail's* support during this year's local elections (*ibid.,* June 3, 1857).

38. April 30, 1860.

39. *Ibid.,* January 19, 1857.

40. *Ibid.,* May 2, 1860.

41. Boyd, *op. cit.,* p. 208.

42. *Daily Mail,* March 3, 13, 1857. No file of the Camden *Republic* has been located.

43. See *supra,* pp. 51-53. Hooper frequently played editorially with other newspaper publishers. For instance, see his replies to M. L. Woods of the Prattville (Alabama) *Statesman,* and to the Milledgeville (Georgia) *Union,* which had called him an "incorrigible wag" (*Daily Mail,* February 9, April 23, 1857).

44. Johnson J. Hooper [of Montgomery, Ala.], *Dog and Gun: A Few Loose Chapters on Shooting. Among Which Will Be Found Some Anecdotes and Incidents* (New York, 1856). This, the first edition, was published by C. M. Saxton & Company, 140 Fulton Street, at 75c. See footnote 49 below.

45. Herbert wrote copiously for the *Spirit* and was one of the best-known "outdoor" men of his time. He died in 1858 (see *ibid.,* XXVIII, 181, May 29, 1858; *Porter's Spirit,* IV, 185, May 22, 1858).

46. I, nos. 5, 8, 14 (February 20, April 21, July 3, 1855) contain chapters III, VI, and X of *Dog and Gun.* Other issues of the *Southern Military Gazette* have not been seen by this writer. The magazine, begun in Montgomery was moved to Atlanta about June 15, 1855.

47. Stockton wrote Hooper (*Dog and Gun,* p. 95) that he was very busy but that he could not refuse to send a chapter on "Snipe Shooting in Florida" to the "'author of Simon Suggs' and 'Editor of Montgomery Mail' . . . Your request is so flattering, you have the gift, as Pliny has it . . . *Adornare verbis, benefacta,* that though little in the mood . . . , I must make the effort."

48. *Daily Mail,* February 2, 3, 1857.

49. By 1861 copies of the book were apparently scarce. *Spirit,* XXXI, 161 (April 20, 1861) contains this note: "W. F. W.—'The enclosure

received. We have not yet been able to find a copy of 'The Dog and the Gun.'"

50. Copies of the two 1856 (Saxton and Judd), the 1858 (Moore), and the 1860 (Saxton, Barker) editions have been seen by this writer. They are believed to be products of the same plates, although the first Judd edition is paper bound with an attractive hunting cover-scene. The second (1871) Judd edition was in print as late as 1876. For a description of Moore's *Rural Hand Books* see *Dog and Gun* (New York, 1860), p. 6 [advertisements]. John C. Phillips, *A Bibliography of American Sporting Books* (Boston, 1930), p. 183, states that the volume was first published by Orange, Judd & Co. [1856] and by A. O. Moore [1858]. It was "a leading book of the period."

51. See, for examples, *Daily Mail*, July 13, August 19, 1857.

52. Pickett's letters "Descriptive and Historical" appeared February 10, 15, 20, 25, March 8, 1858.

53. Sol Smith contributed an essay, "Theatricals in Montgomery Twenty-Eight Years Ago," (February 9, 1858), which was later quoted in the *Spirit*, XXVIII, 77 (March 27, 1858). See also *Daily Mail*, January 8, 1858.

54. Massett wrote Hooper (*ibid.*, March 8, 1858): "'Simon,' when you and I were boys together, and scribbled our yarns for dear W[illiam] T. P[orter] and the jolly old 'Governor'—we were so many thousand miles apart—how little did I think we should ever meet . . ." Massett played in Commerce Hall (Montgomery) and Hooper praised his performances as "the most popular ever offered by any single person in the United States" (*ibid.*, December 9-11, 14, 1859). See also Stephen C. Massett, *Drifting About, or What "Jeems Pipes of Pipesville" Saw-and-Did* (New York, 1858), pp. 25, 58.

55. Woodward's contributions, originally entitled "Old Times in Alabama," began appearing in the *Daily Mail* October 26, 1857. See *supra*, pp. 115-116.

56. Hooper greatly admired Daniel Pratt, the industrialist, and considered his mill at Prattville, Alabama, one of the state's most splendid manufactories (*ibid.*, August 22, 1857).

57. *Ibid.*, May 19, 20, 25, 1857.

58. *Ibid.*, June 23, 1857. The challenge grew out of politics. Cloud had written an article for his paper on the Kansas situation. Hooper replied in the *Mail*, "torturing out a meaning," according to Cloud, which "none but a desperate opponent, regardless alike of truth and intelligence of the public could discover." Hooper demanded retraction of the statement almost daily for more than a week—and was still demanding it when the editorial duel came to an end. And that's as far as the matter got, except that Cloud concluded by saying that he knew

no reason why he should "name a time and a place, beyond the limits of the state" and that he would "fight no duel on such grounds."

59. Hooper joined Masonic Lodge No. 11 (Montgomery) on March 20, 1847, transferred to Solomon Lodge (La Fayette) where, October 31-November 1, 1851, he took the second and third (master) degrees. In 1854, upon his return to Montgomery, he withdrew his membership, i.e., "demitted," but on June 6, 1857, he re-affiliated with the Montgomery chapter and remained in good standing until his death (see *supra,* p. 214, n. 76, and *Annual Return[s] to the Most Worshipful Grand Lodge of Alabama on the Officers and Members of Montgomery Lodge No. 11* [1846-1862] and *Annual Return[s] Made by Solomon Lodge No. 74 to the M. W. Grand Lodge, A.F. and A.M. of Alabama* [1851-1854], MSS. in Masonic Temple Vault, Grand Lodge, Montgomery, Alabama, used here through the courtesy of Mr. Charles Stubinger, grand secretary, Montgomery, Alabama).

60. *Magnum Opus. The Great Book of the University of Comus. The Pandect of our National Hilarities, Confusing Essays upon the Thirteen Divisions of the Rituals; Sketches of the Tredecim Doges, Authors of the Plan, and Monitorial Guide to the Workings of the Fellowship. The Gander-Flight of the Thirteen Doges of Comus* (Louisville, 1886), pp. 7-8, 74-80. The only copy seen is in the University of Kentucky Library. See also Benjamin H. Screws(?), *The 'Loil Legislature of Alabama: Its Ridiculous Doings, and Nonsensical Sayings* (Montgomery, 1868).

61. *Ibid.*, p. 74.

62. See Moore, *op. cit.*, pp. 258ff., and Dorman, *op. cit.*, pp. 137ff, the volumes from which this summary is primarily obtained.

63. *Daily Mail,* July 6, 1857.

64. *Ibid.*, June 28-29, 1857.

65. *Ibid.*, July 31, 1857.

66. Besides Judge for Congress, the *Mail* supported William H. Rives for the Senate and C. H. Molton and J. R. Dillard for the House. They were "billed" as "American and Whig Candidates" (see *ibid.*, June 3ff., 1857).

67. Ulrich B. Phillips, *The Life of Robert Toombs* (New York, 1913), pp. 222-230.

68. *Daily Mail,* July 20, 28, 1857. Toombs, like Yancey, advocated withholding final judgment on Buchanan until after the presidential election.

69. See Tuccoa Cozart, "Henry W. Hilliard," *Transactions of the Alabama Historical Society, 1899-1903* (Montgomery, 1904), IV, 277-299. Hilliard later felt that he had made a mistake in uniting with the Democrats.

70. Quoted by Dorman, *op. cit.*, p. 141.
71. *Daily Mail*, August 12, 1857.
72. *Ibid.*, April 28, 29, 1858.

CHAPTER SEVEN

1. Yancey spoke frequently during the year at political rallies (see *Daily Mail*, May 11, July 14, 17, 19, 1858, for typical meetings at Montgomery, Bethel Church, and Benton).

2. Dorman, *op. cit.*, p. 143; Moore, *op. cit.*, 264ff.; DuBose, *op. cit.*, pp. 437ff.

3. Yancey was not too happy over the *Mail's* support of the League, for his opponents used the fact as evidence that the Leagues were "a combination of defunct Know Nothings and disaffected Democrats whose purpose was to overthrow the Democratic party" (Dorman, *op. cit.*, p. 144). See the *Daily Mail*, April-July, 1858, for evidence of Hooper's increasing interest in Yancey.

4. *Ibid.*, January 25, 1858; Dorman, *op. cit.*, p. 146. See also General William Walker, *The War in Nicaragua* (Mobile, 1860), pp. 429-430.

5. The "Leagues of United Southerners" bore resemblance to the "Southern Rights Associations," which Yancey had sponsored in 1850. The "Leagues" were abolished largely because the Democrats saw "disunion" as the chief idea behind them and were not prepared at the time (1858) for so strong a medicine (Dorman, *op. cit.*, p. 145).

6. Screws, *op. cit.*, II, 192, states that "after the Know-Nothing or American party died out," the *Mail* "became an extreme southern rights paper."

7. *Daily Mail*, August 28, 31, September 5, November 18, 1857.

8. Screws, *op. cit.*, II, 192. In Diary of Mrs. Annie B. Heard, January 16, 1859, this note is recorded: "Mr. Coyne, Mr. Hooper's partner took tea with us [in New Orleans]—a very awkward, dry fellow."

9. *Daily Mail*, March 31, 1858. On this day Hooper editorially thanked "several kind ladies" for bringing the family "corn hoe-cakes and buttermilk."

10. *Ibid.*, December 11, 12, 17, 21, 1857, January 21ff., 1858. As is well known, this was not unusual in Southern newspapers, especially during the late 1850's.

11. Brewer, *op. cit.*, p. 339.

12. In "Montgomery Characters," pp. 112-114. "Horseshoe Ned" was later to "turn journalist" himself (see *infra*, pp. 130-131, 135-136). Woodward's first two letters, dated May 2 and December 9, 1857, and addressed to Hanrick, were ignored in the numbering. They were included in the collection, however.

13. The letters (their dates are given in parentheses) appeared in the *Daily Mail* February 12-13 (December 24, 1857), 18 (January 10,

1858), April 6 (March 21), 9 (March 25), May 6 (April 2, addressed to F. A. Rutherford, Union Springs, Alabama), 24 (April 25, addressed to A. J. Pickett, Montgomery), July 8 (June 13), July 16-17 (June 21, addressed to Pickett), August 11 (June 16, addressed to John Banks, Columbus, Georgia), ? (July 8), August 30 (August 12, addressed to Pickett), October 2 (September 16), and January 8, 1859 (December 25, 1858). Several letters, later included in the collected volume, were not published in the *Daily Mail.*

14. *Ibid.*, August 19, November 23, December 15, 1858; January 4, 1859.

15. *Ibid.*, January 24, 1859.

16. (Montgomery, 1859). The printers were Barrett & Wimbish. The original edition read by this writer is in Newberry Library, Chicago.

17. *Daily Mail,* January 24, February 12, 17, March 17, April 16, 1859. See *ibid.*, February 21, March 1, 1860, for notice of the death of Woodward.

18. See for example, Montgomery *Confederation*, January 25, 1859.

19. Because of its extreme rarity (only nine copies of the original edition are known), the *Reminiscences* were reprinted in April, 1939 (Tuscaloosa and Birmingham, Alabama), with a Preface by Peter A. Brannon, archivist, Alabama State Department of Archives and History.

20. *Daily Mail,* July 13, August 19, 1857, September 13, 15, 1858; *Woodward's Reminiscences,* p. 4. Hooper's Introduction, dated January, 1859, also makes mention of his poor health at the time.

21. *Daily Mail,* March 10, 1858. "Cant-Get-Away Club," according to Louis F. Tasistro, *Random Shots and Southern Breezes* . . . (New York, 1847), I, 235, was a facetious name for nursing organizations which remained at home to take care of yellow fever victims during epidemics (see also Moore, *op. cit.*, pp. 409-410 and Mobile *Daily Register,* July 30, 1875).

22. The other two appeared in *Daily Mail,* April 5, 7, 1858.

23. "Horseshoe Ned" followed him shortly thereafter, arriving in Montgomery June 21 (*ibid.*, June 22, 1858).

24. *Ibid.*, July 17, 19, 1858. As has been noted, Yancey was in these years fighting desperately for control of the state Democratic party.

25. Hooper wrote the editor of the *Spirit,* Edward E. Jones (XXVIII, 475, November 13, 1858), over the signature "Number Eight" that he had been having trouble with his eyes. Jones replied editorially that he hoped he would soon recover (*ibid.*, XXVIII, 541, December 12, 1858). A month later Jones advised Hooper that "The T. R. was forwarded immediately on receipt of order. If not yet come to hand, please say so in your next, and we will send another" (*ibid.*, XXVIII, 577, January 15, 1859).

26. *Daily Mail,* July 17, 30, August 4, 11, 16, 24, 1858. Hooper wrote two essays on Talladega and Shelby Springs (August 4, 12), and Coyne two on his trip to North Alabama (August 18, 24, 1858).

27. *Spirit,* XXVIII, 344 (August 28, 1858) contains a short sketch of Hooper's, entitled "Another Hat-Full Joel," copied from the *Mail.*

28. *Daily Mail,* August 31, September 8, 1858. See *supra,* p. 222, n. 24, and W. Stanley Hoole, "John Gorman Barr: Forgotten Alabama Humorist," *The Alabama Review,* IV, 83-116 (April, 1951).

29. "The arduous labors . . . during the last session of the legislature" were apparently Hooper's reporting, for neither the *Journal of the Sixth Biennial Session of the House of Representatives of the State of Alabama, 1857-'58* (Montgomery, 1858) nor the *Senate Journal* makes any mention of his having had any political responsibility.

30. XXVIII, 475 (November 13, 1858).

31. *Daily Mail,* September 13, 15, 30, 1858. The issue of the 15th contains a letter from Hooper, written from Tuskegee. A few months later Hooper received another pen as a gift from J. Tannenbaum of Montgomery "as a token of my regard for your merits, both as a man and as an editor" (*ibid.,* March 4, 1859).

32. XXIX, 1, 25 (February 1, 26, 1859). "Bourbon" of Gainesville, "Cursor" of Montgomery, and "Justice" of Hayneville were other Alabama contributors.

33. *Ibid.,* XXXI, 65, 305 (March 9, June 22, 1861). The *Spirit* "will be suspended for a time—how long, the undersigned is at present unable to say," wrote Jones. "Business in New York is nearly dead, and money is very scarce. By order of the United States Government we are deprived of Mail communications with our Southern friends . . ."

34. *Daily Mail,* January 4, March 12, 14-16, 1859. The Alleghany Company must not have materialized, for this writer noted no further references to the project. See, however, a long humorous article on "Ducktown" by "Skitt" [H. E. Taliaferro], *Spirit,* XXX, 563, (December 29, 1860).

35. Hooper's enthusiasm for Montgomery's prosperity prompted him to write Editor Edward E. Jones of the *Spirit* "that there is 'a good time' progressing in this, the liveliest, most prosperous and handsomest of Southern towns" (*ibid.,* XXVIII, 475, November 13, 1858).

36. *Montgomery County Conveyances,* O. S. XI, 202-203. The lot was bought from Francis M. and Martha A. Gilmer on February 15, 1859.

37. *Daily Mail,* April 14, 1859.

38. Quoted in *ibid.,* February 2, 1860.

39. *Spirit,* XXIX, 91 (April 2, 1859). See *supra,* p. 107.

40. *Daily Mail,* March 22, April 14, 1859.

41. XXIX, 150, 174 (May 7, 21, 1859).

42. *Porter's Spirit*, VI, 9, 92 (March 5, April 9, 1859) contains articles describing these Mobile races. One is unsigned, the other is signed "Our Own Correspondent." Nothing proves that Hooper supplied them, though the March 5 issue quotes an article about Pfister's Book Store copied from the *Daily Mail.* See also *Spirit*, XXVIII, 342, 487, 510, 536 (August 28, November 20, December 4, 18, 1858) for other similar reports on races at Mobile and Montgomery.

43. *Daily Mail*, March 23, 25, April 7, 12, 1859.

44. XXIX, 210 (June 11, 1859). See also *ibid.*, XXIX, 390 (September 24, 1859) for a report on the Montgomery Fall Races.

45. *Daily Mail*, May 2ff., 1859. The "American and Whig County Convention" met in Montgomery on this date.

46. George Petrie, "William F. Samford, Statesman and Man of Letters," *Transactions of the Alabama Historical Society, 1899-1903* (Montgomery, 1904), IV, 465-485, states that Samford's pen was a complement to Yancey's oratory in the Southern Rights movement, and that together they did much to mold political thinking in the state.

47. Dorman, *op. cit.*, pp. 149-150, 193. In Montgomery County Hooper's friend Thomas J. Judge, a "States Rights Whig," put up an exciting fight for Congress, but "was defeated by a majority of over two hundred."

48. In Montgomery the streets were "full of smoke, fire, dust, hollowing, music, and rockets. The oldest inhabitants [had] never seen anything like it" (*ibid.*, pp. 150-151, quoted from Tuskegee *Republican*, August 4, 1859).

49. Sutton S. Scott, "The Alabama Legislature of 1857-58 and 1859-60," *Transactions of the Alabama Historical Society, 1904* (Montgomery, 1906), V, 43-82.

50. *Acts of the Seventh Biennial Session of the General Assembly of Alabama Held in the City of Montgomery, Commencing on the Second Monday in November, 1859* (Montgomery, 1860), pp. 25, 36-41, 373, 685-687; *Journal of the Seventh Biennial Session of the Senate of the State of Alabama* (Montgomery, 1860), pp. 71, 126-127; and *Journal of the Seventh Biennial Session of the House of Representatives of the State of Alabama* (Montgomery, 1860), p. 474. The Joint Resolution was signed by Governor Moore on February 24, 1860; however, the Senate had introduced it as early as November 30, 1859. Nine military companies were also chartered by this Assembly.

51. *Spirit*, XXIX, 390, 439, 510, 521, 534 (September 24, October 22, December 3, 10, 17, 1860). About *Jonce Hooper* the *Spirit* quipped, "Judge Hunter's Lecomte colt and Major Bacon's *Jonce Hooper* were twin cynosures [in Montgomery]. If you don't hear of both before long,

as bagging lots of 'the needful,' then I am badly mistaken." See *infra*, p. 233, n. 70.

52. To which Thorpe replied (*ibid.*, XXIX, 397, October 1, 1859) that he would "keep a sharp lookout for you."

53. *Ibid.*, XXIX, 421, 439 (October 15, 22, 1859).

54. It is interesting to note that the *Spirit* (XXIX, 576, January 14, 1860) was mightily disturbed by the "unhappy sectional agitation now prevailing." The North, the editors believed, was under great obligation to the South. "Some of the best things, always the most original, produced in this country, are the results of Southern pens. For more than a quarter of a century the columns of the 'Spirit' have teemed with the finest specimens of writing, overflowing with wit and sentiment, playful and profound, a large part of which is destined to become permanent specimens of real American originality, for which we have been largely indebted to Southern correspondents."

The *Spirit* actually fostered a plan of establishing an agency in Richmond where all "Northern businessmen favorable to the South" could sign up so as "Southerners will know the kind of people they patronize North of Mason and Dixon's line" (*ibid.*, XXIX, 612, January 28, 1860).

55. For an invaluable summary of this era see Denman, *op. cit.*, pp. 82ff., and Dorman, *op. cit.*, pp. 154ff. Both studies have been freely used by this writer. See also Walter L. Fleming, *Civil War and Reconstruction in Alabama* (New York, 1905), pp. 1-60. Differing viewpoints of this controversial era may also be seen in Austin L. Venable, "The Conflict Between the Douglas and Yancey Forces in the Charleston Convention," *The Journal of Southern History*, VIII, 226-241 (May, 1942) and Hermione Dannelly, *The Life and Times of Robert Jemison, Jr., during the Civil War and Reconstruction* (unpublished Master's thesis, University of Alabama, 1942), *passim*.

56. *Weekly Mail*, June 8, 1860. Each issue of the *Weekly Mail* is composed of four sheets, at least two of them being merely the "news" sections of the *Daily*. For example, the *Weekly* dated May 9 contains sheets dated May 5, 6, and two additional pages. Hence, an article itself dated May 5 would be included in the May 9 issue of the *Weekly*.

57. *Ibid.*, January 1, May 11, 26, June 19, 1860.

58. Hooper's editorial leadership of the short-lived Southern Rights Opposition party is evident in numerous articles which appeared from the beginning of the organization to its final collapse. See, for best examples, *ibid.*, "The South Comatose," April 27; "The New Party Name," May 4; "Flee From the Wrath to Come!," May 11; "Shall Southern Rights Men Give Up?," "Our Position," May 18; "The Platform of

1856," May 25; "Stand to Principle," June 8; "State Rights Opposition Meeting," June 22; "Mr. Watts' Position," June 29; "State Rights Opposition Convention Adheres to Principle," "State Rights Opposition Convention," July 6; "An United Front to Defeat Lincoln," July 13; "Our Bell and Everett Assailants," July 20; "Breckinridge or a Black Republican," "Is There Nothing Higher Than Party?," July 27; "Opposition Friends of Breckinridge," "Lincoln and Somebody," August 3; "The Half-Year Old Party," August 24; "Address to the State-Rights Opposition Voters of Alabama," September 7, 1860 (Supplement).

59. *Spirit,* XXIX, 588 (January 14, 1860).

60. Hooper's vast interest in the industrial and economic independence of the South is illustrated by the following articles, selected at random from the *Weekly Mail*: "Shad," "The Daily Post," "The Coffee Tree," April 6; "The Western Rail Road Company," April 13; "Tuskegee-Its Improvements," "The Goree Pear," April 20; "The Alabama River and Georgia Lines," "The Polk County Copper Company," April 27; "Argument Against Pugilism," "The Effect on Trade in the South," May 11; "Breaking Up of the Parodi Opera Troupe," May 25; "Newspaper Rights," June 22; "The Harper Establishment," July 6; "Shelby Iron Works," July 13; "A Real Book," July 27; "The Augusta Route-Eating Houses," August 17; "An Infirmary at Tuskegee," August 24, 1860. See Hugh Peter Young, *A Social and Economic History of Montgomery, Alabama 1846-1860* (unpublished Master's thesis, University of Alabama, 1848).

61. Hooper's interest in local civic matters is also evidenced by his appeal to the City Council to close a "Negro Shop kept at the corner known as the Chair Factory, abated as a Nuisance," *Minutes of the City Council of Montgomery* p. 335 (January 2, 1860).

62. *Daily Mail,* January 7, 12, 13, 30, 1860; *Weekly Mail,* January 1, 1860. See also *Wilkes' Spirit,* I, 377 (February 18, 1860), and *Spirit,* XXX, 6 (February 11, 1860).

63. *Daily Mail,* March 6, 1860.

64. XXX, 13 (February 18, 1860).

65. *Daily Mail,* March 19, 1860, quoted from Mobile *Mercury.*

66. *Ibid.,* March 21, 23, 26, 1860; *Weekly Mail,* March 23, 30, 1860; *Spirit,* XXX, 114-115, 126 (April 14, 21, 1860). See also *ibid.,* XXX, 61 (March 17, 1860).

67. *Weekly Mail,* April 6, 1860; *Daily Mail,* March 30, 31, 1861.

68. *Spirit,* XXX, 124 (April 21, 1860), copied from the New Orleans *Cresent,* March 30, 1860.

69. *Daily Mail,* April 5, 7, 8, 9, 11, 16, 1860; *Weekly Mail,* April 6, 13, 20, 1860. Hooper returned to Montgomery on April 16 on "the fine steamer *H. J. King.*"

70. *Wilkes' Spirit,* I, 377, 392 (February 18, 25, 1860); II, 69, 284 (April 7, July 7, 1860); III, 233 (December 15, 1860). *Jonce Hooper* ran frequently in Charleston, Camden (S. C.), and Augusta (Ga.) for $10,000 purses. See *supra,* pp. 123, 230, n. 51.

At this time, in Cassville, Missouri, a correspondent wrote the *Spirit* (XXX, 240, June 23, 1860) as follows: ". . . an old, coverless, and dirty-looking book caught my eye, which, on opening, read as follows: [Hooper's dedication of *Simon Suggs* to William T. Porter quoted]. I proceeded on and found it to be some adventures of Capt. Simon Suggs, late of the Tallapoosa Volunteers. Who of the 'Old Spirit' readers does not remember the humorous adventures of the Captain, published in the good old spirited journal, years and years gone by? Nearly twenty years ago, I recollect almost splitting with laughter in perusing them, and now, having travelled over many portions of the country where the scenes are laid, I appreciate them ten fold more. They came to me like rich old Port, twenty years in bottle, and should the editors be in existence, do, Messrs. Editors, uncork them."

71. *Daily Mail,* March 21, February 2, 18, 1860. A new "Caloric engine" was installed in March (*Weekly Mail,* March 30) and frequent notices of an increasing subscription list appeared currently.

72. *Ibid.,* April 21, 1860.

73. The Montgomery *Confederation,* edited by J. J. Seibels, was convinced that the "Cincinnati Platform and Dred Scott decision [fulfilled] the requirements of our resolutions and our delegates *will not,* then, withdraw [from the Charleston Convention]." Hooper declared this to be "double-dealing politics" and accused the *Confederation* of being content with "stone for bread" and "serpent for fish" (*ibid.,* January 20, 1860).

CHAPTER EIGHT

1. *Proceedings of the Democratic State Convention held in the City of Montgomery, Commencing Wednesday, January 11, 1860* (Montgomery, 1860), *passim.* See also James G. Randall, *The Civil War and Reconstruction* (Boston, 1937), pp. 175ff., and Emerson D. Fite, *The Presidential Campaign of 1860* (New York, 1911), *passim.*

2. See *Proceedings of the National Democratic Convention at Charleston, S. C. Apr. 23, 1860* (Washington, 1860).

3. *Weekly Mail,* April 20, 1860.

4. *Ibid.,* April 27, May 4, 11, 1860; *Daily Mail,* April 23-May 1, 1860.

5. *Weekly Mail,* April 27-May 4, 1860; *Daily Mail,* April 20-May 4, 1860. Hooper realized that opponents of his ardent support of Yancey and secession might lead to a curtailment of *Mail* subscribers, but, he declared, "We cannot yield our right of opinion [although] our position may lead to heavy pecuniary loss . . . *the man and the platform we*

support must freely and without equivocation accord to the South all she justly claims" (*Weekly Mail*, May 14, 18, 1860; *Daily Mail*, May 2, 14, 30, June 4, 1860). See footnote 23 below.

6. *Speech of the Hon. William L. Yancey, of Alabama, Delivered in the National Democratic Convention, Charleston, April 28, 1860, with the Protest of the Alabama Delegation. From the Report of the "Charleston Mercury"* (Charleston, 1860); see also *Proceedings of the National Democratic Convention at Charleston*, pp. 67ff.

7. *Weekly Mail*, May 11-18, 1860; *Daily Mail*, May 11, 13, 1860. The day after Yancey's address Hooper left for Savannah on a "business trip," returning on May 17 (*ibid.*, May 18, 1860).

8. Moore, *op. cit.*, pp. 263-267.

9. *Daily Mail*, June 4, 1860.

10. *Weekly Mail*, June 8, 29, 1860. Both wings first assembled in Baltimore on June 18, however. The "Seceders," finding themselves unwelcome, withdrew and reassembled in Richmond on the twenty-third, at which place they nominated Breckinridge and Lane. The other wing remained in Baltimore and nominated Douglas and H. V. Johnson (after Benjamin Fitzpatrick of Alabama had declined the vice-presidential nomination).

11. *Weekly Mail*, October 26, 1860. Townsend's pamphlet (Charleston, 1860) was a sort of Bible for "Minute Men." The majority of the Oppositionists, like Hooper, ultimately accepted Yancey's leadership and supported Breckinridge, while the minority, including Watts, voted for Bell (see Dorman, *op. cit.*, p. 162; Denman, *op. cit.*, pp. 82-84).

12. *Weekly Mail*, May 11, 18, June 8, 15, 22, 29, July 20, 27, August 3, September 28, October 12, 1860; *Daily Mail*, June 1ff., 1860. These are selected samples—many more could be added.

13. The *Montgomery* arrived in New York, Sunday, June 10 (New York *Times*, June 11, 1860); *Daily Mail*, June 11-14, 1860.

14. *Spirit*, XXIX, 439, (October 22, 1859) contains an article praising the Fifth Avenue Hotel as excellent "for Southern gentlemen."

15. See "The Japanese in New York," New York *Times*, June 19ff., 1860.

16. *Weekly Mail*, June 22, 1860; *Daily Mail*, July 5, 1860.

17. XXX, 117 (June 16, 1860).

18. June 13, 1860.

19. *Proceedings of the [National Democratic] Conventions at Charleston and Baltimore* (Washington, 1860), p. 250. See *Address of the Democracy of Alabama to the National Democratic Convention at Baltimore, June 18th, 1860* (Baltimore, 1860).

20. *Daily Mail*, June 19ff., 1860; *Weekly Mail*, June 22, 1860. "Horseshoe Ned" later served as a Confederate ambassador to the

Indian Nations, persuading them to "fight for the South" (see Richmond *Daily Dispatch*, November 2, 1861).

21. *Daily Mail*, June 22, July 2, 1860.

22. *Weekly Mail*, June 29, July 6, 13, 1860; see also "Southern Union," and "Remove the Douglas Corpse," July 13; "Douglas and Squatter Sovereignty" and "Breckinridge and Lane—Exponents of Your Principles," August 31; "Breckinridgers, Organize!" and "The Tide is Flowing for Him," September 28; "The North Against Us" and "All Coming to Breckinridge! Fresh Disclosures About Negro Equality," October 19; and "An Enemy in Our Camp," October 26, 1860, for other representative Hooper articles.

23. *Daily Mail*, September 4, 1860, states that the *Mail's* politics had lost it 160 subscribers during the past two months and simultaneously gained 335 new ones.

24. *Spirit*, XXX, 280 (July 14, 1860) noted that Hooper, "our friend and correspondent," had reached Montgomery safely and had " 'pitched into' the political campaign with a rush."

25. *Daily Mail*, July 9, 1860, contains this poem, probably by Hooper:

"Unfurl the banners to the air,
And raise the deaf'ning shout,
We bearded Douglas in his lair,
And put him to the rout;
We'll heel the Union where she bleeds—
Let Constitution reign,
And follow truth where'er it leads,
With Breckinridge and Lane.

"Bring out the cannons—let them blaze
From every hill and glen,
And let them thunder forth the praise
Of principles—not men.
Then join the throng—the nation's throng
Who will not fight in vain
And swell the chorus of the song
For Breckinridge and Lane".

26. *Weekly Mail*, September 7, 1860. "Mr. Douglas is to come and speak for us in Montgomery," Hooper wrote. "He could hardly do less. He has spoken of the *clam-bakes* of New England and stated his preference for that species of bivalve, over Southern negroes. It is right that after praising clams so strongly, he should now come and give the 'nigger' his share."

27. *Ibid.*, October 26, 1860. Hooper denounced J. W. Taylor as being "personally disloyal to the South" and the latter replied in an address.

Hooper did not retract what he had said. See also Montgomery *Weekly Advertiser,* October 24, 1860.

28. *Weekly Mail,* November 15, 1860. "The object [of the "Minute Men"] is to organize so as to be ready to offer aid to the State of Alabama, if a Black Republican shall be elected President, and if she fail to dissolve her connection with the Federal Government, then to any other Southern State which, being unwilling to submit to shame, dishonor and death, shall determine to maintain her honor and her rights. Military Companies, preserving their organization, are invited to join."

29. Montgomery *Advertiser,* July 18, 1860.

30. *Weekly Mail,* July 20, 1860; *Daily Mail,* July 17, 1860. Of the author of *Rutledge* (New York, 1860) Hooper wrote, "If Miss Lyons [of Columbia, S. C.] be the writer, the South is to be congratulated on the possession of a genius, in this department, far beyond comparison with any other living American novelist. This is our candid opinion." The author was Miriam Coles Harris.

Hooper's caloric motor, purchased in New York the year before, broke down in November and he replaced it with a steam engine obtained from the Muscogee Works, Columbus, Georgia. When it was put into motion for the first time Hooper "in the presence of a dozen friends christened it 'Separate State Action.' It runs smoothly," he added, "noiselessly, without jar, and with ample power" (*ibid.,* November 16, 1860).

Of Brinley's *Life of William T. Porter* Hooper stated in the *Weekly Mail* "We read this interesting memoir of our dear old friend, almost with tears in our eyes . . . the files of the Old Spirit would furnish ample materials for at least another volume . . ." (*ibid.,* October 19, 1860).

31. *Daily Mail,* July 1ff, 1860. In Florence, Alabama, Yancey spoke to 3,000 people (*Weekly Mail,* August 10, 1860); on October 19 Hooper printed Yancey's entire Cooper Institute (New York) address.

32. See for example, the "Great Mass Meeting in Front of the [Montgomery] Exchange Hotel"; and "Grand Reception of Mr. Toombs . . . A Long Procession—A Thousand People in front of the Exchange" (*ibid.,* August 10, November 2, 1860). See *supra,* p. 110.

33. During this fervent political compaign Hooper still found time to report the activities of the Montgomery Racing Association, of which he was secretary, for the *Spirit* (XXX, 206, 298, 398, 429, 489, July 21, 28, September 22, October 13, November 17, 1860).

34. *Weekly Mail,* September 11, 14, 21, 28, October 12, 1860; *Daily Mail,* September 5-10, 1860. A train wreck between Nashville and Louisville delayed Hooper, but he escaped unhurt.

35. *Ibid.*, November 8, 1860.

36. *Ibid.*, November 5-10, 1860.

37. On December 29, 1860, *Wilkes' Spirit* (III, 264) contained the following paragraph: "To Correspondents: J. J. H. (Montgomery). Please decide the following bets: A bets B that Virginia will go for Breckinridge, $500; B bets A that Virginia will go for Bell, $200. *Answer*—The official action of the state carries the decision. We cannot go behind the record, and that shows that fifteen electors, which is the full complement of Virginia, cast their votes in her name for John Bell. The case is essentially different from that of New Jersey, where a divided electoral vote is cast. Both of the above bets are identical and B, if he be one and the same person, wins $700."

38. *Daily Mail*, November 7, 1860.

39. *Ibid.*, November 10, 1860. "The citizens of Montgomery . . . are invited to meet at Estelle Hall . . . to deliberate upon the condition of the South in the present crisis . . ." Hooper was one of the "Citizens' Committee," as was his partner, Whitfield.

40. *Weekly Mail*, November 30, December 28, 1860; Riley, *op. cit.*, pp. 141ff.; Dorman, *op. cit.*, p. 167.

41. William R. Smith, *The History and Debates of the Convention of the People of Alabama, Begun and Held in the City of Montgomery, on the Seventh Day of January, 1861; in which Is Preserved the Speeches of the Secret Sessions, and Many Valuable State Papers* (Montgomery, 1861), pp. 12-17. The official Executive Document calling for a convention was not written, however, until December 9. The Governor's letter came in answer to a request for action written November 12 by twenty-one citizens of Alabama, among whom were Yancey, Judge, Watts, and S. F. Rice, of Montgomery County, all friends of Hooper. See also *Weekly Mail*, November 9-23, 1860; *Daily Mail*, December 7, 1860.

42. *Weekly Mail*, November 23-30, December 7, 14, 21, 28, 1860; January 4, 1861; *Daily Mail*, December 21ff., 1860.

43. *Ibid.*, December 7, 1860.

44. *Journal of the Convention of the People of Alabama, Held at the City of Montgomery Commencing on the 7th Day of January, 1861* (Montgomery, 1861); Smith, *op. cit.*, pp. 21-22; *Weekly Mail*, January 4ff., 1861.

45. John W. Inzer, "Alabama's Secession Convention, 1861," *The Confederate Veteran*, XXXI, 7-9 (January, 1923). Inzer was a delegate from St. Clair County.

46. Smith, *op. cit.*, p. 33.

47. *Weekly Mail*, January 4-11, 1861. Hooper quoted the following from the Charleston *Mercury*, dated January 9: "The United States

Star of the West, with two hundred fifty men aboard, attempted to enter the harbor to reinforce Major Anderson, was fired into from Morris' Island, hit three times, turned tail and went to sea." An announcement on the 4th of a meeting of the stockholders of the Montgomery "Race Course Association," of which Hooper was secretary, was given most inconspicuous notice.

48. Smith, *op. cit.,* pp. 22-49. Historians are mindful of their great debt to Smith, a delegate to the convention from Tuscaloosa, Alabama, for keeping and later publishing his *History and Debates,* which includes the events of the "Secret Sessions." Otherwise, the proceedings of this momentous "Secession Convention" would doubtless have remained cloudy.

49. For an excellent eye-witness account of these weeks in Montgomery see "The Correspondence of Thomas Reade Rootes Cobb, 1860-1862," *Publications of the Southern History Association,* XI, 147-185, 233-260, 313-328 (May, July, September-November, 1907).

50. Two months later Smith wrote, "The separation is complete and will be perpetuated. I have fought hard against all this—But I have an abiding faith in the ultimate greatness of these Southern States" (letter, William R. Smith to Mansel & Rowland, Montgomery, March 12, 1861, in University of Alabama Library). See also, Anne Easby-Smith, *William Russell Smith of Alabama* . . . (Philadelphia, 1931), pp. 92-124.

51. *Weekly Mail,* January 18, 1861. This flag had previously flown from the *Le Grande,* an Alabama River steamboat.

52. Denman, *op. cit.,* pp. 154-156, shows this distinction by maps.

53. Smith, *op. cit.,* pp. 43-118; Denman, *op. cit.,* pp. 123-153; see also George Petrie, "Montgomery," in L. P. Powell, editor, *Historic Towns of the Southern States* (New York, 1900), p. 404.

54. *Weekly Mail,* January 18, 1861.

55. Inzer, *op. cit.,* p. 9.

56. Smith, *op. cit.,* pp. 119-122.

57. *Ibid.,* p. 268.

58. *Weekly Mail,* January 18 [dated 12], 1861. Former Senator Jeremiah Clemens (in his Memphis, Tennessee, *Enquirer*) severely rebuked Hooper for possessing "the craziest set of politics in the world.' Hooper replied: "We believe that all abolitionists are by nature . . . liars, thieves and cowardly murderers . . ." (*ibid.,* January 16, 1860).

CHAPTER NINE

1. South Carolina had left the Union first, on December 20, followed by Mississippi, Florida, and Alabama on January 9, 10, 11, respectively.

2. Moore, *op. cit.,* pp. 421-422, has been used as a guide in this background summary. See also Georgia Lee Tatum, *Disloyalty in the Confederacy* (Chapel Hill, 1934), pp. 6-8, 54ff.

3. *Weekly Mail*, January 25, 1861. Coyne did not return until February 15.

4. *Ibid.*, January 18, February 1, 8, 15, 1861.

5. *Ibid.*, February 1, 1861.

6. *Ibid.*, January 11, 18, 25, February 8, 1861, for examples.

7. *Ibid.*, February 1, 1861. Hooper replied by thanking Mrs. Hunter, chivalrously adding: "I shall preserve [the flag] with religious care, and transmit it, I trust, to my children . . . While the *daughters* of Alabama are so appreciative of all patriotic endeavor, it is impossible that her sons can be less than *'true'* and *'brave.'* "

8. Moore, *op. cit.*, p. 423.

9. *Weekly Mail*, January 25, 1861. Deputies elected, besides Curry and Chilton, were Richard W. Walker (Lauderdale) and Robert H. Smith (Mobile), "Deputies at Large," and General Colin J. McRae (Mobile), John Gill Shorter (Barbour), Stephen F. Hale (Greene), David P. Lewis (Lawrence), and Dr. Thomas Fearn (Madison), "District Delegates."

10. *Ibid.*, February 1, 8, 1861. See also Albert N. Fitts, "The Confederate Convention," *The Alabama Review*, II, 83-101, 198-210 (April-July, 1949).

11. Texas had seceded February 1, but the delegates had not arrived in Montgomery.

12. *Weekly Mail*, February 8, 1861; Montgomery *Weekly Advertiser*, February 5, 1861; *Tallapoosa Times* (Dadeville), February 14, 1861. Diary of Basil Manly, 1858-1867 (MSS. vol. in University of Alabama Library), p. 36 (February 4, 1861), states: "Judge Chilton then nominated Johnson J. Hooper as Secy of the Congress & he was elected by acclamation." See also W. Stanley Hoole, editor, "The Diary of Dr. Basil Manly, 1858-1867," *The Alabama Review*, IV, 146 (April, 1951).

13. *Journal of the Congress of the Confederate States of America 1861-1865*, I, 16 (Washington, 1904).

14. Samuel Elias Mays, "Sketches from the Journal of a Confederate Soldier," *Tyler's Quarterly Historical and Genealogical Magazine*, V, 37, 144 (July, 1923). Mays added later (p. 144) that "Simon Suggs" was actually Johnson J. Hooper.

15. XXXI, 52 (March 2, 1861). The correspondent also wrote, "The insensate desk, as if for the nonce, imbued with sense and verve, at first seemed to sway, and swerve, and shudder, at the approach of the hideous Jonce, but, by and by, grow firm and still, and quite submissive to the gallant 'Quill.' Jonce deposits the perfect 'negligee" in his comical costume, abandoning himself and throttle to a total absence of everything like 'neck-gear,' and displaying his unequivocal 'Adam's apple' in alto relievo or a bronzed and unwhiskered 'background.'"

The editor of the *Spirit*, however, in the same issue (p. 49) took the correspondent "to task for his allusions to our friend Hooper's personal appearance. 'Jonce' has been getting sort of stuck-up in the handsome line ever since he put up at the Fifth Avenue Hotel in this city, for, to our personal knowledge, several very handsome 'vimmen' that walked by the front of the hotel fell in love with him, but 'Jonce,' we suppose, credited it to their fondness for his genius."

16. The well-known Mary Boykin Chestnut wrote March 5, 1861: "Mr. [Robert] Barnwell and Mr. [William P.] Miles called. They showed me some lines, comic enough . . . This helped to pass an evening call merrily. Also they cited Simon Suggs to the Judge, who is always vaunting his own probity and sneering at the venality of everybody else. Simon was always saying: 'Integrity is the post I ties to.' At camp meeting he got religion, handed round the hat, took the offering to the Lord down into the swamp to pray over it, untied his horse and fled with it, hat, contribution and all" (*A Diary from Dixie*, edited by Ben Ames Williams, Boston, 1949, p. 13).

17. January 31, 1861. Hooper replied in the *Weekly Mail*, February 1, thanking Editor Reid as a "friend and co-laborer in all that relates to our country."

18. *Ibid.*, February 8 [dated 4], 1861.

19. *Ibid.*, February 15 [dated 7], 1861.

20. *Spirit*, XXXI, 65 (March 9, 1861), reported that $30,000 worth of diamonds and other jewels were sent by Tiffany & Co. of New York to Montgomery for the "most distinguished and fashionable of Southern ladies" to wear at the Inauguration Ball.

21. *Journal of the Confederate Congress*, I, 39, 73, 85, 89 and *passim*. See also the *Weekly Mail*, February 15-March 22, 1861, and T. C. DeLeon, *Four Years in Rebel Capitols* (Mobile, 1892), pp. 21-29. Yancey left for Europe about the middle of March (*Weekly Mail*, March 22, 1861).

22. *Journal of the Confederate Congress*, I, 909, 924 (Appendix). See also Montgomery *Weekly Advertiser*, February 27, 1861.

23. *Acts and Resolutions of the First Session of the Provisional Congress of the Confederate States, 1861* (Montgomery, 1861), pp. 5, 22-23.

24. *List of Staff Officers of the Confederate States Army, 1861-1865* (Washington, 1891), lists Hooper as "private secretary to Secretary of War, April, 1861." See also Montgomery *Advertiser*, February 21, 1861.

25. Hooper served as Walker's secretary for a short time only, possibly not more than one month. See *War of the Rebellion*, 1st Series, XII, Pt. 2, 35-36; 4th Series, I, 219, 222-223. These communications are dated April 5, 13, 16-18, 1861.

26. *Acts and Resolutions of the First Session of the Provisional Congress*, pp. 77-78.

27. See, for instance, the *Weekly Mail*, March 22, April 5-12, 1861,

28. *Daily Mail*, February 12, 1861. By March the *Weekly Mail* was flying a large Confederate flag from its masthead. By April 10 the flag bore seven stars.

29. That the *Weekly Mail* was widely quoted at this time is evidenced by this complaint (May 15, 1861): "All we ask is that our contributions to the newspaper intelligence of the day shall receive that recognition to which they are entitled when republished in other papers." The article indicates that the *Mail* was being quoted, particularly in Charleston, without proper acknowledgment.

30. *Ibid.*, April 19 [dated 15], 1861.

31. May 17, 1861. Hooper's name continued to appear on the *Mail's* masthead for several weeks, however.

32. *Journal of the Confederate Congress*, I, 159.

33. Arkansas, North Carolina, and Tennessee seceded May 6, 20, June 8, respectively. On April 24 Virginia entered a military alliance with the Confederate States, but did not legally ratify its Ordinance of Secession until May 28. The other states did not pass ordinances of secession, but they were later represented in the Confederate Congress.

34. *Spirit*, XXXI, 161, 228 (April 20, May 18, 1861) carried two long articles on the "Bombardment of Fort Sumter."

35. *Acts and Resolutions of the Second Session of the Provisional Congress of the Confederate States* (Montgomery, 1861), pp. 3, 5, 36-39, 46, 88.

36. *Ibid.*, p. 98. Act No. 186, approved May 21, 1861: "Relative to the Library of Congress. *The Congress of the Confederate States of America do enact,* That the books purchased by the committee appointed to revise the laws of the United States be delivered to the Secretary of Congress and be retained by him for the use and benefit of the members of Congress; and the secretary sell the furniture and other effects belonging to the government, which shall be turned over to the committee on revision."

37. William M. Robinson, *Justice in Grey: A History of the Judicial System of the Confederate States of America* (Cambridge, 1941), p. 31.

38. DeLeon, *op. cit.*, p. 76.

39. May 11, 1861; see also *Weekly Advertiser*, May 18, 1861.

40. *Acts and Resolutions of the Second Session of the Provisional Congress of the Confederate States*, p. 88; *Journal of the Confederate Congress*, I, 173, 244, 254-257; Huntsville (Alabama) *Democrat*, June 5, 1861.

41. *Weekly Advertiser*, May 25, 1861, gives May 30 as the day the

moving actually began; however, President Davis arrived in Richmond May 29, and it is quite possible that Hooper may have accompanied him and his party.

42. According to *The Montgomery Directory for 1859-'60 . . .* (Montgomery, 1859), p. 48, Hooper and his family lived at the corner of Monroe and Lawrence streets.

43. Richmond *Daily Dispatch,* June 25, 1861. The daughter of a Eufaula, Alabama, widow, missing for several days was announced as follows: "Persons conversant with her whereabouts will please address Johnson J. Hooper, Esq., Secretary of the Confederate Congress, at Richmond . . ."

44. *Ibid.,* June 15, July 13, 1861.

45. *Ibid.,* June 10, 1861.

CHAPTER TEN

1. Richmond newspapers listed names of "Arrivals in the City" with regularity throughout 1861.

2. DeLeon, *op. cit.,* p. 77.

3. *Daily Dispatch,* June 8, 19, 26, 29, 1861. These conditions improved little if any, during the following months (*ibid.,* February 5, 24, 1862).

4. DeLeon, *op. cit.,* pp. 86-87.

5. The Government later (August 28) voted $200 each to certain employees, including Hooper, to help defray the expenses of moving (*Journal of the Confederate Congress,* I, 430).

6. Richmond *Enquirer,* June 10, 1862.

7. *Weekly Mail,* March 22, 1861.

8. *Acts and Resolutions of the Third Session of the Provisional Congress of the Confederate States, Held at Richmond, Va.* (Richmond, 1861).

9. *Daily Dispatch,* July 19, 1861; *Enquirer,* July 22-26, 1861; Huntsville (Alabama) *Advocate,* July 21, 1861, from which this headline was copied.

10. *Acts and Resolutions of the Third Session of the Provisional Congress,* pp. 8, 16, 19, 33, 36.

11. *Ibid.,* pp. 74-75. Hooper, having sold a government iron safe to the Governor of Alabama before leaving Montgomery, was directed to place the sum, $325, to the credit of the contingent fund of Congress. *Journal of the Confederate Congress,* I, 277, states that "two reports on unadjusted accounts of the last session and sale of furniture were received from J. J. Hooper, Secretary, and referred to the Committee on Accounts." At the same time he was authorized to purchase $500 worth of stationery for the use of the Congress.

12. For sample letters and messages of this session as well as others,

see *War of the Rebellion*, 1st Series, LIII, 765, (January 3, 1862); 2nd Series, II, 1207 (August 29, 1861), 1372 (August 23, 1861), 1413 (January 13, 1862), III, 705 (August 17, 1861); 4th Series, I, 99, (February 8, 1861), 320 (May 15, 1861), 865 (January 13, 1862), 901 (January 16, 1862). All are signed "Secretary of Congress." See also *Proceedings on the Announcement of the Death of Hon. John Tyler, January 20th, 1862* . . . by J. J. Hooper, Secretary (Richmond, 1862) and *Proceedings of the Congress on the Announcement of the Death of Col. Francis S. Bartow* . . . By J. J. Hooper (Richmond, 1861).

13. *Journal of the Confederate Congress*, I, 746, 832-833 and *passim*.

14. See *supra*, p. 171.

15. Letter, J. J. Hooper to "2nd Lieut. W. DeB. Hooper, Fort Morgan, Near Mobile, Alabama," Richmond, October 21, 1861, in University of Alabama Library. The letter continues: ". . . For your own sake and that of your name, read diligently military books & observe closely details, in every army as you have opportunity; and above all, learn to spell. You can not imagine how important it is. You could never make a respectable Adjutant without this homely accomplishment. Wherever you doubt about the spelling of a word, refer to a Dictionary and *not* Webster's if you can get any other.

"You will have many temptations to dissipation; you will often feel like indulging a lazy fit; these are the sirens which destroy the promise of hundreds of brilliant young men.

"But above all, my Son, remember that *Truth* is the foundation of all fame and honor — of all that is desirable in life. The liar (I don't fear *your* being one,) is always a coward, morally at least.

"We are all in pretty good health. Your mother was very uneasy about you, till I telegraphed. She now anxiously awaits a letter.

"Your Ma was delighted to hear, by Tom, of your being put on Col. Maury's Staff — but *has* a *Colonel* a Staff? If so, what post is yours?

"Richmond has rumors, every day, of battles expected at Manassas and at Yorktown. Gen. McGruder, at the latter place, I believe expects an attack; and I fear he is ill prepared for it. Our relatives in the 6th and Forney's Alabama Regt., in the 6th Louisiana and Hampton's (S. C.) Legion, were well at last accounts. Your Cousin DeBerniere Roberts, is a Sargeant in the last-named Command.

"It has been quite warm here until today: it is now quite cool. I presume it is becoming unpleasant where you are.

"Do write me some account of your studies, duties &C.&C. Write a long letter; or keep a diary for a week, and send it to me. I wish to know what your opportunities for improvement are.

"Elmore Mayhew is here on his way to Mobile. He has been appointed a Master in the Navy.

"Give my regards to Col. Maury and to Rice and Yancey. I hope you will all have a chance for glory ere long.

"Your Ma and Dolph send love. Write at once. Your affectionate father, J. J. Hooper."

16. January 29, 1862. Coyne continued to edit the *Mail* until November 11, 1863. After several changes of ownership, the paper was merged with the *Advertiser*, May 11, 1871, to become the *Advertiser and Mail*, but by the mid-1880's the *Mail* had been dropped from the title. The Montgomery *Advertiser* is now (1951) in its 123rd year of publication (see *Memorial Record of Alabama*, II, 191-192).

17. *Daily Dispatch*, August 8, 1861, states that the St. Charles Hotel had been converted into a hospital for 160 men and that a hospital for "Alabama wounded" had been established between Leigh and Clay streets.

18. *Ibid.*, May 3, 1861.

19. They were the Richmond Theatre and Franklin and Metropolitan Halls. The *Enquirer*, November 8, 1861, announced the expansion of the Richmond Theatre and arrival of new players. On December 15 Ida Vernon played in *The Honeymoon* and the "Celebrated Zouaves" were performing at Franklin Hall. The theatres prospered until after mid-1862.

20. *Enquirer* and *Daily Dispatch*, November 1, 1861-July 15, 1862, *passim.*

21. J. W. Mallett, "Work of the Ordnance Bureau of the War Department of the Confederate States, 1861-5," *Southern Historical Society Papers*, XXXVII, 12-13 (January, 1909); see also *Enquirer*, January 1-July 1, 1862.

22. *Daily Dispatch* (July 16, 1861) did not agree, however: "'A Short War! A Short War!' Don't you wish you could make it so?" In addition to the *Daily Dispatch* and the *Enquirer* this brief description of war in Richmond is based on Alfred Hoyt Bill, *The Beleaguered City: Richmond, 1861-1865* (New York, 1946), pp. 77-92, a volume highly recommended for its accuracy and readability. See also Ada Sterling, editor, *A Belle of the Fifties: Memoirs of Mrs.* [Clement C.] *Clay, of Alabama . . .* (New York, 1904), pp. 168ff.

23. H. D. Capers, "Recollections of the Confederacy," Gadsden (Alabama) *Leader*, February 7, 1891, quoted in Kelley, *op. cit.*, pp. 240-243. This paper was not seen by this writer (see letters Frank A. Reagan, judge of probate, Etowah County, Gadsden, Alabama, to this writer, August 24, 1948, January 11, 1949, and letter, Lena Martin, librarian, Gadsden Public Library, to this writer, April 4, 1949, in University of Alabama Library). The file of the Gadsden *Leader*, January 11, 1890-February 10, 1893, in the Etowah County Courthouse in 1934, was not

available in 1951. Letter, Father Robert O. Hickman, chancellor, Diocese of Richmond, to this writer, Richmond, Virginia, March 28, 1949, states: ". . . the Powhatan Club was made up of a group of young men of prominence and was located on Eighth Street between Broad and Marshall, and . . . young men went to the club for relaxation. In 1900 the name was changed to Chess, Checker and Whist Club." Letter, Clayton Torrence, director, Virginia Historical Society, to this writer, November 13, 1948, indicates that the Society has no information regarding the Powhatan Club.

24. Garrett, *op. cit.*, p. 526.

25. *Alabama Journal*, February 6, 1849.

26. *Daily Mail*, February 24, 1855.

27. *Enquirer*, June 10, 1862.

28. *Daily Mail*, March 23, 1857; see also May 14, 1855.

29. *Ibid.*, February 15, 1855.

30. *Ibid.*, December 1, 1854.

31. Brewer, *op. cit.*, p. 466.

32. *Daily Dispatch*, December 7, 1861; *Enquirer*, June 10, 1862. Father Andrews, pastor of St. Peter's Cathedral, was himself a convert to Catholicism (see letter, Ray O. Hummell, assistant librarian, Virginia State Library, to this writer, Richmond, February 2, 1949, in University of Alabama Library). Since no death records of St. Peter's Church prior to 1865 exist, it has been impossible to obtain further information regarding his burial (see letter, Father Robert O. Hickman to this writer, Richmond, March 28, 1949).

33. Gadsden *Leader*, February 7, 1891.

34. *Ibid.*, March 10, 1862. See Fleming, *op. cit.*, p. 19, n. 4.

35. *Enquirer*, June 6, 1862.

36. *Daily Dispatch*, April 12, 1862. See also *Facts and Incidents of the Siege, Defense and Fall of Fort Donelson, February, 1862 . . .* (Huntsville, 1863).

37. *Daily Dispatch*, February 24, 1862. See also Bill, *op. cit.*, pp. 93-114, and Robert Selph Henry, *The Story of the Confederacy* (Indianapolis, 1931), pp. 77-99.

38. *Enquirer*, February 21, 1862. President Davis set aside February 28 as a "day of prayer," honoring the new government.

39. *Journal of the Confederate Congress*, I, 17; II, 6-7; Huntsville *Democrat*, March 5, 1862. Nash won over R. C. Downs of Louisiana, A. H. Dawson of Alabama, J. D. Eubanks of Virginia, and Hooper.

40. Gadsden *Leader*, February 7, 1891; *Daily Dispatch*, February 24, 1862.

41. *Ibid.*, June 10, 1862, states upon the occasion of Hooper's death that he was from Montgomery, "at which place his family now reside."

indicating that Mrs. Hooper and Adolph had returned to Alabama at some prior time, perhaps in the Fall or Winter of 1861-1862.

42. See *supra,* p. 243, n. 14.

43. Robinson, *op. cit.,* p. 571. After Hooper's death the work was continued by Major John C. Whitner, of Georgia. Meanwhile, many of the papers had been mislaid or destroyed, thus accounting for "the derangement and loss in the records of the Provisional Congress."

44. *Daily Dispatch,* February 28, 1862.

45. *War of the Rebellion,* 4th Series, III, 1015, 1017. Hooper is said to have left the papers "almost untouched . . . scattered and difficult of access." His successor wrote: "The lamented death of Hon. J. J. Hooper, to whom the work was first assigned, together with the general confusion then existing in Richmond in consequences of the near approach of the enemy and the sending off to other points important Government papers, had doubtless much to do with it. Mr. Hooper had but barely entered upon this work—possibly not long enough to gather up what was necessary for its accurate completion."

46. *Daily Dispatch,* March 22, April 5, May 10, 1862, listed Hooper as having uncalled-for mail in the post office.

47. Gadsden *Leader,* February 7, 1891.

48. *Daily Dispatch,* March 17, 1862, speaks of Lee's appointment as a "great satisfaction," however.

49. In Hooper's copy of the *Book of Common Prayer* (now in the Johnson Jones Hooper Collection, Evans Memorial Library, Aberdeen, Mississippi) is written: "Johnson J. Hooper died in the city of Richmond, Va., at twenty minutes to seven O'clock P. M. on the 7th of June 1862—He would have been 47 years old on the 9th of the same month. His son *Dolph.*" Below is added, "Mark the perfect man and behold the upright, for the end of that man is peace . . . This was your father's book and I hope you will value it as such and go to church and spend the Sabbath evenings in reading good books. *M. M. Hooper.*" Whether Mrs. Hooper was at her husband's bedside is not known. The Montgomery *Daily Mail,* June 14, 1862, states that "Lieut. W. deB. Hooper arrived from Mobile a few days since, and has gone to meet his mother, Mrs. J. J. Hooper, and a younger brother, Adolphus S., at Fayetteville, N. C. Mrs. Hooper will, we learn, probably go to Tuscaloosa for temporary residence. The prayers of many friends attend the family in their sad bereavement."

50. June 10, 1862. See also Mary Brantley Hooper's *Autograph Book* (Johnson Jones Hooper Collection, Evans Memorial Library, Aberdeen, Mississippi).

51. Gadsden *Leader,* February 7, 1891. Hooper was buried in an unmarked grave in Shockhoe Hill Cemetery, Range 2, Section 21, ¼ Sec-

tion 3, Range of Grave 1, "next to alley." His name, age, cause of death ("Lung disease"), and occupation ("clerk") were posted November 15, 1862, in *Interments in the Shockhoe Hill Burying Ground, December 8, 1848-December 31, 1870*, p. 283 (MSS. vol. in Office of the City Home, Richmond, Virginia).

Considerable difficulty was experienced in locating Hooper's grave. Capers, writing in 1891, stated that he had been buried on Hollywood hill which, of course, suggested present-day Hollywood Cemetery. Careful searching of the records there, including *Register of Confederate Dead Interred in Hollywood Cemetery, Richmond, Va.* (Richmond, 1869), failed to produce any evidence. It was later learned that "Hollywood hill" was the name once applied to the general area including both cemeteries. And since Capers wrote from memory he could easily have been confused.

52. See also *Daily Dispatch*, June 28, 1862, quoted from the Milledgeville (Georgia) *Recorder*.

53. Richmond *Daily Examiner*, June 9, 1862: "He was an excellent man, full of genial qualities, and respected by all who knew him."

Enquirer, June 10, 1862: "With sincere sorrow we have to announce that Johnson J. Hooper died at the Richmond House, in this city, on Saturday evening late, after an illness of a few days. Mr. Hooper was widely known as an author, journalist and public official, and not only to our particular profession, but to the literature of the South, his loss is very serious. At the time of his death he was arranging to complete some work which would have been of immense value to the independent literature of our country."

Dispatch, June 10, 1862: "For many years Mr. Hooper has been well known throughout this country as a racy and brilliant writer of everyday sketches, and as a political editor. Among his earlier writings were some admirable sketches for the old *Spirit of the Times*, which, at the time, attracted considerable attention. His first book was *Simon Suggs*, a work inimitable of its kind, and which has obtained a world-wide reputation for keen wit and genuine satire. For several years past Mr. Hooper has been connected with the Montgomery (Ala.) *Mail*, which paper he conducted up to a little more than a year ago. When the Provisional Congress met in Montgomery, Mr. Hooper was elected Secretary, and held that office during the Provisional year. He was about forty years of age, a man of great talent, of unbounded liberality, and beloved by all who knew him."

54. June 10, 1862.

EPILOGUE

1. In the summary of editions, anthologies, and *critiques* which forms this brief "Epilogue" the writer stakes no claim to definitiveness.

Rather, he lists those which he has personally examined and considers fair reflection of Hooper's reputation and popularity over a period of a century. Undoubtedly, there are other anthologies and criticisms and, perhaps, other editions. Those given are intended to be *representative*, therefore, but not inclusive.

2. See *supra*, pp. 56ff., 72ff., 92, 105ff., 114ff.

3. See *supra*, pp. 56ff., 75, 214, n. 73. It is interesting to note that Montrose J. Moses, *The Literature of the South* (New York, 1910), p. 236, completely confused the two characters by saying that "Hooper won renown by developing the son of *Simon Suggs*, whom Baldwin sketched in 'Flush Times.'" Of course, the opposite was true.

4. (Philadelphia, 1846, 1847, 1858), p. viii.

5. *Op. cit.*, I, 21-40, 131, 144, 257-261. Other editions appeared in 1866 and 1873.

6. (London, 1853), pp. 5-16.

7. (Richmond, 1855?), pp. 89-92. The volume bears no date, but in an advertisement (p. xxiv) signed by the publisher, J. W. Randolph, the evidence is clear that the year was 1855.

8. (Philadelphia, 1857), pp. 37, 546.

9. (New York, 1858), I, 325-331, 371. There was another edition in 1866.

10. *Weekly Mail*, June 28, 1862. Quoted from the Milledgeville (Georgia) *Recorder*. See Eugene Current-Garcia, "Newspaper Humor in the Old South, 1835-1855," *The Alabama Review*, II, 102-121 (April 1949).

11. See Blair, *Native American Humor* (*1800-1900*), pp. 102-103.

12. See Fred Lewis Pattee, *A History of American Literature Since 1870* (New York, 1915), pp. 25ff.

13. *North American Review*, CII, 591-592 (April, 1866).

14. Carl Van Doren, *The American Novel* (New York, 1921), p. 158.

15. *Native American Humor* (*1800-1900*), p. 104. Blair's penetrating analysis (pp. 104ff.) of post-Civil War humor has been freely used by this writer.

16. S. S. Cox, "American Humor," *Harper's Magazine*, L, 690-701 (April, 1875).

17. Meine, *op. cit.*, p. xxx.

18. Walter Blair, "Burlesques in Nineteenth-Century American Humor," *American Literature*, II, 236-247 (May, 1930); see also his "The Popularity of Nineteenth-Century American Humorists," *ibid.*, III, 175-194 (May, 1931).

19. "A Retrospect of American Humor," *The Century Illustrated Monthly Magazine*, LXIII, 59-60 (November, 1901).

20. *The Greatest Pages of American Humor* (New York, 1936), p. 69.

21. Robert E. Spiller and others, editors, *Literary History of the United States* (New York, 1948), I, 609.

22. Will D. Howe, "Early Humorists," in William P. Trent and others, editors, *The Cambridge History of American Literature* (New York, 1918), II, 158.

23. Blair, *Native American Humor (1800-1900)*, pp. 102-108, 557-560.

24. See *supra*, pp. 127-128, 138, n. 43, 142-144, 157. *Simon Suggs' Adventures. Late of the Tallapoosa Volunteers. Together with "Taking the Census," and Other Alabama Sketches. With a Portrait of Captain Simon Suggs.* With ten Illustrations by Darley (Philadelphia, 1881), was issued by T. B. Peterson. The 1928 edition was published by the Americus (Georgia) Book Company.

25. *Magnum Opus*, p. 74.

26. Aswell,*op. cit.*, p. 390. The direct source of Thackeray's tribute to Hooper this writer has failed to find. Howe, *op. cit.*, II, 153, states that *Simon Suggs* "was admired by Thackeray"; *The Pocket Book of Early American Humorists* (Boston, 1907), p. 78, that "Thackeray praised this book *[Simon Suggs]* highly . . ."; C. Alphonso Smith, "Johnson Jones Hooper," in Edwin A. Alderman and Joel Chandler Harris, editors, *Library of Southern Literature* (Atlanta, 1907), VI, 2491, that "Thackeray praised the book *[Simon Suggs]*"; and Bret Harte (Kozlay, *op. cit.*, p. 22) states, without mentioning Hooper specifically, that the humor of the Old South and West "was recognized by the greatest English humorist that the world had known . . . ." Other similar references, all secondary, have been seen by this writer. See also Annie Mae Hollingsworth, "Johnson Jones Hooper: Statesman and Humorist," *The Alabama Historical Quarterly*, I, 257-260 (Fall, 1930).

27. See *supra*, pp. 186-187.

28. See *supra*, pp. 28-30.

29. *Op. cit.*, pp. 16, 530.

30. *The Literature of Roguery* (Boston, 1927), I, 2-6.

31. Blair, *Native American Humor (1800-1900)*, pp. 86-87. In this connection it is interesting to recall that Hooper gave his sister-in-law, Sarah Brantley, a copy of *Don Quixote* (see *supra*, p. 45, n. 32). Lucy L. Hazard, "The American Picaresque" in James F. Willard and Colin B. Goodykoontz, editors, *The Trans-Mississippi West* (Boulder, 1930), p. 198, says: "To find the American picaro we must follow the American pioneer . . . . The qualities fostered by the frontier were the qualities indispensable to the picaro: nomadism, insensibility to danger, shrewdness, nonchalance, gaiety . . ." See also Constance Rourke, *op. cit.*, p. 69; Percy H. Boynton, *Literature and American Life* (Boston, 1936), pp. 614-615; V. L. O. Chittick, *Thomas Haliburton Chandler*

(*"Sam Slick"*): *A Study in Provincial Toryism* (New York, 1924), pp. 536-537.

32. "American Literary Comedians," *Harper's New Monthly Magazine,* LXXX, 783-793 (April, 1890).

33. *Op. cit.,* II, 153.

34. *The Compromises of Life and Other Lectures and Addresses Including Some Observations on Certain Downward Tendencies of Modern Society* (New York, 1903), pp. 78-79.

35. Letter, Thomas D. Clark to this writer, Lexington, Kentucky, December 22, 1948; Thomas D. Clark, *The Southern Country Editor* (New York, 1948), p. 124.

36. See, for examples, Montgomery *Daily Advertiser,* December 5, 1863, in which one of Hooper's legal anedoctes is compared to those of Abraham Lincoln, and Aberdeen (Mississippi) *Examiner,* July 29, 1875, and Mobile *Daily Register,* July 30, 1875, in which he is praised as "a writer and editor familiar to all our readers."

37. W. H. Milburn, D. D., "Philip J. Neely and Alabama Five and Fifty Years Ago," *Methodist Quarterly Review,* XV, 295-313 (January, 1894). "I must not leave Montgomery without a word concerning a most interesting and delightful man, Johnson J. Hooper, who came to the fair little city about the time I left it to edit a newspaper, the *Mail,* and was known to the readers of that day as the author of 'Simon Suggs' and other humorous pieces. He was by birth a 'Tar Heel,' as the people of North Carolina liked to call themselves, and well represented the unpretending, modest, yet brave and chivalrous stock of the ancient commonwealth . . . A rich vein of humor is characteristic of the race, and this was also finely illustrated by Mr. Hooper . . . Delicacy, refinement, and honor were so unaffectedly genuine with him that no amount of provocation, although he was very nervous and sensitive, ever betrayed him into act or utterance that was not most considerate and kindly. His breeding was from the heart, not learned in the dancing school. Those who knew him best used to call him the 'Fool of Quality,' so ideal was his chivalry and yet so real. He was always hard up, never collected a debt, though he failed not to pay his own. He was a victim to neuralgia at the time when he was working hardest. The fragments he has left show that if he had had leisure he would have written books of rare humor and racy of the soil. A competent judge declares, 'He was the wittiest man I ever knew, and to know him at his best was to see him as I did, with the members of his family. The memorials of his genius are few and scanty, for hard at work upon a daily newspaper, and launched on the stormy sea of politics in a most exciting time, he found no scope for literature; yet he wrought zealously to the last, even when he was known to be a dying man;

and so passed away 'with a most voiceless thought sheathing it as a sword.'"

38. Opelika (Alabama) *Post*, January 15, 1897. The speaker was Colonel C. S. Scott, and the occasion an address in Auburn, Alabama.

39. P. 339.

40. Pp. 39ff.

41. (New York, 1888), pp. 598-610. Reprinted (1906) in three volumes. See DeVoto, *Mark Twain's America*, p. 256, n. 16.

42. Pp. 162-165, 449.

43. (Nashville, 1903), II, 505-524.

44. (New York, 1906), p. 169.

45. (Boston, 1907), pp. 78-96. No editor is given.

46. (New York, 1907), pp. 881-894.

47. (New York, 1907), "Shillaber to Mark Twain," pp. 31-48.

48. (Atlanta, 1907), VI, 2489-2506.

49. (New York, 1929), pp. 94-128.

50. *Op. cit.*, pp. 274-276, 530-534.

51. Pp. 308-325.

52. Pp. 3-38, 175-182, 241-248, 273-277, 299-301, 325-334, 425-435.

53. (Caldwell, 1946), pp. 166-171, 235-265.

54. (New York, 1947), pp. 106-111, 168-169.

55. *Op. cit.*, p. xv.

56. *Native American Humor (1800-1900)*, p. 162.

57. *Mark Twain's America*, p. 257.

58. *Ibid.*, p 255.

59. *Ibid.*, p. 256, n. 15.

60. See Richmond *Times-Dispatch*, January 18, 1951. The men were Franklin J. Meine, Monroe F. Cockrell, and Alfred W. Stern of Chicago, and Walter B. Jones of Montgomery, and James F. Sulzby, Rucker Agee, William H. Brantley, Jr., Allen Rushton, George R. Stuart, and Seale Harris, Sr., of Birmingham, and this writer.

BIBLIOGRAPHY

BOOKS AND ARTICLES

Abernethy, Thomas P., *The Formative Period in Alabama, 1815-1828.* Montgomery, 1922.

An Accompaniment to Mitchell's Reference and Distance Map of the United States . . . together with . . . an Account of the Actual and Perspective Internal Improvements throughout the Union. . . . Philadelphia, 1834.

Address of the Democracy of Alabama to the National Democratic Convention at Baltimore, June 18th, 1860. Baltimore, 1860.

Alderman, Edwin A., "Address . . . on the Life of William Hooper, 'The Prophet of American Independence.'" Chapel Hill, 1894.

——, and Joel Chandler Harris, editors-in-chief, *Library of Southern Literature.* 16 vols. Atlanta, 1907.

"Artemus Ward; his Travels," *North American Review,* CII, 586-592 (April, 1866).

Aswell, James R., editor, *Native American Humor.* New York, 1947.

Baldwin, Joseph Glover, *Flush Times in Alabama and Mississippi.* New York, 1853.

——, *Party Leaders, Sketches of Thomas Jefferson, Alex'r Hamilton, Andrew Jackson, Henry Clay, John Randolph, of Roanoke, Including Notices of Many other Distinguished American Statesmen.* New York, 1855.

Barr, James, editor, *The Humour of America.* London, 1893.

Bill, Alfred Hoyt, *The Beleaguered City: Richmond, 1861-1865.* New York, 1946.

Blair, Walter, "Burlesques in Nineteenth-Century American Humor," *American Literature,* II, 236-247 (May, 1930).

——, *Horse Sense in American Humor.* Chicago, 1942.

——, *Native American Humor (1800-1900).* New York, 1937.

——, "The Popularity of Nineteenth-Century American Humorists," *American Literature,* III, 175-194 (May, 1931).

——, *Tall Tale America.* New York, 1933.

——, and Franklin J. Meine, *Mike Fink: King of Mississippi Keelboatmen.* New York, 1933.

Blue, M. P. [and others], *City Directory and History of Montgomery, Alabama with a Summary of Events in that History, Calendarically Arranged, besides Other Valuable and Useful Information.* Montgomery, 1878.

Book of Common Prayer. Philadelphia, 1841. Copy inscribed "J. J. Hooper from his Mother," in Johnson Jones Hooper Collection, Evans Memorial Library, Aberdeen, Mississippi.

Botkin, B. A., editor, *A Treasury of American Folklore.* New York, 1944.

Boyd, Minnie Clare, *Alabama in the Fifties.* New York, 1931.

Boynton, Percy H., *Literature and American Life.* Boston, 1936.

Brannon, Peter A., "Jons Hooper's Influence in Early State Literature," Montgomery *Advertiser*, Centennial Edition, March 15, 1928.

——, "Little Journeys Through Alabama," *Alabama Highways*, IV, 3-6 (April, 1930).

Brewer, Willis, *Alabama: Her History and Resources, and Public Men, from 1540 to 1872.* Montgomery, 1872.

Brinley, Francis, *Life of William T. Porter.* New York, 1860.

Brown, John Howard, *Biographical Sketches.* Boston, 1915. Reprinted from *Twentieth Century Biographical Dictionary of Notable Americans.*

Buck, Paul H., "The Poor Whites of the Ante-Bellum South," *American Historical Review*, XXXI, 41-54 (October, 1925).

Burke, Thomas A., editor, *Polly Peablossom's Wedding; and Other Tales.* Philadelphia, 1851.

——, editor, *Polly Peablossom's Wedding; and Other Tales.* Philadelphia, n.d.

Burr, J. G., "A Fragmentary History of Johnson Hooper," in James Sprunt, *Chronicles of the Cape Fear River.* Raleigh, 1914.

Burton, William E., *Cyclopedia of Wit and Humor.* 3 vols. New York, 1858.

Caldwell, Erskine, *Tobacco Road.* New York, 1932.

Capers, H. D., "Recollections of the Confederacy," Gadsden (Alabama) *Leader*, February 7, 1891.

Chandler, Frank W., *The Literature of Roguery.* 2 vols. Boston, 1927.

Chestnut, Mary Boykin, see Williams, Ben Ames.

Chittick, V. L. O., *Ring-Tailed Roarers: Tall Tales of the American Frontier, 1830-1860.* Caldwell, 1946.

——, *Thomas Chandler Haliburton ("Sam Slick"): A Study in Provincial Toryism.* New York, 1924.

Clark, Thomas D., *The Southern Country Editor.* New York, 1948.

Clemens, Samuel L., *Mark Twain's Library of Humor.* New York, 1888. Reprinted in 3 vols., 1906.

Cole, Arthur C., *The Whig Party in the South.* Washington, 1913.

"The Correspondence of Thomas Reade Rootes Cobb, 1860-1862," *Publications of the Southern History Association,* XI, 147-185, 233-260, 313-328 (May, July, September-November, 1907).

Cox, S. S., "American Humor," *Harper's Magazine,* L, 690-701 (April, 1875).

Cozart, Tuccoa, "Henry W. Hilliard," *Transactions of the Alabama Historical Society, 1899-1903,* IV, 277-299. Montgomery, 1904.

Cromwell, O., *Directory or Guides to the Residences and Places of Business of the Inhabitants of the City of Charleston and Its Environs: Prefaced with a Description of Our Various Public Buildings, and Other Local Information* [1829]. Charleston, 1828.

Current-Garcia, Eugene, "Newspaper Humor in the Old South, 1835-1855," *The Alabama Review,* II, 102-121 (April, 1949).

Dannelly, Hermione, *The Life and Times of Robert Jemison, Jr., during the Civil War and Reconstruction* (unpublished Master's thesis, University of Alabama, 1942).

Davidson, James Wood, *The Living Writers of the South.* New York, 1869.

Davis, William Watson, "Ante Bellum Southern Commercial Conventions," *Transactions of the Alabama Historical Society,* V, 153-202. Montgomery, 1906.

DeLeon, T. C., *Four Years in Rebel Capitols.* Mobile, 1892.

Denman, C. P., *The Secession Movement in Alabama.* Montgomery, 1933.

DeVoto, Bernard, "Frontier America," *The Saturday Review of Literature,* V, 1067 (June 1, 1929).

——, *Mark Twain's America.* Boston, 1932.

——, "The Matrix of Mark Twain's Humor," *The Bookman,* LXXIV, 172-178 (October, 1931).

Dictionary of American Biography. 20 vols. New York, 1928-1936.

Dorman, Lewis, *Party Politics in Alabama from 1850 to 1860.* Montgomery, 1935.

Dorson, Richard M., *Jonathan Draws the Long Bow.* Cambridge, 1946.

Dowling, D. J., *Dowling's Charleston Directory, and Annual Register for 1837 and 1838.* Charleston, 1837.

DuBose, John Witherspoon, *The Life and Times of William Lowndes Yancey: A History of Political Parties in the United States, from 1834 to 1864; Especially as to the Origin of the Confederate States.* Birmingham, 1892.

Easby-Smith, Anne, *William Russell Smith of Alabama, His Life and Works; Including the Entire Text of the Uses of Solitude.* Philadelphia, 1931.

Ellison, Rhoda Coleman, *A Check List of Alabama Imprints, 1807-1870.* University, Alabama, 1946.

——, "Early Alabama Interest in Southern Writers," *The Alabama Review,* I, 101-110 (April, 1948).

Ellison, W. W., "Noted Author Once Lived in La Fayette, Ala.," Columbus (Georgia) *Ledger Magazine,* June 19, 1927.

Facts and Incidents of the Siege, Defense and Fall of Fort Donelson, February, 1862. Complied from Official Documents, Published by Resolutions of the Confederate States' Congress. Huntsville, 1863.

Feare, Varian, "In Search of a Book, a Man, an Inn," Birmingham *News-Age Herald Magazine,* October 6, 1935.

Fite, Emerson D., *The Presidential Campaign of 1860.* New York, 1911.

Fitts, Albert N., "The Confederate Convention," *The Alabama Review,* II, 83-101, 189-210 (April-July, 1949).

Fitzgerald, O. P., *Judge Longstreet: A Life Sketch.* Nashville, 1891.

Fleming, Walter L., *Civil War and Reconstruction in Alabama.* New York, 1905.

Garrett, William, *Reminiscences of Public Men in Alabama for Thirty Years.* Atlanta, 1872.

Goldsmith, Morris, *Directory and Strangers' Guide, for the City of Charleston and Its Vicinity, from the Fifth Census of the United States.* Charleston, 1831.

Griswold, Rufus W., *The Prose Writers of America.* Philadelphia, 1857.

Haliburton, Thomas C., editor, *Traits of American Humor, By Native Authors.* 3 vols. London, 1852.

Harris, Joel Chandler, editor, *American Wit and Humor by One Hundred of America's Leading Humorists.* New York, 1907.

Harris, Miriam Coles, *Rutledge.* New York, 1860.

Hazard, Lucy L., "The American Picaresque," in James F. Willard and Colin B. Goodykoontz, editors, *The Trans-Mississippi West.* Boulder, 1930.

Henry, Robert Selph, *The Story of the Confederacy.* Indianapolis, 1931.

Holliday, Carl, *A History of Southern Literature.* New York, 1906.

Hollingsworth, Annie Mae, "Johnson Jones Hooper, Alabama's Mark Twain, Champion of the Creeks," Montgomery *Advertiser,* March 23, 1931.

——, "Johnson Jones Hooper: Statesman and Humorist," *The Alabama Historical Quarterly,* I, 257-260 (Fall, 1930).

Hoole, W. Stanley, editor, "Advice to an Overseer: Extracts from the 1840-1842 Plantation Journal of John Horry Dent," *The Alabama Review,* I, 50-63 (January, 1948).

——, editor, "The Diary of Dr. Basil Manly, 1858-1867," *The Alabama Review,* IV, 127-149 (April, 1951).

——, "John Gorman Barr: Forgotten Alabama Humorist," *The Alabama Review*, IV, 83-116 (April, 1951).

——, *Sam Slick in Texas*. San Antonio, 1945.

Hooper, Archibald Maclaine, "Life of William Hooper, Signer of the Declaration of Independence," Hillsboro (North Carolina) *Recorder*, November 13, 20, 27, December 4, 1822.

——, "Abridgement of the Memoirs of Maj. Gen. Robert Howe, of North Carolina," *The North-Carolina University Magazine*, II, 209-221 (June, 1853).

Hooper, Johnson J., *Adventures of Captain Simon Suggs, Late of the Tallapoosa Volunteers; Together with "Taking the Census," and Other Alabama Sketches*. By the author of "Widow Rugby's Husband." With a Portrait of Simon Suggs, from Life, and Ten Original Illustrations by Darley. Philadelphia: T. B. Peterson and Brothers, 1851.

——, "Dog and Gun," *Southern Military Gazette*, I, nos. 5, 8, 14 (February 20, April 21, July 3, 1855).

——, *Dog and Gun; A Few Loose Chapters on Shooting. Among Which Will be Found Some Anecdotes and Incidents*. New York: Orange & Judd Co., 1856.

——, *Ibid.*, New York: C. M. Saxton & Co., 1856.

——, *Ibid.*, New York: A. O. Moore, 1858.

——, *Ibid.*, New York: C. M. Saxton, Barker & Co., 1860.

——, *Ibid.*, New York: C. M. Saxton, 1863.

——, *Ibid.*, New York: Orange & Judd Co., 1871.

——, "The 'Frinnolygist' at Fault," *Wheler's Southern Monthly Magazine* (Athens, Georgia), N. S. II, 25-28 (January, 1850).

——, "The Georgia Major," *Harper's New Monthly Magazine*, X, 133 (December, 1854).

——, "How Widder Westbrook 'Took' the Sheriff," *The Southern Times* (Montgomery), March 31, 1855.

——, *Read and Circulate: Proceedings of the Democratic and Anti-Know-Nothing Party in Caucus; or the Guillotine at Work, at the Capital, during the Session of 1855-'56*. Montgomery, Alabama: Barrett & Wimbish, 1855.

——, *A Ride with Old Kit Kuncker, and Other Sketches, and Scenes of Alabama*. Tuscaloosa, Alabama: M. D. J. Slade, 1849.

——, "Simon Becomes Captain," *The South Carolinian* (Columbia), June 26, 1845.

——, *Simon Suggs' Adventures. Late of the Tallapoosa Volunteers. Together with "Taking the Census," and Other Alabama Sketches.* With a Portrait of Captain Simon Suggs. By Johnson J. Hooper, (of La Fayette, Alabama.) Author of "Widow Rugby's Husband." With

Ten Illustrations by Darley. Philadelphia: T. B. Peterson & Brothers, 1881.

——, *Simon Suggs' Adventures. Late of the Tallapoosa Volunteers. Together with "Taking the Census," and Other Alabama Sketches.* With a Portrait of Captain Simon Suggs. By Johnson J. Hooper (of La Fayette, Alabama.) Author of "Widow Rugby's Husband." With Eight Illustrations by Darley. Americus, Georgia: Americus Book Company, 1928.

——, *Simon Suggs' Adventures and Travels. Comprising all the Scenes, Incidents and Adventures of His Travels, in a Series of Sketches of His Life; with Widow Rugby's Husband, and Twenty-Six Other Humorous Tales of Alabama.* Being the Most Laughable and Side-Splitting Stories that Have Ever Appeared in Print. With Seventeen Illustrations from Original Designs from Darley. Philadelphia: T. B. Peterson, 1856.

——, *Some Adventures of Captain Simon Suggs, Late of the Tallapoosa Volunteers; Together with "Taking the Census," and Other Alabama Sketches.* By a Country Editor. With a Portrait from Life, and Other Illustrations, by Darley. Philadelphia: Carey & Hart, 1845, 1846, 1848.

——, *Ibid.*, Philadelphia: A. Hart, 1850.

——, *Ibid.*, Philadelphia: Getz & Buck, 1851, 1852.

——, *Ibid.*, New York: Stringer & Townsend, 1851.

——, "A Three Days' Hunt in Alabama," *The American Penny Magazine*, I, 387-388 (July 26, 1845).

——, "A Visit to the Ugly Man's," "Sloshin' About," "Shifting the Responsibility," "In Favor of the Hog," "Another Hatful Joel," *Yankee Notions, or Whittlings from Jonathan's Jack-Knife*, II, 310, 311 October, 1853); III, 205 (July, 1854); V, 125, 263 (April, September, 1857); VII, 358 (December, 1858).

——, *The Widow Rugby's Husband, A Night at the Ugly Man's, and Other Tales of Alabama.* By Johnson J. Hooper, author of "Adventures of Capt. Simon Suggs." With Engravings from Original Designs by Elliott. Philadelphia: A. Hart (Late Carey & Hart), 1851, 1853.

——, *Ibid.*, Philadelphia: T. B. Peterson, 1856.

——, [co-author], see *Magnum Opus.*

——, [editor], see Woodward, Thomas S.

Howe, Will D., "Early Humorists," in William P. Trent and others, editors, *The Cambridge History of American Literature.* 4 vols. New York, 1918.

Hubbell, Jay B., "Cavalier and Indentured Servant in Virginia Fiction," *The South Atlantic Quarterly*, XXVI, 22-39 (January, 1927).

Hudson, Arthur Palmer, *Humor of the Old Deep South.* New York, 1936.

Hundley, D. L., *Social Relations in our Southern States.* New York, 1860.

Inzer, John W., "Alabama's Secession Convention, 1861," *The Confederate Veteran,* XXXI, 7-9 (January, 1923).

Jack, Theodore H., *Sectionalism and Party Politics in Alabama, 1819-1842.* Menasha, Wisconsin, 1919.

Jerdan, William, editor, *Yankee Humor, and Uncle Sam's Fun.* London, 1853.

Journal of the Convention of the People of the State of Alabama, Held At the City of Montgomery Commencing on the 7th Day of January, 1861. Montgomery, 1861.

Kelley, Marion, *The Life and Writings of Johnson Jones Hooper* (unpublished Master's thesis, Alabama Polytechnic Institute, 1934).

Kozlay, Charles M., *The Lectures of Bret Harte.* Brooklyn, 1909.

Landrum, Grace Warren, "Notes on the Reading of the Old South," *American Literature,* III, 60-71 (March, 1931).

——, "Sir Walter Scott and His Literary Rivals in the Old South," *American Literature,* II, 256-276 (November, 1930).

Leacock, Stephen, *The Greatest Pages of American Humor.* New York, 1936.

"Letter from Hooper to Meek," unidentified newspaper clipping, owned by Anne H. Augustus, Macon, Mississippi.

Link, Samuel Albert, *Pioneers of Southern Literature.* 2 vols. Nashville, 1903.

Longstreet, Augustus Baldwin, *Georgia Scenes, Characters, Incidents, etc. in the First Half Century of the Republic.* Augusta, 1835.

Lukens, Henry Clay, "American Literary Comedians," *Harper's New Monthly Magazine,* LXXX, 783-793 (April, 1890).

McIlwaine, Shields, *The Southern Poor-White from Lubberland to Tobacco Road.* Norman, Oklahoma, 1939.

McMillan, Malcolm Cook, "The Selection of Montgomery as Alabama's Capital," *The Alabama Review,* II, 79-90 (April, 1948).

McRee, Griffith J., "The Late Archibald Maclaine Hooper," *University of North Carolina Magazine,* IV, 57-62 (March, 1855).

Magnum Opus. The Great Book of the University of Comus. The Pandect of our National Hilarities, Comprising Essays upon the Thirteen Divisions of the Rituals; Sketches of the Tredecim Dodges, Authors of the Plan, and Monitorial Guide to the Workings of the Fellowship, The Gander-Flight of the Thirteen Doges of Comus. Louisville, 1886.

Mallett, J. W., "Work of the Ordnance Bureau of the War Department of the Confederate States, 1861-5," *Southern Historical Society Papers,* XXXVII, 12-13 (January, 1909).

Martineau, Harriet, *Society in America.* 2 vols. New York, 1837.

Massett, Stephen C., *Drifting About, or What "Jeems Pipes of Pipesville" Saw-and Did.* New York, 1858.

Masterson, James R., *Tall Tales of Arkansaw.* Boston, 1943.

Mays, Samuel Elias, "Sketches from the Journal of a Confederate Soldier," *Tyler's Quarterly Historical and Genealogical Magazine,* V, 37, 144 (July, 1923).

Meek, A. B., *Songs and Poems of the South.* New York, 1857.

Meine, Franklin J., editor, *Tall Tales of the Southwest.* New York, 1937.

———, see Blair, Walter.

Milburn, W. H., "Philip J. Neeley and Alabama Five and Fifty Years Ago," *Methodist Quarterly Review,* XV, 295-313 (January, 1894).

The Montgomery Directory, for 1859-'60. Containing the Names of the Inhabitants, Business Directory, Street Directory, and an Appendix of Much Useful Information. Montgomery, 1859.

Moore, Albert Burton, *History of Alabama.* University, Alabama, 1934.

Moses, Montrose, J., *The Literature of the South.* New York, 1910.

Mott, Frank Luther, *A History of American Magazines, 1741-1850.* New York, 1930.

Nott, Henry Junius, *Novellettes of a Traveller.* New York, 1834.

Owen, Thomas McAdory, *History of Alabama and Dictionary of Alabama Biography.* 4 vols. Chicago, 1921.

Owsley, Frank L., "The Pattern of Migration and Settlement on the Southern Frontier," *The Journal of Southern History,* XI, 147-176 (May, 1945).

——, *Plain Folk of the Old South.* Baton Rouge, 1949.

Pattee, Fred Lewis, *A History of American Literature Since 1870.* New York, 1915.

Petrie, George, "Montgomery," in L. P. Powell, editor, *Historic Towns of the Southern States.* New York, 1900.

——, "William F. Samford, Statesman and Man of Letters," *Transactions of the Alabama Historical Society, 1899-1903,* IV, 465-485. Montgomery, 1904.

Phillips, John C., *A Bibliography of American Sporting Books.* Boston, 1930.

Phillips, Ulrich B., *A History of Transportation in the Eastern Cotton Belt to 1860.* New York, 1908.

——, *Life and Labor in the Old South.* Boston, 1929.

——, *The Life of Robert Toombs.* New York, 1913.

Pocket Book of Early American Humorists, A. Boston, 1907.

Porter, B. F., "My Home, My Dear Loved Home, Written for J. J. Hooper," poem in unidentified clipping in Johnson Jones Hooper Collection, Evans Memorial Library, Aberdeen, Mississippi.

Porter, William T., editor, *The Big Bear of Arkansas, and Other Sketches, Illustrative of Character and Incidents in the South and South-West.* Philadelphia, 1845.

——, editor, *A Quarter Race in Kentucky, and Other Tales.* Philadelphia, 1846.

Posey, Walter B., "Alabama in the 1830's as Recorded by British Travellers," *Birmingham-Southern College Bulletin,* XXXI, 1-47 (December, 1838).

Power, Tyrone, *Impressions of America during the Years 1833, 1834, and 1835.* 2 vols. London, 1836.

Proceedings of the Congress on the Announcement of the Death of Col. Francis S. Bartow, of the Army of the Confederate States, and Late a Delegate in the Congress from the State of Georgia. Published by Order of the Congress, By J. J. Hooper, Secretary. Richmond, 1861.

Proceedings of the Democratic State Convention held in the City of Montgomery, Commencing Wednesday, January 11, 1860. Montgomery, 1860.

Proceedings of the [National Democratic] Conventions at Charleston and Baltimore. Washington, 1860.

Proceedings of the National Democratic Convention at Charleston, S. C., April 23, 1860. Washington, 1860.

Proceedings on the Announcement of the Death of Hon. John Tyler, January 20th, 1862. Published by Order of the Congress, by J. J. Hooper, Secretary. Richmond, 1862.

Randall, James G., *The Civil War and Reconstruction.* Boston, 1937.

Register of the Confederate Dead Interred in Hollywood Cemetery, Richmond, Va. Richmond, 1869.

Riley, B. F., *Makers and Romance of Alabama History.* N. p., [1915?].

Robb, John S. ("Solitaire"), *Streaks of Squatter Life and Far Western Scenes. A Series of Humorous Sketches Descriptive of Incident and Character in the Wild West.* Philadelphia, 1846.

Robinson, William M., *Justice in Grey: A History of the Judicial System of the Confederate States of America.* Cambridge, 1941.

Rollins, [?], *The Method of Teaching and Studying the Belles Lettres.* London, 1761. Copy inscribed "A. M. Hooper to Johnson J. Hooper," in Johnson Jones Hooper Collection, Evans Memorial Library, Aberdeen, Mississippi.

Rourke, Constance, *American Humor: A Study of National Character.* New York, 1931.

Rutherford, M. L., *The South in History and Literature.* Atlanta, 1907.

Scott, Sutton S., "The Alabama Legislature of 1857-58 and 1859-60," *Transactions of the Alabama Historical Society, 1904,* V, 43-82. Montgomery, 1906.

Screws, Benjamin H. (?), *The 'Loil' Legislature of Alabama: Its Ridiculous Doings, and Nonsensical Sayings.* Montgomery, 1868.

Screws, W. W., "Alabama Journalism," in *Memorial Record of Alabama.* 2 vols. Madison, 1893.

Smith, Sol., "Theatricals in Montgomery Twenty-Eight Years Ago," Montgomery *Daily Mail,* February 9, 1858.

Smith, William R., *The History and Debates of the Convention of the People of Alabama, Begun and Held in the City of Montgomery, on the Seventh Day of January, 1861, in which Is Preserved the Speeches of the Secret Sessions, and Many Valuable State Papers.* Montgomery, 1861.

Smithers, Nellie, *Library of Humorous American Works* (unpublished Master's thesis, Columbia University, New York, 1936).

Southern and South-Western Sketches. Fun, Sentiment and Adventure. Edited by a Gentleman of Richmond. Richmond, [1855?].

Speech of the Hon. William L. Yancey, of Alabama, Delivered in the National Democratic Convention, Charleston, April 28, 1861, with the Protest of the Alabama Delegation. From the Report of the "Charleston Mercury." Charleston, 1860.

Spiller, Robert E., and others, editors, *Literary History of the United States.* 3 vols. New York, 1948.

Sterling, Ada., editor, *A Belle of the Fifties: Memoirs of Mrs.* [Clement C.] *Clay, of Alabama, Covering Social and Political Life in Washington and the South, 1853-66, Put into Narrative Form by Ada Sterling.* New York, 1904.

Stewart, Samuel Boyd, *Joseph Glover Baldwin* (unpublished Ph. D. thesis, Vanderbilt University, Nashville, 1941).

Taliaferro, H. E. ("Skitt"), "Ducktown," *The Spirit of the Times,* XXX, 563 (December 29, 1860).

——, *Fisher's River (North Carolina) Scenes and Characters.* New York, 1859.

Tandy, Jeannette, *Crackerbox Philosophers in American Humor and Satire.* New York, 1925.

Tasistro, Louis Fitzgerald, *Random Shots and Southern Breezes, containing Critical Remarks on the Southern States and Southern Institutions, with Semi-Serious Observations on Men and Manners.* 2 vols. New York, 1842.

Tatum, Georgia Lee, *Disloyalty in the Confederacy.* Chapel Hill, 1934.

Townsend, John, *The South Alone Should Govern the South.* Charleston, 1860.

Trent, W. P., "A Retrospect of American Humor," *The Century Magazine,* LXIII, 59-60 (November, 1901).

Twentieth Century Biographical Dictionary of Notable Americans. 10 vols. Boston, 1904.

Van Doren, Carl C., *The American Novel.* New York, 1921.

Venable, Austin L., "The Conflict Between the Douglas and Yancey Forces in the Charleston Convention," *The Journal of Southern History,* VIII, 226-241 (May, 1942).

Wade, John Donald, *Augustus Baldwin Longstreet, a Study of the Development of Culture in the South.* New York, 1924.

Walker, General William, *The War in Nicaragua.* Mobile, 1860.

Watterson, Henry, *The Compromises of Life and Other Lectures and Addresses Including Some Observations on Certain Downward Tendencies of Modern Society.* New York, 1903.

——, *Oddities in Southern Life and Character.* Boston, 1883.

Wheeler, John H., *Historical Sketches of North Carolina, from 1584 to 1851.* 2 vols. Philadelphia, 1861.

Whitaker, Fanny Hooper, "The Hooper Family," *The North Carolina Booklet,* V, 39-71 (July, 1905).

Wilder, Marshall P., editor, *The Wit and Humor of America.* 10 vols. New York, 1907.

Williams, Ben Ames, editor, Mary Boykin Chestnut, *A Diary from Dixie.* Boston, 1949.

Williams, Clanton W., editor, "Presidential Election Returns and Related Data for Ante-Bellum Alabama," *The Alabama Review,* I, 279-293 (October, 1948); II, 63-73 (January, 1949).

Wilt, Napier, *Some American Humorists.* New York, 1929.

Woodward, Thomas S., *Woodward's Reminiscences of the Creek, or Muscogee Indians, Contained in Letters to Friends in Georgia and Alabama.* Montgomery, 1859. Reprinted with a Preface by Peter A. Brannon, Tuscaloosa and Montgomery, 1939.

Yonge, J. E. D., "The Conservative Party in Alabama, 1848-60," *Transactions of the Alabama Historical Society,* IV, 501-526. Montgomery, 1904.

Young, Hugh Peter, *A Social and Economic History of Montgomery, Alabama, 1846-1860* (unpublished Master's thesis, University of Alabama, 1948).

DOCUMENTS

Acts and Resolutions of the First Session of the Provisional Congress of the Confederate States, 1861. Montgomery, 1861.

Acts and Resolutions of the Second Session of the Provisional Congress of the Confederate States, 1861. Montgomery, 1861.

Acts and Resolutions of the Third Session of the Provisional Congress of the Confederate States, Held at Richmond, Va. Richmond, 1861.

Acts of the Fourth Biennial Session of the General Assembly of Alabama, Held in the City of Montgomery, Commencing on the Second Monday in November 1853. Montgomery, 1854.

Acts of the Seventh Biennial Session of the General Assembly of Alabama, Held in the City of Montgomery, Commencing on the Second Monday in November, 1859. Montgomery, 1860.

Acts Passed at the Annual Session of the General Assembly of the State of Alabama, Begun and Held in the City of Tuscaloosa, on the First Monday in December, 1845. Tuscaloosa, 1846.

Acts Passed at the First Biennial Session of the General Assembly of the State of Alabama, Begun and Held in the City of Montgomery, on the First Monday in December, 1847. Montgomery, 1848.

Chambers County Administrator's Guardian and Will Record, IV [December 3, 1849], recopied in *Chambers County Will Record,* I-II.

Chambers County Appearance Docket, January Term, 1842; ibid., Spring Term, 1849-Spring Term, 1855.

Chambers County Bar Trial Docket, October Term, 1843; ibid., April-October Terms, 1845; ibid., November Term, 1846-Fall Term, 1849.

Chambers County Bond Book of Public Officials, 1833-1841.

Chambers County Circuit Court Minutes, Spring Term, 1850-Fall Term, 1853, VI, VII.

Chambers County Circuit Court Trial Docket, November Term, 1846.

Chambers County Commissioners Court Record, April, 1833-November, 1837.

Chambers County Deed Record, February 8, 1833-July 7, 1837, I; *ibid., 1837-1839,* II; *ibid., April 23, 1844-October 9, 1844,* VI; *ibid., November 15, 1854-June 12, 1857,* XII; *ibid., July 15, 1857-October 3, 1860,* XIII.

Chambers County Estray Book, 1833-1839.

Chambers County Minutes of Chancery Court, 1842-1862.

Chambers County Minutes of Circuit Court, 1833-1837, I; *ibid., October Term, 1844-Fall Term, 1849,* V; *ibid., Spring Term, 1850-Fall Term, 1853,* VI.

Chambers County Orphans Court Record, 1837-1838, III; *ibid., 1845-1849.*

Chambers County Orphans Court Trial Docket, November Term, 1843-June Term, 1847.

Chambers County Record of Marriages, November 8, 1839-September 19, 1843, II.

Chambers County State Docket, 1834-1836.

Chambers County Trial Docket, April Term, 1843-October Term, 1844; ibid., October Term, 1845.

Chambers County Will Record, I-II.

Clay, C. C., *A Digest of the Laws of the State of Alabama Containing all the Statutes of a Public and General Nature, in Force at the close of the Session of the General Assembly, in February, 1843.* Tuscaloosa, 1843.

Journal of the Congress of the Confederate States of America, 1861-1865. 7 vols. Washington, 1904.

Journal of the House of Representatives of the General Assembly of the State of Alabama, Begun and Held in the City of Tuscaloosa, on the First Monday in December, 1845. Tuscaloosa, 1846.

Journal of the House of Representatives of the State of Alabama, at the First Biennial Session Begun and Held in the City of Montgomery, on the First Monday in December, 1847. Montgomery, 1848.

Journal of the Senate of the State of Alabama, at the First Biennial Session Begun and Held in the City of Montgomery, on the First Monday in December, 1847. Montgomery, 1848.

Journal of the Seventh Biennial Session of the House of Representatives of the State of Alabama, Session of 1859-60, Held in the City of Montgomery. Montgomery, 1860.

Journal of the Seventh Biennial Session of the Senate of the State of Alabama, Session of 1859-'60, Held in the City of Montgomery. Montgomery, 1860.

Journal of the Sixth Biennial Session of the House of Representatives of the State of Alabama, Session of 1857-'58, Held in the City of Montgomery. Montgomery, 1858.

Journal of the Sixth Biennial Session of the Senate of the State of Alabama, Session of 1857-'58, Held in the City of Montgomery. Montgomery, 1858.

List of Staff Officers of the Confederate States Army, 1861-1865. Washington, 1891.

Seventh Census of the United States: 1850. Washington, 1851.

Sixth Census or Enumeration of the Inhabitants of the United States, as Corrected at the Department of State, in 1840. Washington, 1841.

Tallapoosa County Bench Trial Docket, Fall Term, 1838; ibid., 1844-1849 [Spring Term, 1844].

Tallapoosa County Bond Book [1839-1848], II.

Tallapoosa County Bond Book of County Officers, 1849-1859.

Tallapoosa County Chancery Court Trial Docket, May Term, 1848-May Term, 1851; ibid., May Term, 1844-November Term, 1854; ibid., May Term, 1852-November Term, 1853.

Tallapoosa County Circuit Court Minutes, E, [1850].

Tallapoosa County Deed Record Book, February 4, 1835-June 20, 1842, A; *ibid., 1843-1844,* C; *ibid., 1844-1846,* D; *ibid., 1848-1849, F.*

Tallapoosa County Record Book, 1834-1839, A; *ibid., 1839-1842,* B.

Tallapoosa County Record of Circuit Court, Fall Term, 1834-Spring Term, 1836.

Tallapoosa County Records Docket, 1854-1855.

Tallapoosa County Subpoena Docket [1851-1859].

Tallapoosa County Trial Docket, 1839-1841; ibid., Spring Term, 1841; ibid., Fall Term, 1841; ibid., Spring Term, 1842; ibid., Spring Term, 1844; ibid., Spring Term, 1844-1849.

Tuomey, Michael, *First Biennial Report on the Geology of Alabama.* Tuscaloosa, 1850.

The War of the Rebellion: A Compilation of the Official Records of the Union and Confederate Armies. 128 vols. Washington, 1880-1901.

MANUSCRIPTS

The Alabama Standard Account Book [La Fayette] *1842.* MSS. owned by W. B. Wood, Jr., Lafayette, Alabama.

Annual Returns Made by Solomon Lodge No. 74 [La Fayette, Alabama] *to the M. W. Grand Lodge, A. F. and A. M. of Alabama* [1851-1854]. MSS. in Masonic Temple Vault, Grand Lodge of Alabama, Montgomery.

Annual Return [s] to the Most Worshipful Grand Lodge of Alabama on the Officers and Members of Montgomery Lodge No. 11, [1846-1862]. MSS. in Masonic Temple Vault, Grand Lodge of Alabama, Montgomery.

Autograph Album of Mary Brantley Hooper. MSS. vol. in Johnson Jones Hooper Collection, Evans Memorial Library, Aberdeen, Mississippi.

Boyle & La Wall & Co. Tailors' Records [La Fayette, 1851]. MSS. ledger owned by W. B. Wood, Jr., Lafayette, Alabama.

Capias Warrant—"[Johnson J.] Hooper State's Attorney, February 27-28, 1851, Chambers County Circuit Spring Term, 1851." Case of "The State *vs* Jere Harris & Smith Drinkard." Owned by W. B. Wood, Jr., Lafayette, Alabama.

Carey & Hart Record Books, II-IV (August 25, 1845-March 6, 1850). MSS. vols. in the Historical Society of Pennsylvania, Philadelphia.

Coat-of-arms bookplate of Johnson J. Hooper, motto: "nil conscire sibi," inscribed to "Sarah Brantley from Johnson J. Hooper," owned by Anne H. Augustus, Macon, Mississippi.

[Dadeville, Ala.] *Index to the Map of the Town of Dadeville,* [1838-1840]. MSS. vol. in Tallapoosa County Courthouse, Dadeville, Alabama.

Diary of Annie Brantley [Mrs. Thomas R.] Heard, February 24, 1858-October, 1863, owned by Anne H. Augustus, Macon, Mississippi.

Diary of Joseph A. Johnson, September 10-October 3, 1837, owned by C. S. Johnson, Jacksonville, Florida.

Diary of Basil Manly, 1858-1867, in University of Alabama Library.

Interments in the Shockhoe Hill Burying Ground, December 8, 1848-December 31, 1870. MSS. vol. in the office of the City Home, Richmond, Virginia.

Ledger (unidentified) in Chambers County Courthouse, Lafayette, Alabama.

Ledger (unidentified) in Tallapoosa County Courthouse, Dadeville, Alabama.

Letter, Anne H. Augustus to Lawrence M. Foster, Macon, Mississippi, June 11, 1945, in University of Alabama Library.

Letter, Kate (Brantley) Augustus to George B. Augustus, Jr., Macon, Mississippi, March 18, 1884, owned by Anne H. Augustus, Macon, Mississippi.

Letters, Green D. Brantley to Ann B. Heard, La Fayette, Alabama, December 25, 1842; Alsea K. Brantley, La Fayette, Alabama, August 11, 18 [?]; Elizabeth [Mrs. Green D.] Brantley, Walnut Hill, Arkansas, April 27, 1849, owned by Anne H. Augustus, Macon, Mississippi.

Letter, George E. Brewer to Peter A. Brannon, Columbus, Georgia, October 15, 1919, in possession of addressee, State Department of Archives and History, Montgomery, Alabama.

Letter, Richard C. Foster, president, University of Alabama, to Miss Caroline A. Hooper, University, Alabama, February 26, 1938, in University of Alabama Library.

Letters, Ann B. Heard to Green D. Brantley, Mobile, Alabama, December 19, 1848; Elizabeth [Mrs. Green D.] Brantley, Cahawba, Alabama, July 3, 18 [?], Mobile, Alabama, January 18, December 26, 1845; Kate Brantley, "Saturday Noon," n. d.; Amelia M. Brantley, Mobile, December 3, 18 [?]; Sarah J. Brantley, New Orleans, May 6, 1853, February 15, 1861, May 4, 1862; "My Dear Sister" [Sarah J. Brantley?], La Fayette, Alabama, January 21, 1850, owned by Anne H. Augustus, Macon, Mississippi.

Letter, Caroline A. Hooper to Marie Bankhead Owen, Birmingham, Alabama, November 28, 1932, in Alabama State Department of Archives and History, Montgomery.

Letters, Johnson J. Hooper to Alsea K. Brantley, La Fayette, Alabama, October 7, 1849; Mrs. T. R. Heard, Montgomery, Alabama, August 22, 1850; and Sarah J. Brantley, Montgomery, Alabama, April 9, 1854, in the possession of Miss Anne H. Augustus, Macon, Mississippi; Johnson J. Hooper to William DeBerniere Hooper, Richmond, October 21, 1861, in University of Alabama Library; and Hooper to Joseph A. Johnson, Charleston, South Carolina and Chambers Court

House, Alabama, October 3, 1838 and n.d., owned by C. S. Johnson, Jacksonville, Florida.

Letters, Mary Mildred [Mrs. J. J.] Hooper to Mrs. Annie B. Heard, Abdeen, Mississippi, November 24, 18[?]; Mrs. Kate B. Augustus, Macon, Mississippi, December 1, 18[?], owned by Miss Anne H. Augustus, Macon, Mississippi.

Letters, Joseph A. Johnson to James Moore, Russellville and Shreveport, Louisiana, September 30, November 18, 1837, owned by C. S. Johnson, Jacksonville, Florida.

Letter, Samuel Lover to Johnson Jones Hooper, Montgomery, Alabama, February 25, 1847, in Johnson Jones Hooper Collection, Evans Memorial Library, Aberdeen, Mississippi.

Letter, Catherine Moore to James Moore, Ouachita Parish, Louisiana, August 1, 1837, owned by C. S. Johnson, Jacksonville, Florida.

Letters, Jackson Moore to James Moore, Maplesville, Alabama, June 8 and Jefferson County, Mississippi, June 28, 1837, owned by C. S. Johnson, Jacksonville, Florida.

Letter, James Moore to Jackson Moore, Dudleyville, Alabama, September 3, 1837, owned by C. S. Johnson, Jacksonville, Florida.

Letter, Joel Riggs to Green D. Brantley, Montgomery, Alabama, June 3, 1848, owned by Miss Anne H. Augustus, Macon, Mississippi.

Letter, William R. Smith to Rowland & Munsell, Montgomery, March 12, 1861, in University of Alabama Library.

Letters to W. Stanley Hoole, in University of Alabama Library: Willie L. [Mrs. James A.] Anderson, Tuscaloosa, Alabama, January 1, 1949; Anne H. Augustus, Macon, Mississippi, June 11, 1945, April 2, 21, May 27, 1949; Dorothy C. Barck, librarian, New York Historical Society, New York, July 29, 1946; Peter A. Brannon, Alabama State Department of Archives and History, Montgomery, April 30, 1946; Lewis C. Branscomb, associate director of libraries, Ohio State University, Columbus, September 29, 1948; Clarence S. Brigham, director, American Antiquarian Society, Boston, January 20, 1947; Clara Mae Brown, reference librarian, Joint University Libraries, Nashville, October 11, 1948; Thomas D. Clark, University of Kentucky, Lexington, Kentucky, December 28, 1948; Olan V. Cooke, assistant librarian, University of North Carolina Library, Chapel Hill, February 15, 1946, March 7, 1949; Jack Dalton, associate librarian, University of Virginia, Charlottesville, August 3, November 18, 1948; Leslie W. Dunlap, acting chief, General Reference and Bibliography Division, Library of Congress, Washington, August 14, 1947; Rhoda C. Ellison, Chapel Hill, North Carolina, February 20, 1945; Ernest L. Hettich, acting director of libraries, New York University, New York, January 17, 1946; Robert O. Hickman, chancellor, Diocese of Richmond,

Virginia, March 28, 1949; Henry Lea Hudson, Lea & Febiger, Publishers, Philadelphia, January 28, 1947; Ray O. Hummell, Jr., assistant librarian, Virginia State Library, Richmond, February 2, 1949; Marion Kelley, Mississippi State College, February 28, 1946; Guy R. Lyle, director of libraries, Louisiana State University, Baton Rouge, March 7, 1949; D. M. McKeithan, Department of English, University of Texas, Austin, March 23, 1946; Mrs. Emma W. MacMillan, librarian, Wilmington (North Carolina) Public Library; Miss Lena Martin, librarian, Gadsden (Alabama) Public Library, April 4, 1949; Franklin J. Meine, editor-in-chief, *American Peoples Encyclopedia*, Chicago, February 5, 1946, March 24, April 27, May 4, 1949; Michael Mulvoy, Newman Catholic Center, University, Alabama, January 26, 1949; Joe O. Naylor, president, The Naylor Company, San Antonio, Texas, January 17, 1949; Pearl C. Partridge, Boligee, Alabama, July 22, 1948; Miss Lucille Peacock, librarian, Evans Memorial Library, Aberdeen, Mississippi; Gordon N. Ray, Widener Library, Harvard College, Cambridge, Massachusetts, March 25, 1946; Frank A. Reagan, judge of probate, Etowah County, Gadsden, Alabama, August 24, 1948, January 11, 1949; Paul North Rice, chief, Reference Department, New York Public Library, New York, July 30, 1946, November 12, 1948; Esther Claire Robertson, newspaper librarian, Louisiana State University, Baton Rouge, March 7, 1949; Henry L. Savage, archivist, Princeton University Library, Princeton, New Jersey, February 4, May 2, 1947, June 3, April 8, 1948; Mary L. Thornton, librarian, North Carolina Collection, University of North Carolina, Chapel Hill, April 5, 1946; Clayton Torrence, director, Virginia Historical Society, Richmond, November 13, 1948; R. N. Williamson, 2nd, director, Historical Society of Pennsylvania, Philadelphia, July 22, 1946, February 5, 1947; C. S. Johnson, Jacksonville, Florida, February 7, 14, 19, 27, 1951.

Magistrate's Execution, Green D. Brantley, J. P., to Thomas K. Smith, April 19, 1841, executed February 22, 1842, owned by Anne H. Augustus, Macon, Mississippi.

Minute Book Solomon's Lodge No. 74, La Fayette, Alabama, December 27, 1848-June 1, 1855. MSS. vol. owned by W. B. Wood, Jr., Lafayette, Alabama.

Minutes of the City Council of Montgomery, Alabama, June 2, 1856-September 10, 1860. MSS. vol. in University of Alabama Library.

Montgomery (Alabama) *County Conveyances* O. S., VII, XI, XII.

Parish Register, St. John's Church, Montgomery, in Alabama State Department of Archives and History, Montgomery.

Poems by Sarah J. Brantley. MSS vol. owned by Anne H. Augustus, Macon, Mississippi.

Receipts, "Chambers Tribune, Holifield and Hooper," dated November 9, 1852; "Chambers Tribune, Phillips and Prather," dated August 12, 1853, owned by W. B. Wood, Jr., Lafayette, Alabama.

Roster of Cemeteries and of Persons in Marked Graves in Monroe County, Mississippi, in Evans Memorial Library, Aberdeen, Mississippi.

Secretary Book No. 1 Concord Chapter No. 37 [Royal Arch Masons] *La Fayette, Alabama, June 19, 1848-April 22, 1865.* MSS. owned by W. B. Wood, Jr., Lafayette, Alabama.

United States Census (Sixth), 1840, Alabama, I, VII; *ibid.,* (Seventh), 1850, Alabama, II, [Original MSS. Returns].

MAGAZINES AND NEWSPAPERS

Aberdeen (Mississippi) *Examiner.*

Alabama Daily State Gazette (Montgomery).

Alabama Highways (Montgomery).

Alabama Journal (Montgomery).

The Alabama Historical Quarterly (Montgomery).

The Alabama Review (University).

American Historical Review (Washington).

American Literature (Durham).

American Penny Magazine (New York).

Birmingham (Alabama) *News-Age Herald Magazine.*

Birmingham-Southern College Bulletin (Birmingham).

The Bookman (New York).

Cape-Fear Recorder (Wilmington, North Carolina).

The Century Illustrated Monthly Magazine (New York).

Chambers County Tribune (La Fayette, Alabama).

Clarke County Democrat (Grove Hill, Alabama).

Columbus (Georgia) *Ledger Magazine.*

The Commercial (Wilmington, North Carolina).

The Confederate Veteran (Nashville).

The Courier (Charleston, South Carolina).

Dadeville (Alabama) *Banner.*

Dadeville (Alabama) *Record.*

Dallas Gazette (Cahawba, Alabama).

DeBow's Review and Industrial Resources, Statistics, etc. (New Orleans).

East Alabamian (La Fayette, Alabama).

Flag of the Union (Tuscaloosa, Alabama).

Florence (Alabama) *Gazette.*

Gadsden (Alabama) *Leader.*

The Harbinger, Devoted to Social and Political Progress (New York).

Harper's New Monthly Magazine (New York).

Hillsboro (North Carolina) *Recorder.*

Huntsville (Alabama) *Democrat.*
Huntsville (Alabama) *Southern Advocate.*
Journal of Southern History (Baton Rouge).
The Knickerbocker, or New York Monthly Magazine.
The Literary World, A Journal of Science, Literature, and Art (New York).
Little Scissors (New York).
Macon Republican (Tuskegee, Alabama).
Methodist Quarterly Review (Nashville, Tennessee).
Mobile (Alabama) *Daily Advertiser.*
Mobile (Alabama) *Daily Register.*
Mobile (Alabama) *Register and Journal.*
Mobile (Alabama) *Weekly Register.*
Montgomery (Alabama) *Advertiser and State Gazette.*
Montgomery (Alabama) *Daily Advertiser.*
Montgomery (Alabama) *Daily Alabama Journal.*
Montgomery (Alabama) *Daily Mail.*
Montgomery (Alabama) *Daily Messenger.*
Montgomery (Alabama) *Daily Confederation.*
Montgomery (Alabama) *Tri-Weekly Mail.*
Montgomery (Alabama) *Weekly Advertiser.*
Montgomery (Alabama) *Weekly Alabama Journal.*
Montgomery (Alabama) *Weekly Mail.*
New Orleans *Delta.*
New Orleans *Commercial Times.*
New Orleans *Daily Picayune.*
New York *Herald.*
New York Mirror: A Journal of Literature, News and the Fine Arts.
New York *Times.*
North American Review (Boston).
North Carolina Booklet (Raleigh).
The North-Carolina University Magazine (Chapel Hill).
Opelika (Alabama) *Post.*
The People's Press and Wilmington (North Carolina) *Advertiser.*
Porter's Spirit of the Times; a Chronicle of the Turf, Field Sports, Literature and the Stage (New York).
Publications of the Southern History Association (Washington).
Richmond (Virginia) *Daily Dispatch.*
Richmond (Virginia) *Daily Examiner.*
Richmond (Virginia) *Enquirer.*
Richmond (Virginia) *Whig and Public Advertiser.*
Saturday Review of Literature (New York).
St. Louis (Missouri) *Reveille.*

Savannah (Georgia) *News.*

Savannah (Georgia) *Republican.*

The South Atlantic Quarterly (Durham).

South Carolinian (Columbia).

Southern Historical Society Papers (Richmond).

Southern Military Gazette (Montgomery, Alabama, and Atlanta, Georgia).

Southern Times (Montgomery, Alabama).

The Spirit of the Times; a Chronicle of the Turf, Agriculture, Field Sports, Literature and the Stage (New York).

Talladega (Alabama) *Reporter.*

Tallapoosa Times (Dadeville, Alabama).

Transactions of the Alabama Historical Society (Tuscaloosa; Montgomery).

Troy (Alabama) *Independent American.*

Tyler's Quarterly Historical and Genealogical Magazine (Richmond).

Wetumpka (Alabama) *Dispatch.*

Wetumpka (Alabama) *State Guard.*

Wetumpka (Alabama) *Whig.*

Wheler's Southern Monthly Magazine (Athens, Georgia).

Wilkes' Spirit of the Times, A Chronicle of the Turf, Field Sports, Literature, and the Stage (New York).

Wilmington (North Carolina) *Advertiser.*

The World We Live In (New York).

Yankee Notions, or Whittlings from Jonathan's Jack-Knife (New York).

INDEX